1880 CENSUS:

FAYETTE COUNTY, TENNESSEE

Head-of-Household Index

Samuel Sistler

JANAWAY PUBLISHING, INC.
Santa Maria, California
2012

1880 Census Fayette County, Tennessee
Heads-of-Household Index

Originally published, Nashville, 2003

Reprinted by:

Janaway Publishing, Inc.
732 Kelsey Ct.
Santa Maria, California 93454
(805) 925-1038
www.JanawayGenealogy.com

2010, 2012

ISBN: 978-1-59641-115-9

Made in the United States of America

DIRECTIONS

The entries are arranged alphabetically by head of household. In general this is just a head of household index. Also included are individuals whose surname differed from that of the household head.

Each entry includes name, age, and a stamped page number from the original schedules (this is the number in the upper right-hand corner of every other page). A person's sex, (m) or (f) is given if it is in question. The symbol (B) identifies black or mulatto families. The symbol (I) was supposed to identify Indians (Native Americans), but actually was used by enumerators to represent various racial mixtures.

Samuel Sistler
2003

ABAGE, Granville 27* (B) (389)
ABBOTT, Charles 79?* (421)
ABERNATHY, Anne 37* (B) (414)
ABERNATHY, Dan 23* (433)
ABERNATHY, Henry 19* (B) (428)
ABERNATHY, Lucius? 21 (B) (426)
ABERNATHY, Minerva 11* (B) (426)
ABERNATHY, _____ 62 (f), (432)
ABINGTON, Blount 23* (B) (352)
ABINGTON, Haywood 21 (B) (351)
ABINGTON, Mathew 75 (B) (377)
ABINGTON, _____cy 50 (m) (B) (387)
ABRAMFIELD, Gus 10* (B) (420)
ADAIR, Wm. 50 (B) (420)
ADAMS, Catherin 66* (181)
ADAMS, Charles 35 (B) (167)
ADAMS, George W. 29, (406)
ADAMS, Gus 24 (B) (289)
ADAMS, J. M. 50 (m), (304)
ADAMS, JAmes 45* (B) (273)
ADAMS, James 50 (B) (482)
ADAMS, Mary 44, (414)
ADAMS, Matilda 40* (424)
ADAMS, Spot 49 (m)* (465)
ADAMS, Sterling 57 (B) (398)
ADAMS, Thomas 16* (346)
ADAMS, W. 28 (m)* (488)
ADAMS, Wm. J. 46, (183)
ADAMS, Wright 61 (B) (169)
ADAMS?, _____ 51 (m) (B) (300)
ADARH?, Rose 13* (B) (498)
ADDINGTON, _____ 20 (f)* (B) (418)
ADDISON, Davy 55 (B) (436)
ADKINS, Albert 20* (B) (178)
ADKINS, Henry 49? (B) (262)
ADKINS, Wm. 37 (B) (171)
ADKISON?, Albert 25* (B) (252)
ADLETTA, Phillip 50, (295)
ADLUM, Mary L. 25, (291)
AENIOUS?, H. 50 (m) (B) (489)
AENIOUS?, Squire 47 (B) (489)
AIKEN, Frank 30, (277)
AILMOND?, Granvil 52, (207)
AIRS, Nedd 25 (B) (398)
ALBERT, Edda 10 (m)* (B) (493)
ALBRIGHT, Alley 30 (m) (B) (374)
ALBRIGHT, George 40, (222)
ALBRIGHT, Wilson 23 (B) (355)
ALEN, JAck 16* (B) (213)
ALEN, Manuel 21* (B) (204)
ALEN, Tom 30 (B) (206)
ALEN?, Rose 20* (B) (425)
ALERSON, Louis 35* (B) (477)
ALEXANDER, Arther 34 (B) (370)
ALEXANDER, Betta 25 (B) (403)
ALEXANDER, Charley 30? (B) (326)
ALEXANDER, Dann 32 (B) (402)

ALEXANDER, Fillis 22 (f) (B) (405)
ALEXANDER, Henry 30 (B) (403)
ALEXANDER, Henry 40* (B) (399)
ALEXANDER, Henry 46 (B) (391)
ALEXANDER, Ike 32 (B) (334)
ALEXANDER, J. 20 (m)* (B) (291)
ALEXANDER, JAne 62* (333)
ALEXANDER, James W. 35, (412)
ALEXANDER, Joe 21* (B) (344)
ALEXANDER, John 43, (408)
ALEXANDER, Louis 24 (B) (404)
ALEXANDER, Oliver 26* (B) (217)
ALEXANDER, S. J. 46 (m), (406)
ALEXANDER, Sarah 16* (B) (347)
ALEXANDER, Taylor 31* (430)
ALEXANDER, Thomas M. 35, (406)
ALEXANDER, Thornton 45 (B) (199)
ALEXANDER, Tom 26 (B) (265)
ALEXANDER, Uria 40* (433)
ALEXANDER, W. J. 43 (m), (314)
ALEXANDER, _ 35 (m), (165)
ALEXANDER?, Joe 21* (B) (316)
ALFORD, O. K. 40 (m)* (477)
ALLBRIGHT, Julia 22* (B) (377)
ALLBRIGHT, L. A. 22 (m)* (440)
ALLBRIGHT?, Willie 18* (436)
ALLEN, Albert jr. 34* (B) (237)
ALLEN, Albert sr. 70?* (B) (237)
ALLEN, Ben 65* (B) (414)
ALLEN, Bob 45? (B) (318)
ALLEN, Cage 16* (B) (421)
ALLEN, Cazada 45 (f)* (B) (382)
ALLEN, Clarence 27, (434)
ALLEN, Ellen 17* (B) (475)
ALLEN, Fed 22 (m) (B) (301)
ALLEN, Frank 25* (B) (414)
ALLEN, George 87* (413)
ALLEN, Gus 39* (429)
ALLEN, Harry? 30? (B) (244)
ALLEN, Horace 39* (181)
ALLEN, Ike 33 (B) (248)
ALLEN, J. 35 (m)* (B) (495)
ALLEN, J. B. 33 (f)* (342)
ALLEN, Jackson 22* (B) (405)
ALLEN, Jackson 50, (291)
ALLEN, Jeff 36 (B) (497)
ALLEN, Jefferson 28 (B) (454)
ALLEN, John 44 (B) (485)
ALLEN, Leer 55 (f)* (B) (216)
ALLEN, Lucinda 50 (B) (268)
ALLEN, MAttie A. _ (B) (179)
ALLEN, Maggie 50 (B) (167)
ALLEN, Robert 54* (413)
ALLEN, Sam 24* (B) (425)
ALLEN, Sam H. 65* (B) (297)
ALLEN, Sophia 27* (B) (483)
ALLEN, Thomas 19 (B) (423)
ALLEN, Werter 23* (B) (383)
ALLEN, Wm. 47, (437)

ALLEN, Wm. 57, (413)
ALLEN, Wm. H. 44* (168)
ALLEN, _____ 48 (m), (434)
ALLEN, tom? 55 (B) (244)
ALLEN?, Eva 21* (434)
ALLEN?, Garnett 29 (B) (300)
ALLEN?, Richard 75* (B) (420)
ALLEY, Antney 45 (m) (B) (378)
ALLEY, Charles? 15* (B) (370)
ALLIN, Milie 50 (B) (397)
ALLIN, Thos. D. 33, (441)
ALLIN, Wm. 30* (443)
ANA, Julie 21* (B) (433)
ANDERS, J. N. 32 (m), (476)
ANDERS, P. H. 43 (m)* (206)
ANDERS, R. A. 55 (m), (476)
ANDERSON, Adam 55* (B) (194)
ANDERSON, Arther 22 (B) (248)
ANDERSON, Ben 25 (B) (450)
ANDERSON, Bill 26* (B) (222)
ANDERSON, Billie 60 (B) (448)
ANDERSON, C. W. 29 (m), (406)
ANDERSON, Clay 22* (B) (388)
ANDERSON, Daniel 47 (B) (448)
ANDERSON, Davy 29* (B) (250)
ANDERSON, Edward 35, (388)
ANDERSON, Elbert 23 (B) (176)
ANDERSON, Eliza 5 (B) (273)
ANDERSON, George 22* (B) (171)
ANDERSON, Hal 34 (B) (284)
ANDERSON, Henry 21* (B) (414)
ANDERSON, Henry 25 (B) (445)
ANDERSON, J. 52 (m), (468)
ANDERSON, James 24?* (393)
ANDERSON, James 40* (B) (367)
ANDERSON, Jeff 13* (B) (399)
ANDERSON, John 45* (B) (168)
ANDERSON, Joseph 70, (369)
ANDERSON, Lewis 13* (B) (441)
ANDERSON, Logan M. 42* (460)
ANDERSON, Lou 12 (f) (B) (333)
ANDERSON, Lucy 23?* (B) (217)
ANDERSON, Lucy 51* (B) (432)
ANDERSON, M. 40 (m) (B) (496)
ANDERSON, M. 55 (f)* (B) (470)
ANDERSON, Mack 13* (B) (273)
ANDERSON, Morris 50 (B) (176)
ANDERSON, Myra 50* (B) (424)
ANDERSON, Robt. 32 (B) (437)
ANDERSON, Sawney? 47 (m) (B) (360)
ANDERSON, Wyatt 45 (B) (283)
ANDERSON, _iram 45 (m)* (B) (251)
ANDERTON, C. C. 46 (m)* (293)
ANDREWS, Joseph 26* (253)
ANDREWS, Wm. 21, (274)
ANDREWS, _. H. 65 (m)* (206)
ANGEL, Wm.? 33 (B) (449)
ANNIS, Sue 42, (319)
ANNSTON?, Leanna 25 (B) (484)
ANTHONY, Ann E. 39, (357)
ANTHONY, Charles W. sr. 55, (357)
ANTHONY, James M. 34, (362)
ANTHONY, John 9* (B) (347)
ANTHONY, Lee 28 (m)* (B) (355)
ANTHONY, Lewis 27* (B) (365)

ANTHONY, M. 14 (m)* (B) (499)
ANTHONY, Nick 55 (B) (357)
ANTHONY, Peter 36* (B) (354)
ANTHONY, Samuel T. 36* (366)
ANTHONY, V. S. 21 (m)* (483)
ANTHONY, Wm. 18* (361)
APLEBERRY?, Wm. 33* (338)
APPERSON, _____p 51 (m) (B) (183)
ARCHBELL, Spenser 19* (B) (211)
ARCHBELL?, Davy 29 (m) (B) (216)
ARCHBELL?, _. R. 60 (m), (216)
ARCHER, Nathan 14* (B) (211)
ARCHER, Stallings 26 (m)* (B) (329)
ARCOWOD?, J. J. 25 (m), (488)
ARMER, Sarah 19* (387)
ARMON, Covington 30, (442)
ARMOR, Isham 25* (B) (242)
ARMOR, Perrie 18* (B) (428)
ARMOUR, Dave 29 (B) (194)
ARMOUR, Ed 40 (B) (491)
ARMOUR, George 35* (B) (492)
ARMOUR, Jane 48 (B) (490)
ARMOUR, Jas. H. 6* (B) (172)
ARMOUR, Joseph J. 29, (351)
ARMOUR, L. 40 (m)* (B) (489)
ARMOUR, Margaret 45 (B) (182)
ARMOUR, S. 23 (m) (B) (491)
ARMOUR, Sally 56* (B) (195)
ARMSTRONG, Aggie? 80 (f)* (B) (481)
ARMSTRONG, E. 33 (m) (B) (311)
ARMSTRONG, George 20* (B) (175)
ARMSTRONG, Henry 21* (368)
ARMSTRONG, J. 30 (m) (B) (458)
ARMSTRONG, J. H. 26 (m) (B) (216)
ARMSTRONG, Lasslie 25 (m)* (175)
ARMSTRONG, Patsy 53* (B) (161)
ARMSTRONG, Ridly 34 (f)* (163)
ARMSTRONG, Sandy 55 (m) (B) (169)
ARMSTRONG, Sarah 24* (B) (169)
ARMSTRONG, Susan 55* (B) (171)
ARMSTRONG, T.? 20 (m)* (B) (499)
ARMSTRONG, Virginia 20* (163)
ARNOLD, Jim 23 (B) (256)
ARROWOOD, M.? 23 (m)* (501)
ARTIN?, Wm. 56?* (328)
ARTISON, Arrey 28 (m)* (B) (356)
ARTISON, Marion 38 (B) (353)
ARTISON, Noah 72 (B) (356)
ARWOD, Charles 13* (232)
ARWOOD, John C. 28, (253)
ARWOOD, Vance E. 20* (232)
AR____, _____ 62 (f)* (B) (242)
ASCUE, Edmond 65* (B) (243)

1

ASCUE, Sam 21 (m)* (B) (478)
ASHFORD, H. 72 (m), (472)
ASKEN, Richard 27* (B) (425)
ASKEW, B. F. 40 (m)* (302)
ASKEW, B. R. 37 (m) (B) (368)
ASKEW, George 21 (B) (434)
ASKEW, Isaac 45 (m) (B) (303)
ASKEW, Wm. 54* (B) (425)
ASKEW, ____ __ (m) (425)
ASKEW?, Dolley 44 (f)* (B) (302)
ATKINS, Dave 50* (B) (481)
ATKINS, George W. 7?* (B) (178)
ATKINS, James 28 (B) (451)
ATKINS, John 40 (B) (298)
ATKINS, Sam 36 (B) (217)
ATKINS, Thomas 22* (B) (177)
ATKINSON, B. F. 51 (m)* (487)
ATKINSON, R. D. 30 (m), (185)
AULDRIDGE, Henrietta 22 (B) (162)
AUSTIN, Charlie 25 (B) (222)
AUSTIN, Minor 32* (B) (188)
AVANT?, Jo 50 (m) (B) (496)
AVERETT, P. H. 60 (f), (220)
AVERITTE, G. T. 30 (m), (329)
AVERITTE, Wiley D. 24* (197)
AVERITTE, Wm. 30* (198)
AVERY, Jere 23 (m)* (B) (351)
A___, Caledonia 18* (B) (351)
A____, W. 34 (m) (B) (321)
A_____, Alex jr. 27 (B) (192)
BABB, John 31 (B) (361)
BAGBY, Jack 30 (B) (382)
BAGBY, Matilda 60 (B) (382)
BAGLAND, Step__ 100 (m)* (B) (248)
BAIL, Frank 28 (B) (220)
BAILEE, Hiram 44, (432)
BAILESS, Samuel 20* (432)
BAILEY, Bettie 15* (B) (349)
BAILEY, Catherine 29 (B) (190)
BAILEY, Eliza 56* (B) (163)
BAILEY, Finkler 35 (m)* (346)
BAILEY, Fred 55* (B) (279)
BAILEY, George 26* (B) (431)
BAILEY, Georgia 34?* (232)
BAILEY, Henry __ (B) (190)
BAILEY, John 28, (329)
BAILEY, John 41 (B) (491)
BAILEY, John W. 25* (168)
BAILEY, Leanna 70* (B) (231)
BAILEY, Lewis 34 (B) (347)
BAILEY, Madison 24 (B) (431)
BAILEY, Richard 21 (B) (347)
BAILEY, Singleton 51* (B) (348)
BAILEY, Sol 45* (B) (288)
BAILEY, Thomas 30 (B) (430)
BAILEY, Tony 28 (B) (184)
BAILEY, Wm. 24, (185)
BAILY, Albert 48 (B) (246)
BAILY, John G. 36* (297)
BAILY, Joseph 21 (B) (490)
BAILY, Richard 40 (B) (436)
BAILY, Sarah J. 24* (183)
BAIRD, Henry 22 (B) (495)
BAIRD, Jake 29 (B) (487)
BAIRD, Jim? 60 (B) (488)
BAIRD, Mary 82* (B) (495)
BAIRD, Pheb.? 45 (f)* (B) (202)

BAIRD, R. 15 (m)* (B) (488)
BAIRD, R. H. 47 (m), (487)
BAIRD, West 22?* (B) (193)
BAIRD, Wiley 30 (B) (193)
BAIRD?, H. 50 (f) (B) (486)
BAIRD?, Moses 52 (B) (501)
BAKER, Amy? 50* (B) (167)
BAKER, Henry 22* (167)
BAKER, J. F. 39 (m)* (315)
BAKER, Jones 80 (B) (471)
BAKER, Nellie 89* (291)
BAKER, Samuel 25* (B) (402)
BAKER, Samuel 50 (B) (401)
BAKER, Simon 56? (B) (229)
BAKER, Tomas 43 (B) (297)
BALDWIN, E. 48 (m)* (B) (264)
BALDWIN, Edder 25 (m)* (431)
BALDWIN, Feriby 12 (m)* (B) (263)
BALDWIN, Green? 20* (B) (431)
BALDWIN, Julia 50, (427)
BALDWIN, Nelson 45 (B) (263)
BALDWIN, Ruseel 26* (449)
BALDWIN, Thos. 50 (B) (450)
BALDWIN, Washington 35 (B) (363)
BALDWIN, Will 28 (B) (450)
BALDWYN, Gaston 27, (426)
BALEY, J. 83 (f)* (B) (492)
BALEY, Wm. T. 28* (406)
BALIE, Fannie 40 (B) (449)
BALL?, Pirtle 22 (m)* (B) (208)
BALLARD, Ed 26 (B) (215)
BALLARD, George 33, (273)
BALLARD, Horatio 24* (389)
BALLARD, Retter 7 (f)* (B) (217)
BALLARD, Toney 60* (B) (278)
BALLARD, Wm. 36, (198)
BALLEW, Margaret 45 (B) (435)
BALTHROP, Elbert 50, (195)
BALY, Tony 28* (B) (490)
BAN?, Ned 59 (B) (424)
BANE, R. E. 40 (f)* (315)
BANKS, Alexander 26* (B) (206)
BANKS, Duncan 29* (B) (367)
BANKS, Joseph 35 (B) (256)
BANKS, Nancy 9* (B) (267)
BANKS, Ransom 48* (B) (446)
BANKS, Walker 20* (B) (377)
BANKS, Will 12* (B) (206)
BARBER, Frank 21 (B) (375)
BARBER, George 29* (B) (425)
BARBER, James 30 (B) (425)
BARBER, John 45* (B) (166)
BARD, Amsted 26 (B) (486)
BARD, Simon 24* (B) (494)
BARDEN, Wm. 21* (276)
BARDEW?, James? __ (B) (297)
BARKER, Clary 65 (f)* (164)
BARLY, Sophia 38 (B) (244)
BARNES, Jeremiah 30 (B) (365)
BARNETT, Wilson 47* (417)
BARNS, Ishan 35 (m) (B) (474)
BARNWELL, Ben F. 52, (369)
BARRET, Al_a 27 (m)* (B) (437)
BARRET, Henry 17* (B) (435)
BARRETT, Wm. 25 (B) (435)
BARRETTE, Ben 45 (B) (484)
BARRINGER, Calvin 33* (437)

BARRON, Albert 27 (B) (405)
BARROUS, J. F. 21 (m)* (480)
BARROW, Edward 16* (B) (346)
BARROW, W. _. 40 (m), (326)
BARROWS, Benjamin F. 48* (359)
BARTLETT, Rebecca E. 46* (351)
BARTLETTE, Manuel 60 (B) (322)
BARTON, James 20* (253)
BASKERVILLE, Dick 60* (B) (225)
BASKERVILLE, George 33* (231)
BASKERVILLE, Gus 29 (B) (231)
BASKERVILLE, Henry 36* (B) (231)
BASKERVILLE, John 60 (B) (231)
BASKERVILLE, Johnson 46 (B) (231)
BASKERVILLE, Lilly 85* (B) (225)
BASKERVILLE, Richard 36 (B) (231)
BASKERVILLE, Robert 34* (B) (232)
BASKEVILLE?, Mirtle? 50* (B) (264)
BASLEY, Lucy 8* (B) (348)
BASS, James 27 (B) (362)
BASS, Jerry 52* (B) (478)
BASS, Mary J. 31, (393)
BASSENGALE, C. 35 (m)* (293)
BATEMAN, John 57, (437)
BATES, Alford 23 (B) (374)
BATES, Fannie 25* (B) (375)
BATES, Frank 70 (B) (376)
BATES, Henry 21 (B) (374)
BATES, Tip 19 (m)* (B) (375)
BATS, E. 8 (f)* (B) (500)
BATTLE, Hester 35* (B) (284)
BATTLE, J. B. 42 (m) (B) (460)
BATTLES, Andrew 18* (B) (326)
BATTLES, Ben 23 (B) (326)
BATTLES, Easter 20* (B) (341)
BATTS, A. W. 35 (m), (484)
BAUGH, Edward 25 (B) (360)
BAUGH, John 40, (414)
BAUGH, John 43 (B) (482)
BAUGH, ____ 60 (f)* (B) (422)
BAXTER, Nathaniel 58, (407)
BAXTER, W. S. 36 (m)* (482)
BAXTER?, Joe 35* (B) (318)
BAXTER?, ____ 30 (m) (B) (172)
BAYLAN, Bettie 40* (B) (265)
BAYLEY, Jake 20* (B) (466)
BAYLEY, Tom 25* (B) (468)
BAYLEY, Wash 30* (B) (389)
BAYLON, Dave 38* (B) (264)
BAYLON, Gey? 15 (m)* (B) (265)
BAYLON?, Jane 25? (B) (264)
BEAL, Enoch 44* (B) (440)
BEAL, T. L. 41 (m)* (478)
BEAL, Wm. 45, (478)
BEAMAN, Scott 35 (B) (475)
BEAN, Sim 31 (B) (300)
BEARD, Alex 25* (B) (372)
BEARD, Annis 40 (f)* (B) (292)

BEARD, Ellen 22* (B) (337)
BEARD, JAck 39 (B) (292)
BEARD, Jack 30, (411)
BEARD, John 60, (411)
BEARD, Lewis 20* (B) (257)
BEASLEY, Amy 30* (B) (290)
BEASLEY, Henry 40, (284)
BEASLEY, Issom 59, (279)
BEASLEY, James 45 (B) (336)
BEASLEY, James 48 (B) (405)
BEASLEY, James D. 84* (387)
BEASLEY, John 17* (B) (473)
BEASLEY, Lonzo 26 (m)* (B) (284)
BEASLEY, Lula 14* (B) (284)
BEASLEY, Reuben 29 (B) (255)
BEASLEY, Ruben 30 (B) (274)
BEASLEY, Sam 63 (B) (255)
BEASLEY, Sam 63 (B) (276)
BEASLEY, Scott 20* (B) (284)
BEASLEY, Thos. J. 38, (279)
BEASLEY, Wm. 20* (B) (317)
BEASLEY, Wm. 20* (B) (342)
BEASLY, George 71, (442)
BEASLY, J. 50 (m)* (B) (499)
BEASLY, Jack 24* (B) (496)
BEASLY, Jack 35 (B) (465)
BEASLY, Sarah 14* (B) (256)
BEASON, Koley 30 (m) (B) (384)
BEAVERS, Clabe 55* (B) (294)
BEAVERS, Ellen 50 (B) (276)
BEAVERS, Florence 30* (B) (285)
BEAVERS, Geo. 27, (277)
BEAVERS, S. 67 (m)* (278)
BEAVERS, Thos. 25* (277)
BECK, Julea 31 (B) (445)
BECK, Peter 30 (B) (338)
BECKHAM, J. 65 (m), (268)
BEDAULT?, Moses 16* (B) (335)
BEDAUX, Tom 9* (B) (320)
BEDFORD, John 42* (368)
BEDIFORD, Clark 27, (432)
BELFORD, Manerva 58* (B) (339)
BELGER, Rosa 45 (B) (339)
BELK, Lucius 24, (306)
BELL, Abraham 59, (305)
BELL, Anderson 46* (B) (460)
BELL, Boshel 22 (m) (B) (391)
BELL, Ellis 15* (B) (249)
BELL, Frank 28 (B) (359)
BELL, George 60 (B) (391)
BELL, Giles 47 (B) (460)
BELL, Gloster 51 (B) (207)
BELL, Gracy 80 (B) (460)
BELL, J. K. P. 36 (m), (331)
BELL, Jas. 20 (B) (497)
BELL, John 36 (B) (163)
BELL, Lee 4 (f), (468)
BELL, Lizza 28* (B) (498)
BELL, Lucy 39?* (B) (387)
BELL, Millie 25 (f) (B) (471)
BELL, Sallie 50 (B) (460)
BELL, Spencer 35 (B) (497)
BELL, Thomas 25 (B) (456)
BELL, Wallace 48 (B) (162)
BELL, Wm. A. 44* (167)
BELT, Hanna 38* (B) (422)
BENNETT, Eugene 32, (433)
BENNETT, Jerry 72 (m), (477)

2

BENNETT, Joseph 26* (B) (352)
BENNETT, Noel 30, (481)
BENNETT, Z. L. 78 (m)* (488)
BENSON, James 61* (432)
BENSON, Jery 21 (m)* (B) (393)
BENSON, John 32 (B) (281)
BENSON, Samuel 21* (B) (374)
BENSON, Simon 27 (B) (177)
BENTLEY, Charles 40* (B) (184)
BENTON, J. 29 (m)* (B) (498)
BENTON, St.? 60 (m) (B) (498)
BENY, James 30* (B) (309)
BERKINS, Lucy 18* (B) (414)
BERRY, Andy 40 (B) (420)
BERRY, Emily 41* (B) (263)
BERRY, Hannah 25* (B) (174)
BERRY, James 50* (B) (366)
BERRY, Jefferson 6* (B) (310)
BERRY, Lorson? 59 (m) (B) (453)
BERRY, Samuel 27* (B) (437)
BERY, Abe 55* (373)
BERY, Joe 26* (B) (437)
BESS, Wm. 35 (B) (288)
BESTEDER, Ben 53* (B) (382)
BETTIS, JAckson? 50 (B) (464)
BEUMAN?, John 33* (B) (433)
BIARD?, Sallie 60 (B) (463)
BIAS?, Sam 55 (B) (463)
BIBB, Tom 20* (B) (405)
BIGGERS, JAmes 32* (281)
BIGGERS, John W. 35* (287)
BIGGS, Jack 40 (B) (356)
BILBUGLEY, Lucius 25 (B) (264)
BILLINGLY, Drawford 24* (B) (260)
BILLINGLY, Florance 25 (m) (B) (232)
BILLINGLY, Frank 54 (B) (233)
BILLINGLY, Ransom 48 (B) (232)
BILLINGSLY, Tucker 60 (B) (260)
BILLS, Felix 40 (B) (458)
BINAM, Tom 30 (B) (403)
BING, Edward 34, (382)
BING, George 63, (382)
BIOUS?, Joe 60 (B) (480)
BIRD, Albert 32 (B) (283)
BIRD, Dennis 30* (B) (282)
BIRD, Harry 35 (B) (282)
BIRD, Louis 26 (B) (282)
BIRD, W. M. 51 (m), (474)
BIRD?, B. F. 43 (m)* (315)
BIRDING, Samuel 31* (299)
BIRDSONG, Sam 55 (B) (258)
BISHOP, Chaney 20 (f) (B) (363)
BISHOP, Edd 24 (B) (341)
BISHOP, Emma 30* (B) (479)
BISHOP, Henry 21 (B) (210)
BISHOP, Horace 11* (B) (270)
BISHOP, Jerey 63 (m) (B) (210)
BISHOP, Sally 28* (B) (216)
BISHOP, W. J. 54 (m), (478)
BISHOP, Willis 47 (B) (341)
BISMAN?, Henry 80* (324)
BIVENS?, Sofia 30* (160)
BLACK, Aaron 35* (B) (447)
BLACK, Dinah 40 (B) (430)
BLACK, Harry 70? (B) (246)
BLACK, Hogan 60* (B) (475)
BLACK, Ida 15* (B) (460)

BLACK, John 39* (370)
BLACK, John M. 43, (370)
BLACK, Jones 24, (471)
BLACK, Julian 50 (m)* (B) (443)
BLACK, Mary 60* (291)
BLACK, Sallie 50* (B) (430)
BLACK, Winfield 26, (198)
BLACKMAN, Gober 30 (m) (B) (373)
BLACKWELL, Peter 75 (B) (216)
BLADES, Mary 48? (B) (167)
BLADES, Wm. 29 (B) (181)
BLADES?, Willie 13 (m)* (B) (186)
BLADLEY, Jim 20* (B) (294)
BLAIN, Alexander M. 26, (365)
BLAIN, Dick 32 (B) (359)
BLAIN, Nathaniel 60, (365)
BLAIN, Wm. N. 24, (364)
BLAIR, Columbia 40 (f) (B) (255?)
BLAKE, Edmond 52 (B) (387)
BLAKE, Eliza 65* (163)
BLAKE, W. _. 22? (m)* (324)
BLAKELY, Fabie 35 (f)* (B) (388)
BLAKEMORE, Henry 21* (B) (212)
BLAND, Amy 50* (278)
BLAND, Chas. 57, (278)
BLAND, Felix 45* (B) (285)
BLAND, Lucius 49* (B) (282)
BLAND, Lucy 75* (B) (273)
BLAND, M. 19 (m)* (B) (497)
BLAND, Riley 53 (B) (293)
BLAND?, Zack 39?* (B) (270)
BLANE, Lillie 50 (B) (395)
BLANKENSHIP, Eli 64, (176)
BLANTON, Castille 43 (m)* (422)
BLAYDES, Benn? 55 (m) (B) (308)
BLAYDES, Wm. 38* (B) (307)
BLEDSOE, Aggie 38 (f)* (280)
BLEDSOE, C. 20 (f)* (B) (307)
BLEDSOE, Edd 28 (B) (329)
BLEVIN, Sam 32 (B) (171)
BLOCK, Biddie 80 (f)* (B) (467)
BLOCK, Jacob 37* (268)
BLOUND, Jack 53 (B) (355)
BLOUNT, Jesse 55 (B) (357)
BLR, Alice 18* (204)
BLUNT, Louis 40 (B) (405)
BL_____, Harriet 40* (B) (329)
BOALS, John 80 (B) (193)
BOALS?, A. O. 27 (m)* (466)
BOATS?, John W. 70, (181)
BOBBETT, Coleman 25 (B) (350)
BOBBETT, Florence 6* (414)
BOBBITT, A. J. 22 (m), (478)
BOBBITT, Anna D. 4* (406)
BOBBITT, Arthur C. 10* (345)
BOBBITT, Cornelia 16* (B) (359)
BOBBITT, Geo. Ann 15* (B) (485)
BOBBITT, John G. 19* (406)
BOBBITT, Louis C. 30, (406)
BOBBITT, Sallie O. 35, (411)
BOBBITT, Thomas H. 13* (411)
BOBBITTE, J. G. 25 (m)* (481)

BOBO, J. W. 55 (m)* (285)
BODO_, Sallie 40* (B) (166)
BODY, Sanford 28* (B) (298)
BOGGS, Samuel 37* (191)
BOLDEN, Wm. 46 (B) (464)
BOLDIN, John 30 (B) (451)
BOLDS, Wash 12* (B) (213)
BOLDWIN, Tim 41 (B) (456)
BOLES, Jane 16* (B) (441)
BOLETER?, Jerry 22* (B) (426)
BOLFORD?, Balam 25 (m) (B) (238)
BOLIN, Albert 25* (B) (246)
BOLIN, Dina 69* (B) (250)
BOLIN, Mathew 25* (B) (247)
BOLIN, Shaderic 65* (B) (247)
BOLIN, Tempy 29 (f)* (B) (240)
BOLIN, Wren 31* (B) (251)
BOLING, Andrew 53 (B) (421)
BOLING, Mary 30* (B) (426)
BOLING, Ned 28 (B) (238)
BOLING, Patience 37 (B) (240)
BOLING, Thomas 56, (424)
BOLTON, Canda 8* (B) (397)
BOLTON, John 22 (B) (397)
BOLTON, Jordan 58 (B) (397)
BOMAN, Julie 25* (B) (167)
BOMAR, Jack 12* (299)
BOMAR, Wm. 26* (299)
BOMEN, B. B. 27 (m)* (325)
BOND, Harriet 10* (B) (269)
BOND, Mary F. 61* (350)
BOND, _____ 73 (m), (195)
BONDERANT, R. 24 (m), (301)
BONDURANT, J. 46 (m), (301)
BONDURANT, V. 49 (m) (B) (298)
BONDURANT, __ 30 (f)* (296)
BONE, Champ 18* (305)
BONE, Dudly 23* (B) (240)
BONE, George 72* (B) (240)
BONE, Louis 42* (B) (240)
BONE?, Charlotte 77* (B) (300)
BONE?, Henry 50 (B) (298)
BONNAR?, Douglas 58* (460)
BONNER, Colmon 55* (B) (229)
BONNER, Henry 25 (B) (232)
BONNER, Stpehen? 23* (B) (265)
BONNER, Tom 25* (B) (263)
BONNER, W. T. 10 (m)* (161)
BONURANT, P. M. 51 (m), (302)
BOOK, Harriett 60 (B) (427)
BOOKER, Alex 23 (B) (276)
BOOKER, Elijah __* (B) (198)
BOOKER, G__ 36 (m) (B) (332)
BOOKER, John 45* (B) (348)
BOOKER, Lucinda 17* (B) (197)
BOOKER, Lydia 50* (B) (194)
BOOKER, Thos. 30 (B) (276)
BOOKOUT?, John? 28, (494)
BOON, Edward? 60* (B) (215)
BOON, James 25 (B) (481)
BOON, Ransom? 21* (B) (234)
BOON?, Wash 45 (B) (393)
BOONE, Jonas 25 (B) (257)
BOONE, Yancey 20* (B) (353)
BOOTHE, John 25, (490)
BOOTHE, Wm. 33, (488)
BORDEAUX, Andy 54* (B) (320)

BORDEAUX, Malinda 16* (B) (320)
BORDING?, J. G. 53 (m), (307)
BOREGARD, John 35 (B) (451)
BORRAN, Thomas 65* (306)
BORRAN, Thomas jr. 28* (306)
BOSS, George 23 (B) (417)
BOSS, Lucy 15* (187)
BOSTICK, G.? 50 (m)* (B) (492)
BOSTICK, John 66* (183)
BOSTICK, Lane 58 (m)* (489)
BOSTICK, Mary J. 48* (346)
BOSWELL, Albert D. 32, (412)
BOSWELL, Alf 20 (B) (329)
BOSWELL, Dickson S. 66, (412)
BOSWELL, Easter 8 (f)* (B) (330)
BOSWELL, Fannie 4* (B) (395)
BOSWELL, James S. 28, (406)
BOSWELL, Lucy 50, (394)
BOSWELL, Rebecca 6* (B) (399)
BOSWELL, Simon? 49 (B) (331)
BOSWELL, Thomas 20, (406)
BOSWELL, Thomas L. 64* (406)
BOSWELL, Winston 25 (B) (346)
BOSWELL, Wm. 30 (B) (403)
BOTS, Edmon 76 (B) (470)
BOTTLE, Bettie 28* (305)
BOTTS, Mary 45 (B) (439)
BOUNDS, Dick 35* (B) (403)
BOUNDS, J. 13 (f)* (476)
BOUNDS, P. 34 (f), (415)
BOUNDS, Tilmon 40* (B) (414)
BOURDEAUX, T. 78? (f)* (331)
BOWDEN, Ad 20 (f)* (344)
BOWDEN, Ad 21 (f)* (316)
BOWDEN, Carrie? 10* (254)
BOWDEN, Sam 16?* (268)
BOWEN?, Henry 53* (B) (160)
BOWERS, Ella 26* (B) (311)
BOWERS, Felix 31* (B) (311)
BOWERS, Henry 33* (B) (309)
BOWERS, L. 23 (m)* (B) (190)
BOWERS, Lucy 77* (B) (192)
BOWERS, Luke __ (B) (179)
BOWERS, Marge 22 (m)* (B) (347)
BOWERS, Miles 18* (B) (191)
BOWERS, Owen 53 (B) (192)
BOWERS, Rebecka 65* (B) (483)
BOWERS, Sally 23 (B) (192)
BOWERS, Sarah 35* (B) (186)
BOWERS?, Rebecca 49?* (B) (166)
BOWLEN, Calvin 35 (B) (379)
BOWLEN, Mit 30 (m) (B) (379)
BOWLEN, Stephen 45 (B) (379)
BOWLES, Carrie 40* (B) (208)
BOWLES, G.? D. 70 (m), (335)
BOWLES, M. T. 35 (m), (335)
BOWLES, Wiley 46 (B) (208)
BOWLING, Jery 20 (m)* (B) (369)
BOWLING, ___dy W. 37 (m), (385)
BOWLS, Andrew 23* (B) (209)
BOWLS, D. F. 33 (m), (305)
BOWLS, Jef 20* (B) (209)
BOWLS, Nelson 45* (B) (277)
BOWLS, Wm. 23* (305)

3

BOWMAN, Joe 38?, (272)
BOYACAN, Pompy 74* (B) (212)
BOYAD, S. C. 33 (f)* (213)
BOYD, A. 20 (m)* (B) (311)
BOYD, Alfred 17* (B) (367)
BOYD, Alfred 8/12* (B) (267)
BOYD, Amy 12* (B) (186)
BOYD, Anna 40 (B) (405)
BOYD, Betsey 50* (B) (255?)
BOYD, Bettie 75?* (B) (380)
BOYD, Charles 24 (B) (297)
BOYD, Edmund 21 (B) (200)
BOYD, Eliza 42* (B) (289)
BOYD, Eliza 50, (169)
BOYD, Elizabeth 14* (315)
BOYD, Elizabeth 75, (183)
BOYD, Henry 16* (B) (167)
BOYD, John 34 (B) (256)
BOYD, John W. 22? (B) (300)
BOYD, Julia 58* (163)
BOYD, Lewis 26 (B) (228)
BOYD, M. A. 15 (f)* (B) (342)
BOYD, MAttie W. 19 (f)* (234)
BOYD, Martin 45* (B) (344)
BOYD, Martin 51?* (B) (316)
BOYD, Mit 15 (f)* (B) (317)
BOYD, Rasmus 56* (B) (240)
BOYD, Richard 22* (B) (242)
BOYD, Robert 20 (B) (300)
BOYD, Sam 27? (B) (296)
BOYD, Tom 16 (B) (323)
BOYD, W. H. 23 (m)* (477)
BOYD, Wm. H. 34, (184)
BOYD, ____ 2 (m)* (B) (338)
BOYD, ____ 27 (m)* (B) (311)
BOYD, ____ 39 (m), (201)
BOYD, __ayden 29 (m)* (183)
BOYD?, Sallie 50 (B) (240)
BOYD?, Winnie 60* (B) (235)
BOYED, Addie? _* (492)
BOYED, Alaxan 31 (m)* (B) (491)
BOYED, B. K. 41 (m), (490)
BOYED, Jess 38 (m)* (B) (493)
BOYLAND, Americus? 55 (m)* (B) (227)
BOYLAND, Elliot 10* (B) (230)
BOYLAND, Emily 30 (B) (227)
BOYLAND, George 46 (B) (226)
BOYLAND, Isaiah 26 (B) (227)
BOYLAND, Ivison 56* (B) (226)
BOYLAND, Jim 2* (B) (228)
BOYLAND, Jim 22 (B) (230)
BOYLAND, Manned? 30 (f) (B) (227)
BOYLAND, Millie 50* (B) (230)
BOYLAND, Ness 60 (m) (B) (227)
BOYLAND, Weldond E. 48 (m)* (226)
BOYLAND, Wm. 23* (B) (226)
BOYLE, Reuben 75* (B) (202)
BOYLE, Rogers 33 (B) (193)
BO____, An 37 (f)* (495)
BRACKEN, Charles 55 (B) (164)
BRACKEN, David 54 (B) (199)
BRACKEN, George 46 (B) (167)
BRACKEN, James 39 (B) (178)
BRACKEN, Samuel 31* (187)
BRACKEN, Tom 38 (B) (210)

BRACKIN, JErry 25 (m)* (B) (229)
BRACKIN, Jerry 51 (B) (243)
BRADEN, B. P. 55 (m), (281)
BRADEN, Dove 28 (m)* (B) (269)
BRADEN, Fanny 30* (B) (276)
BRADEN, Frank 35* (B) (275)
BRADEN, Geo. 30* (B) (286)
BRADEN, JAs. P. 32* (287)
BRADEN, Jack 22 (B) (269)
BRADEN, Jos. P. 72* (287)
BRADEN, Maria 65* (B) (273)
BRADEN, Mat 55 (m)* (B) (269)
BRADEN, Ruben 22* (B) (284)
BRADFORD, Chris 37 (B) (420)
BRADFORD, Louisa 15* (B) (312)
BRADFORD, P. P. 19 (m)* (302)
BRADSHER, R. H. 66 (m)* (319)
BRADSHER, Steve? 39 (m), (319)
BRADY, Benn 26 (B) (384)
BRADY, Green 45* (B) (384)
BRAGG, Anna 16* (B) (360)
BRAIS?, Alexander 35* (B) (312)
BRAME, Charles 23?* (426)
BRANBERRY, _. L. 43 (m), (406)
BRANCH, A. 19 (m) (B) (500)
BRANCH, Bell 22, (441)
BRANCH, Ben 22 (B) (473)
BRANCH, David 68 (B) (171)
BRANCH, Etham? 27 (m)* (288)
BRANCH, George 22* (B) (296)
BRANCH, George 25 (B) (472)
BRANCH, Jack 40 (B) (473)
BRANCH, Margrate 30 (B) (249)
BRANCH, Nelson 25 (B) (445)
BRANCH, R. 22 (m)* (B) (500)
BRANCH, Rose 19* (B) (500)
BRANCH, T. J. 44 (m)* (467)
BRANCH, Walter 5* (B) (366)
BRANCH, Wm. 30 (B) (456)
BRANCH, ____ 46 (m)* (B) (418)
BRANDON, Wm. 52, (244)
BRANNAN, Alex 30* (190)
BRANNAN, Hue 17* (331)
BRANNON, Geo. 17* (191)
BRANSCOMB, A. 2 (f)* (B) (500)
BRANSCOMBE, Mack? 25* (B) (448)
BRANSCOMBE, Mark 30 (B) (452)
BRANSCOMBE, Mic? 55 (m) (B) (452)
BRANSKOMB, James 23 (B) (459)
BRANT?, Henry 14* (B) (419)
BRAODNOY, Sarah 40 (B) (281)
BRAODWAY?, A. 53 (m) (B) (269)
BRASHER, Linda 28* (B) (434)
BRASWELL, Bart 21* (B) (310)
BRASWELL, Eli 32 (B) (351)
BRASWELL, J. F. 42 (m)* (304)
BRASWELL, T.? 19 (f)* (B) (310)
BRASWELL, W. M. 45 (m)* (B) (305)

BRATCHER, J. 50 (m)* (B) (303)
BRATTOCK, Alice 28* (B) (435)
BRAXTER, Cary 47* (B) (436)
BRESHURS, Jack 36, (419)
BREWER, Charles 45* (B) (366)
BREWER, Cilvia 16 (f)* (B) (259)
BREWER, Clara 18* (B) (193)
BREWER, David 50 (B) (261)
BREWER, Elisha 50 (B) (495)
BREWER, James 50 (B) (292)
BREWER, James jr. 21 (B) (284)
BREWER, K. 63 (m)* (B) (259)
BREWER, Wm. 53* (B) (241)
BREWER?, Deed 22 (m) (B) (263)
BREWER?, Henry 54* (B) (259)
BREWER?, K. 35 (m) (B) (259)
BREWER?, Matthew __ (B) (259)
BREWSTER, Ed 55 (B) (415)
BRIDGES, York 90 (B) (326)
BRIDGETT, George 40 (B) (455)
BRIDGEWATER, Jack 22 (B) (171)
BRIDGEWATER, NElson 29 (B) (176)
BRIERS, Wint 32 (m) (B) (278)
BRIGGS, Peter 62 (B) (430)
BRIGS, Henry 22* (B) (431)
BRIMLY, Tom 45* (B) (399)
BRINKLY, Thos. W. 37* (196)
BRINLEY, Lou 9 (f)* (B) (382)
BRITMAN, Littie 27 (f)* (B) (380)
BRITMAN, Louis 60* (B) (382)
BRITT, Thomas 26* (315)
BRITTON, Wm. E. 35, (202)
BROADNER, Israel 28 (B) (175)
BROADNOY, Dick 45 (B) (289)
BROADNOY, Martin __ (B) (289)
BROADNOY?, Jim 53 (B) (271)
BROADNOY?, Wilson 22* (B) (270)
BROADWAY, Frank 60* (269)
BROCHIN, Robert 21 (B) (423)
BROCK, John 60, (376)
BROCK, Wm. 21* (417)
BROCK, Wm. 31, (410)
BROCK, Young 57, (417)
BROCK?, Henry 24 (B) (443)
BROCK?, Martha 7?* (B) (419)
BRODEN, Colbert 28* (B) (268)
BRODEN, Horace 21* (B) (268)
BRODLE, B. B. 30 (m)* (300)
BROGDON?, Emeline 3_ (B) (213)
BROILS, Ephrum 27* (B) (332)
BROILS, Nancy 60* (B) (323)
BROILS, ____ 34 (m) (B) (325)
BROM, Laura 14* (B) (316)
BROMLEY?, A. J. 65 (m), (476)
BRONSON, Minnia 9* (B) (162)
BROOKE, Wm. 30* (433)
BROOKS, Albert 38* (B) (434)
BROOKS, Arch 40 (B) (365)
BROOKS, Calami? 27 (m) (B) (161)
BROOKS, Edwin 51 (B) (197)
BROOKS, Elizabeth 77, (389)
BROOKS, John 21?* (B) (164)
BROOKS, Joseph 44* (B) (199)
BROOKS, Joseph 50 (B) (452)

BROOKS, Mollie 10* (B) (280)
BROOKS, Topsie 24 (f)* (B) (340)
BROOKS, Vandy 12 (m)* (392)
BROOM, Anna 15* (B) (323)
BROOM, Britt 38 (B) (308)
BROOM, Hannie? 16 (f)* (322)
BROOM, Julious 28 (B) (323)
BROOM, Peter 4_* (323)
BROOM, Susan 50 (B) (384)
BROOM, W. D. 49 (m)* (315)
BROOM?, Thomas 53* (279)
BROOMFIELD, John 50 (B) (273)
BROOMFIELD, Lizzie 11* (B) (273)
BROOMFIELD, Taylor 27 (B) (283)
BROOTTER?, Charles 40* (B) (483)
BROWER?, Wm. 27 (B) (445)
BROWN, Aaron 25* (B) (178)
BROWN, Alfred W. 30* (349)
BROWN, America 25, (456)
BROWN, Belton 29 (B) (290)
BROWN, Charles 24 (B) (353)
BROWN, Charley 27* (456)
BROWN, Collin 25* (B) (345)
BROWN, Cornelia 14* (B) (166)
BROWN, Daniel 45* (B) (353)
BROWN, Delia 25* (B) (470)
BROWN, Dick 30* (B) (295)
BROWN, Ed 36 (B) (282)
BROWN, Edmond 35* (B) (282)
BROWN, Edward 24* (B) (426)
BROWN, El 9 (f)* (B) (218)
BROWN, Ellen 28* (B) (424)
BROWN, Ely 28* (B) (340)
BROWN, Emanuel 15* (B) (187)
BROWN, Emily 42* (B) (434)
BROWN, George 28 (B) (362)
BROWN, George 32* (B) (355)
BROWN, Grandison 29* (B) (261)
BROWN, H. A. 18 (f)* (328)
BROWN, HArriett 68* (B) (231)
BROWN, Hardy 56* (B) (352)
BROWN, Harry 30 (B) (234)
BROWN, Isaiah? 35* (B) (271)
BROWN, JAmes 28* (469)
BROWN, James 27 (B) (469)
BROWN, James 30 (B) (474)
BROWN, Jane 40* (B) (447)
BROWN, Jeruselem 39 (f)* (B) (167)
BROWN, Jessee 30 (m) (B) (187)
BROWN, Jim 30* (B) (346)
BROWN, Jim? 21* (B) (267)
BROWN, Joe 48 (B) (257)
BROWN, John 11* (B) (374)
BROWN, John 12* (B) (390)
BROWN, John 13* (B) (352)
BROWN, John 21 (B) (162)
BROWN, John 30 (B) (375)
BROWN, John 35?, (250)
BROWN, John 37* (B) (394)
BROWN, John 40* (432)
BROWN, John 54* (B) (263)
BROWN, John B. 56* (B) (167)
BROWN, John M. 32, (407)
BROWN, John W. 31* (246)
BROWN, John jr. 26* (B) (168)

BROWN, Joseph 35 (B) (364)
BROWN, Julia A. 50 (B) (405)
BROWN, Laura 14* (344)
BROWN, Lindsy 58 (m) (B) (227)
BROWN, Lucinda C. 59* (349)
BROWN, Lucy 23 (B) (166)
BROWN, MAndy 75* (B) (479)
BROWN, Malinda 23? (B) (200)
BROWN, Martha 31* (B) (167)
BROWN, Mary 17* (495)
BROWN, Mary 50* (B) (461)
BROWN, Mill 27* (B) (321)
BROWN, Milly 75* (B) (355)
BROWN, Monroe 50* (B) (367)
BROWN, Napoleon 25* (B) (172)
BROWN, Nathaniel 4_ (B) (297)
BROWN, Paul 57* (B) (164)
BROWN, Pricilla 70* (226)
BROWN, Queen 25 (B) (359)
BROWN, Ransom 28 (B) (178)
BROWN, Ridly 27 (B) (312)
BROWN, Robert 22* (B) (397)
BROWN, Robt. 25* (B) (165)
BROWN, Rosanna 27* (B) (177)
BROWN, Sallie 17* (B) (270)
BROWN, Sam 60* (B) (270)
BROWN, Squire 53 (B) (161)
BROWN, Thomas 39, (231)
BROWN, W. 33 (m)* (B) (266)
BROWN, Willie 19 (B) (405)
BROWN, Willie 7 (m)* (B) (420)
BROWN, Willis 27 (B) (438)
BROWN, Wm. 21* (B) (352)
BROWN, Wm. 33, (428)
BROWN?, Wash 23* (B) (386)
BROWNE, Wash? 73 (B) (449)
BROWNING, Richard 50* (B) (423)
BROWNLEE, Adam 55 (B) (353)
BRUCE, Lizzie 22 (B) (360)
BRUMLEY, Joe 50* (B) (217)
BRUMLEY, John 25* (B) (218)
BRUMLEY, Lear 65 (f)* (B) (217)
BRUMMIT, Albert 29, (411)
BRUSTER, Martin 60* (B) (473)
BRUTEN?, John K. 37, (193)
BRYACAN?, Peter 55 (B) (215)
BRYANT, Ben 19* (223)
BRYANT, Edward 45, (192)
BRYANT, George 4_* (192)
BRYANT, Henderson 21* (B) (200)
BRYANT, James 42 (B) (192)
BRYANT, Lemma 19 (f) (B) (365)
BRYANT, MAry 25* (B) (201)
BRYANT, Mary 13* (B) (400)
BRYANT, Riley 35* (B) (168)
BRYANT, Th. 35 (m), (409)
BRYANT, Virginia 30* (191)
BRYANT, Wm. 48* (202)
BRYANT?, _____ 11 (f)* (B) (191)
BR__T, Andrew 78?, (191)
BR___T, Caroline 33? (B) (191)
BR___T, M. 24 (m) (B) (191)
BUCHANAN, John 41* (240)
BUCHANAN, Sam 35 (B) (418)
BUCK, Thomas 27* (236)

BUCKHANAN?, Tom 35* (B) (452)
BUCKLEY, MArtha 13* (277)
BUCKLEY, Wiley 40, (278)
BUCKLEY?, Joe 23, (278)
BUFORD, Austin 35 (B) (463)
BUFORD, J. C. 66 (m), (467)
BUFORD, _____ 48 (f) (B) (464)
BUGG, George 2* (B) (263)
BULL, Lizzie 35* (B) (431)
BULL, Stephen 50* (432)
BULLERD, Lizzie 25* (B) (260)
BULLOCK, Edmund 65* (B) (173)
BULLOCK, George 23 (B) (175)
BULLOCK, Isaac 50* (B) (338)
BULLOCK, John 33? (B) (201)
BULLOCK, Len 31* (200)
BULLOCK, Lewis 15?* (B) (190)
BULLOCK, Neely 40 (f)* (B) (217)
BULLOCK, Robt. S. 38, (200)
BULLOCK, _____ 20? (m)* (B) (324)
BULOCK, Roda 26* (B) (215)
BULOCK, Tom 35* (B) (210)
BULOCK?, LEwis 40* (213)
BUMPAS, Albert 28 (B) (253)
BUMPASS, Robert 19* (B) (256)
BUMPUSS, George 59* (161)
BUMPUSS, Wily? 50* (B) (338)
BURCHAM, _. D. 28 (m)* (285)
BURCHUM, J. D. 38 (m), (337)
BURDYNE, A. __ (m)* (B) (190)
BURDYNE, R. 25 (m) (B) (190)
BURFOOT, Bettie 18* (374)
BURFORD, Danel 25* (B) (208)
BURFORD, Henry _ (B) (200)
BURGES, Robert 30* (B) (378)
BURGESS, Alfred 24, (195)
BURGIS?, Willie 18 (m)* (B) (391)
BURJES?, Amsted 37 (B) (375)
BURK, Charles 46 (B) (389)
BURK, Fletcher 75 (B) (391)
BURKE, Wm. 49 (B) (353)
BURNET, Henry 55 (B) (331)
BURNETT?, J. E. 46 (m), (476)
BURNETTE, John 28 (B) (394)
BURNETTE, Lewis 28 (B) (394)
BURNETTE, Louis 30* (B) (405)
BURNS, Robert 37* (B) (376)
BUROUGH, Fed 23 (m) (B) (245)
BUROUS, Harriette 37* (B) (165)
BURRASS, Wm. 23 (B) (455)
BURRELL, Maria 50 (B) (463)
BURROW, Andrew 24 (B) (303)
BURROW, Antheny 66 (B) (310)
BURROW, Calib 32?* (B) (297)
BURROW, Ellen 50, (277)
BURROW, Fannie 16* (B) (309)
BURROW, Levy 52 (B) (311)
BURROW, Peyton 22 (B) (296)
BURROW, Robert 22* (277)
BURROW, Ruben 29* (277)
BURROW, Solomon 58 (B) (350)
BURROW, Wm. H. 27* (278)
BURRUS?, Caroline 23* (B) (170)
BURT, Eli 21, (409)
BURT, P. M. 74 (f)* (280)

BURTON, Anthony? 46 (B) (308)
BURTON, Ben 73* (B) (167)
BURTON, Chas. 25 (B) (278)
BURTON, Jim 15* (B) (295)
BURTON, Littleton 60* (B) (196)
BURTON, Louisa 32* (B) (166)
BURTON, Marthia? 63, (475)
BURTON, Thomas 47* (B) (359)
BURTON, Wm. 17* (163)
BURTON?, _____ 56 (f), (166)
BURT__, Wm. 45 (B) (251)
BUSY, West 23* (B) (414)
BUTCHER, M. 56 (m) (B) (497)
BUTH, Andrew? 26, (424)
BUTLER, Alex 19* (B) (270)
BUTLER, Charles 30 (B) (460)
BUTLER, Ed _3* (B) (290)
BUTLER, F. E. 27 (m)* (298)
BUTLER, George 37* (B) (494)
BUTLER, Susan 40 (B) (183)
BUTLER, Walter? L. 8/12* (B) (183)
BUTTERSWORTH?, Lana 21 (f)* (B) (165)
BUTTERWORTH, Leana 17* (B) (168)
BUTTLE, W. B. 24 (m), (279)
BUTTS, Danuel? 62 (m), (372)
BU_____, _____ (m)* (B) (207)
BYAR, Gradison? 28 (B) (463)
BYRD, Cicero 27 (B) (435)
BYRUM, Charles 45 (B) (356)
B___TON, Cynthia 31, (412)
B____, Edin 24 (B) (449)
B____, N. O. 26 (m), (471)
CABIN, Martha 40 (B) (179)
CABLER, Horace 36* (B) (163)
CADA?, H. 26 (m)* (B) (325)
CAGE, John 22* (B) (292)
CAIN, George 25 (B) (240)
CAIN, John 30, (441)
CAIN?, Edwin 21* (443)
CALAWAY, Susan 30* (B) (392)
CALB___, Jack _3 (B) (226)
CALDWELL, Eliza 22* (B) (400)
CALDWELL, Essick 65 (m)* (B) (340)
CALDWELL, Peter 47 (B) (186)
CALDWELL, V. C. 19 (f)* (335)
CALLAWAY, Alex 10* (B) (430)
CALLAWAY, Ben 28 (B) (287)
CALOWAY, Becca 17* (B) (233)
CAMBELL, Richmdon 51* (B) (433)
CAMP, George W. 30, (406)
CAMPBELL, Albert? 46 (B) (216)
CAMPBELL, Buck 30 (B) (448)
CAMPBELL, Ella? 21* (476)
CAMPBELL, Hary 20 (B) (216)
CAMPBELL, Mary 49* (364)
CAMPBELL, Tyson 24, (168)
CAMPBELL, W. J. 49 (m), (216)
CAMPBELL, W.? 19 (m) (B) (262)
CAMPBELL?, Emeline 35 (B) (212)
CANADA, John B. 62, (350)
CANADY, Alfred 28* (B) (457)
CANDLE?, Peter 55 (B) (335)
CANIPE, John W. 42, (179)

CANNON, Jenna 12?* (486)
CANNON, R. 29 (m)* (502)
CANNON, S. 44 (m), (496)
CANNON, _usan? 60 (f)* (B) (255?)
CANNON?, D. 17 (m)* (501)
CANON, W. J. 53 (m)* (255?)
CAPS, Juty 7 (f)* (B) (222)
CARAWAY, Edward 39, (194)
CARAWAY, Ida J. 5* (198)
CARAWAY, John B. 34, (229)
CARAWAY, Mar___ 15 (f)* (B) (392)
CARAWAY, Tom 19?* (B) (168)
CARAWAY, Wm. 29* (230)
CARDEM?, Caroline 26* (368)
CARGILL, Wyley 45* (388)
CARKSEY, John 31 (B) (219)
CARL, Henry 50, (410)
CARL?, J. E. 50 (m), (311)
CARLETON, Tom 17* (324)
CARLTON, July 9* (B) (249)
CARMON, Nora 51, (161)
CARMON?, Tom 41* (427)
CARNES, Amanda 55* (B) (169)
CARNES, Claracy 68* (B) (174)
CARNES, Stephen J. 51* (169)
CARNES?, Lucy 49* (B) (195)
CARNEY, Asbery 24* (B) (224)
CARNEY, Gorge 25* (B) (215)
CARNS, Peter? 25 (B) (209)
CARNS, _____ 24 (m)* (B) (209)
CARNS, _____ 30 (m)* (B) (210)
CARNS?, Sandy 37 (m)* (B) (321)
CARNY, Ed 30* (B) (223)
CARNY, P. D. 37 (m)* (160)
CARPAN?, C. Wilson 60* (B) (227)
CARPENTER, Allice 33* (B) (162)
CARPENTER, Amanda 34 (B) (163)
CARPENTER, Amy 76* (B) (172)
CARPENTER, Findal? 70 (m), (187)
CARPENTER, Gilbert 56 (B) (173)
CARPENTER, Isom 48 (B) (421)
CARPENTER, JErry J. 22 (m) (B) (185)
CARPENTER, JEsse 40 (m)* (B) (199)
CARPENTER, Jeff 19, (410)
CARPENTER, Jerry 61 (m) (B) (185)
CARPENTER, Joe 22* (B) (242)
CARPENTER, John 30, (407)
CARPENTER, Lena 35?* (B) (172)
CARPENTER, M. 7 (m)* (B) (164)
CARPENTER, Marty 50 (f)* (372)
CARPENTER, Moses 28* (B) (185)
CARPENTER, Nat 59 (m) (B) (187)
CARPENTER, Oner? 55 (m) (B) (339)

5

CARPENTER, Robbin 46* (B) (172)
CARPENTER, Rosa 22* (B) (368)
CARPENTER, STephen 47* (393)
CARPENTER, Sim 24, (385)
CARPENTER, Tulip? 15 (f)* (B) (185)
CARPENTER, Will 34* (B) (428)
CARPENTER, ____ 35 (f) (B) (199)
CARPENTER, ____ 7 (m)* (B) (471)
CARR, Andy 32 (B) (450)
CARR, Billie 20* (429)
CARRAWAY, James 28 (B) (376)
CARRAWAY, Jerry 53 (m) (B) (285)
CARRAWAY, Sam 26* (B) (281)
CARRAWAY, W. T. 69 (m)* (287)
CARROL, G. W. 59 (m), (304)
CARROL, Sallie 18* (286)
CARROL, Townsend 56 (B) (292)
CARROLL, J. A. 26 (m), (339)
CARROLL, Josh 17* (B) (460)
CARROLL, L. H. 33 (m), (296)
CARTER, Anderson 23* (340)
CARTER, B. J. 35 (m) (B) (285)
CARTER, Bob 36* (B) (164)
CARTER, Bourous 41 (m), (244)
CARTER, Dabney 25 (365)
CARTER, Henryetta 24* (B) (167)
CARTER, Ike 38 (B) (216)
CARTER, J. S. 45 (m)* (167)
CARTER, JOhn 35* (B) (287)
CARTER, James 34 (B) (360)
CARTER, James T. 34, (362)
CARTER, John 18* (B) (289)
CARTER, John 20* (B) (404)
CARTER, Lize 22 (m) (B) (237)
CARTER, Mary 48, (407)
CARTER, Perry 33 (B) (286)
CARTER, Preston 18* (B) (391)
CARTER, S. A. 29 (m)* (329)
CARTER, Samuel 26 (B) (365)
CARTER, Silas 39 (B) (355)
CARTER, W. 10 (m)* (B) (498)
CARTER, W. F. 53 (m), (329)
CARTER, Washington 29 (B) (348)
CARTER, Washington? 60* (B) (312)
CARTER, Wm. 54, (244)
CARTER?, Willie 83* (B) (254)
CARTRELL, Andrew 63 (B) (249)
CARTRELL, Berry 26* (B) (250)
CARTRELL, John 20* (B) (250)
CARTWRIGHT, Demps 56 (m)* (317)
CARTWRIGHT, Demps 56 (m)* (342)
CARTWRIGHT, Demsy 65 (m) (B) (401)
CARTWRIGHT, Dick 58 (B) (320)
CARTWRIGHT, G. 21 (m) (B) (320)
CARTWRIGHT, G. 23 (m)* (B) (312)

CARTWRIGHT, Gloss 25 (m) (B) (400)
CARTWRIGHT, Harriet _0 (B) (323)
CARTWRIGHT, Haywood 27* (B) (317)
CARTWRIGHT, Haywood 27 (B) (342)
CARTWRIGHT, John 42* (341)
CARTWRIGHT, Lewis 60* (B) (320)
CARTWRIGHT, Louis 25* (B) (320)
CARTWRIGHT, Nelson R. 85* (347)
CARTWRIGHT, S. W. 67 (f)* (323)
CARTWRIGHT, Sam 28 (B) (401)
CARTWRIGHT, Walter 21* (B) (346)
CARUTH, Erastus C. 40, (393)
CARUTHERS, Dee 28 (B) (430)
CASH, Alford 35* (B) (388)
CASH, Mary 30* (B) (380)
CASH?, Abert 50 (B) (299)
CASSAL?, Lyda 82* (324)
CASSELBURY, Louis 31 (B) (478)
CASSELS, David 50* (B) (372)
CASTLES, George 25* (B) (401)
CASTLES, Thomas 61, (411)
CATES, Hamilton 58* (B) (186)
CATES, James 30* (188)
CATES?, Charles 33* (346)
CATRON, Adam 50 (B) (246)
CATRON, Isham 36?* (B) (246)
CATRON, Richard 55 (B) (244)
CATRON?, Stephen? 63? (B) (246)
CATRUN, John 35, (244)
CATRUN, ____ 20 (m)* (243)
CAUGH___, Ellen 43* (170)
CAUSY, James A. 55, (223)
CAYTON, Charles 19* (B) (379)
CECIL, C. C. 27 (m), (284)
CENTER, Sallie 20* (282)
CHAFFIN, D. L. 55 (m)* (449)
CHAFFIN, Harris 70* (B) (341)
CHAMBERS, Amelia 29 (B) (490)
CHAMBERS, Ben 63, (490)
CHAMBERS, D. 45 (m), (496)
CHAMBERS, E. G. 70 (m), (275)
CHAMBERS, Frank 25, (490)
CHAMBERS, G.? 32 (m)* (B) (487)
CHAMBERS, H. 23 (f) (B) (496)
CHAMBERS, Harriett 14* (B) (265)
CHAMBERS, Jas. T. 21* (162)
CHAMBERS, Jemima 66* (419)
CHAMBERS, John 64, (409)
CHAMBERS, M. L. 47 (m), (411)
CHAMBERS, S. J. 25 (m), (490)
CHAMBERS, Z.? M. 32 (m)* (488)
CHAMBLESS, W. 20 (m)* (314)
CHAMPION, S. E. 33 (m), (476)
CHAPEL, Dora _* (B) (428)
CHAPIN, James 53* (B) (164)
CHAPMAN, JAmes 35* (287)
CHAPMAN, Jane 18* (B) (378)

CHAPPEL, Curtis 50 (B) (422)
CHAPPEL, D. 24 (m)* (500)
CHAPPEL, Eli 27, (501)
CHAPPEL, Morris C. 36* (362)
CHAPPEL, R. 21 (m)* (486)
CHAPPEL, Wm. 32?* (486)
CHAPPIL, C. 24 (m)* (486)
CHAPPIL, C. 28 (m), (486)
CHAPPIL, L. 36 (m), (486)
CHAPPIN, Lorney? 35 (m), (341)
CHAPPIN, M. J. 56 (f)* (341)
CHAPPIN, Susan 54?* (341)
CHASHEW, John 25 (B) (402)
CHEAIRS, Manuel 30 (B) (356)
CHEAIRS, Peyton 33 (B) (364)
CHEATAM, Wm. 29* (B) (422)
CHECK, Wm. 17* (436)
CHENY?, J. B. 49 (m), (300)
CHENY?, J. R. 59 (m)* (298)
CHERRY, SAllie B. 40* (259)
CHICK, Fred 48, (373)
CHILTON, Charles 51* (166)
CHITTS, Wm. C. 24, (200)
CHOLMERS, Oliver 31 (B) (372)
CHRISTIAN, Allen 40 (B) (439)
CHRIST____, ____ 37 (m), (160)
CHUM, Milton 23* (B) (219)
CHUNN, Ceazer 41 (B) (215)
CINDLE, Frank 40* (477)
CININGER?, Jack 27* (167)
CLACK, George 59 (B) (492)
CLAFTEN, M. 32 (m), (491)
CLAPP, H. C. 40 (m), (337)
CLARA, _. 52 (m) (B) (320)
CLARK, Adline 28 (B) (399)
CLARK, B. 42 (m)* (471)
CLARK, Bob 40* (B) (339)
CLARK, David 58, (428)
CLARK, H. 35 (m), (212)
CLARK, Jordan 27* (B) (418)
CLARK, Margaret 80, (197)
CLARK, Sarah P. 56* (392)
CLARK, Thomas 50 (B) (449)
CLARK, Wash 19* (B) (502)
CLARK, Wordlow 24 (B) (424)
CLARKE, Abe 53 (B) (286)
CLARKE, Austin 48 (B) (282)
CLARKE, Bass 10 (m)* (B) (255)
CLARKE, Frank 40 (B) (274)
CLARKE, Gilbert 32* (294)
CLARKE, HArrison 57 (B) (262)
CLARKE, Judge 38 (B) (262)
CLARKE, Sarah 60* (B) (278)
CLARKE, Tom 45* (B) (282)
CLARKE, Wm. 35 (B) (278)
CLAXTON, Jas. R. 52, (280)
CLAXTON, War__ 45 (m), (248)
CLAY, Charity 40* (B) (461)
CLAY, Clinton 30* (B) (475)
CLAY, Esquire? 37 (m)* (B) (391)
CLAY, Henry 45 (B) (474)
CLAY, James A. 43* (347)
CLAY, Jim 30 (B) (276)
CLAYTON, Columbus C. 25* (253)
CLEAR, John 29 (B) (313)
CLEAR, R. 70 (m) (B) (313)
CLEAVES, B. 20 (m)* (B) (301)

CLEAVES, Ben 45 (B) (316)
CLEAVES, Ben 45 (B) (344)
CLEAVES, Charlie 14* (B) (311)
CLEAVES, Joe 26 (B) (307)
CLEAVES, John 58* (305)
CLEAVES, Lilburn 45 (B) (347)
CLEAVES, R. 19 (m)* (B) (307)
CLEAVES, Richard 46 (B) (308)
CLEAVES?, Redick 17* (165)
CLEER, M. 35 (m), (322)
CLEER, Robt. 28 (B) (319)
CLEERE, J. L. 50 (m)* (344)
CLEEVES, Allen 23 (B) (321)
CLEEVES, George _0 (B) (323)
CLEEVES, Henry 27* (B) (305)
CLEEVES, James 16* (332)
CLEEVES, Jerry 60 (m)* (B) (300)
CLEEVES, M. E. 62 (f)* (332)
CLEEVES, Mattie 22 (f)* (322)
CLEEVES, Nathaniel 42 (B) (322)
CLEEVES, Sallie __ (B) (321)
CLEEVES, Steven 46 (B) (341)
CLEEVES, Willis 70 (B) (320)
CLEEVES, Wilson 42 (B) (320)
CLEEVES?, Rinda 38 (f)* (B) (318)
CLEMENTS, James L. 55* (B) (345)
CLEM__, Wm. 35 (B) (255?)
CLENNON, Bern 28 (m)* (B) (479)
CLERY, Young 22 (B) (370)
CLIFF, Catherine 8* (B) (500)
CLIFTON, Annis 60 (f)* (B) (286)
CLIFTON, Henry 25* (329)
CLIFTON, James 27 (B) (450)
CLIFTON, Robert 57, (280)
CLINE?, Bowlen 30 (f) (B) (319)
CLINGMAN, Andy 37* (B) (473)
CLING__NEL, Tom 50 (B) (472)
CLINTON, Osa 25 (f)* (B) (494)
CLI____MON, Clou? 80 (f)* (B) (475)
CLOPTON, L. 25 (m)* (494)
CLOYD, Emanuel 22* (B) (168)
CLOYD, George 37 (B) (171)
CLOYD, Sarah E. 45, (184)
CLOYED, W. 18 (m)* (B) (497)
CLUTTS, John 28, (190)
CLUTTS, Thomas 26, (201)
CL__, J. L. 50 (m)* (316)
COAL, ____tte 30 (m) (B) (462)
COATNEY, Anthney 26* (B) (481)
COATS, Esther 24* (B) (193)
COBB, Candis _* (161)
COBB, Chesley 65 (B) (340)
COBB, Frank 23 (B) (162)
COBB, M. B. 43 (f), (300)
COBB, Ollie? 25 (f)* (B) (482)
COBB, Perceval 6* (B) (176)
COBB?, ____ 28 (m) (B) (170)
COBEN?, Headly 45* (302)
COBLES, Franklin 15* (B) (309)
COBURN, Abraham 36* (B) (352)
COBURN, Jonas 38* (B) (352)
COBURN, Levi 45 (B) (351)
COBURN, Mitchell 40 (B) (351)

COBURN, Rachel 90* (B) (352)
COBY, Elenora 18* (B) (352)
COCKE, Calvin 23, (281)
COCKE, Ennis 35 (B) (238)
COCKE, Fanny 40, (274)
COCKE, Henry 30 (B) (238)
COCKE, Henry 50 (B) (281)
COCKE, Isaack 78* (B) (237)
COCKE, JAmes H. 55* (253)
COCKE, Jim 26 (B) (237)
COCKE, L. V.? 36 (f), (187)
COCKE, Robin 60 (m) (B) (192)
COCKE, Thos. 65* (169)
COCKE, W. H. 32 (m)* (266)
COCKRAN, Silas 60 (423)
COCKRAN, W.? S. 29 (m)* (160)
CODY, F. M. 46 (m), (301)
CODY, Thomas 47, (298)
COE, Billy 20 (B) (230)
COE, Billy 70?* (B) (226)
COE, Ephram 53 (B) (250)
COE, Fed 25 (m)* (B) (230)
COE, Francis 27, (265)
COE, Haywood 19* (B) (290)
COE, Henry 65* (B) (230)
COE, Josephene 27 (B) (250)
COFFEE, Andrew J. 34, (348)
COFFEE, Joel 76, (411)
COFFER, Fannie 22* (302)
COFFER, R. 5 (m)* (302)
COFFEY, H. 78 (m), (204)
COFFIE, W. H. 37 (m), (481)
COGBILL, Carles 69 (m)* (389)
COLE, Allen 25* (283)
COLE, Amanda 74?* (297)
COLE, Angeline 12* (B) (269)
COLE, Ben 22* (B) (484)
COLE, Bettie 12* (B) (274)
COLE, Caroline 42* (B) (306)
COLE, Clem 35 (m) (B) (394)
COLE, E. E. 38 (f)* (263)
COLE, I. C. 28 (m)* (B) (317)
COLE, I. C. 28 (m)* (B) (342)
COLE, Isham 72* (B) (254)
COLE, J. _. 13 (m)* (323)
COLE, Luella 12* (B) (261)
COLE, Robert 35 (B) (283)
COLE, Sam? 25 (B) (296)
COLE, Thomas 45 (B) (355)
COLE, Washington 54 (B) (314)
COLE, Wm. 63* (427)
COLEMAN, C. 19 (f)* (B) (311)
COLEMAN, Chas. 25 (B) (257)
COLEMAN, Henry 42* (B) (325)
COLEMAN, Jason 22* (B) (262)
COLEMAN, Jim 47 (B) (281)
COLEMAN, Joe 54 (B) (332)
COLEMAN, Robert 38* (B) (187)
COLEMAN, Sam 24* (B) (324)
COLIER, John 53 (B) (246)
COLLIER, Byrd 10* (287)
COLLIER, Henry 23* (B) (285)
COLLIER, Joseph 32 (B) (273)
COLLIER, Nevia 5 (f)* (295)
COLLIER, Susan 100?* (B) (357)
COLLIER, Wm. 45 (B) (354)
COLLINS, C. W. 41 (m)* (B) (186)
COLLINS, John 30* (B) (186)
COLTON, Edward 20 (B) (414)

COMMINGS, George 35 (B) (383)
COMO, Sam 31 (m) (B) (333)
COMO?, James 50 (B) (396)
COMPTON, B. 25 (m)* (501)
CONAWAY, Mather 23 (f)* (B) (282)
CONDIT, Taylor 15* (B) (437)
CONKIE, Nellie 50 (B) (441)
CONLEY, Ann 50* (B) (382)
CONLEY, Henry 22 (B) (436)
CONLEY, Henry 5* (B) (428)
CONLEY, Julia A. 35* (380)
CONLEY, Mike 50* (276)
CONLY, Wm. 22 (B) (366)
CONN, G.? M. 29 (m)* (492)
CONNER, Andrew 66, (408)
CONNER, Elizabeth 45, (202)
CONNER, John 27* (202)
CONNER, Willie _ (f)* (B) (267)
CONNETTE?, Bill 55, (335)
CONOLLY, Delphy 70 (f)* (B) (444)
COOK, Charles 22* (B) (376)
COOK, Harett 57* (B) (216)
COOK, Henry 74* (B) (267)
COOK, J. A. 35 (m)* (280)
COOK, J. D. 33 (m), (204)
COOK, J. H. 2_* (208)
COOK, Lee J. 50, (409)
COOK, Levinia 55, (407)
COOK, Losson 21 (m), (480)
COOK, Robert H. 51, (380)
COOK, Wm. H. 23, (409)
COONS, John 22, (264)
COOPER, Allen 19* (B) (321)
COOPER, Amer___ 50 (m) (B) (262)
COOPER, Della 22* (B) (355)
COOPER, Dora 23* (B) (352)
COOPER, Floid 28 (B) (330)
COOPER, George 65* (B) (379)
COOPER, JErry 45* (B) (169)
COOPER, Joe 13?* (B) (321)
COOPER, John 52* (B) (421)
COOPER, Mary 48* (B) (262)
COOPER, Newton F. 30, (407)
COOPER, Sallie 20 (B) (358)
COOPER, Stephen 26* (B) (262)
COOPER?, Abe 30* (B) (267)
COOPER?, John 50 (B) (453)
COPPAGE, Andey 30 (B) (216)
CORBEL, Henry __ (B) (418)
CORE, Buck 78* (B) (170)
CORE?, Green 27* (B) (223)
CORGILL?, Wm. W. 58, (387)
CORNELIUS, G. 10 (m)* (B) (312)
CORRETHERS?, Handy 35 (B) (439)
CORTTAR?, Sterlin? 55 (m) (B) (248)
COSBY, Carry 56 (m) (B) (244)
COSBY, George 22* (187)
COSSETTE, Wm. 51 (B) (465)
COTHER, Wm. 49 (B) (288)
COTHRAN, E. G. 39 (m), (291)
COTHRAN, John 30, (291)
COTHRAN, Porter 26* (291)
COTRAR?, Becca 50 (B) (238)
COTRAR?, Jinnie 75* (B) (238)

COTTON, Cosselle 50 (m) (B) (421)
COTTON, Isaac 45 (B) (422)
COULTER, Anna 18* (B) (354)
COUNON?, Charley 18* (B) (256)
COURSLER, James 57 (B) (388)
COUSIN, Henry 20* (B) (483)
COVEY, Dock 20* (B) (354)
COVINGTON, John 21* (247)
COVINGTON, Thomas 23, (195)
COVINGTON, _. G. 29 (m)* (167)
COWAN, Alexander 18* (B) (364)
COWAN, Alice 30 (B) (365)
COWAN, Buck 56 (B) (364)
COWAN, John 30, (192)
COWAN, John 33* (433)
COWAN, John 34* (426)
COWAN, Moses 73, (191)
COWAN, Pink? 27 (m), (202)
COWPER, John 42* (B) (174)
COWSAR?, Robt. 27* (163)
COX, Adline 19* (B) (405)
COX, Alice 35* (339)
COX, Ambrose 55 (B) (404)
COX, Andrew 50* (B) (338)
COX, Charles 21* (B) (311)
COX, Elsey 75 (f)* (293)
COX, Frank 12* (B) (404)
COX, George 18* (477)
COX, George 59 (B) (358)
COX, Hannah 40* (B) (305)
COX, JAmes 27* (468)
COX, James 28* (419)
COX, James? N. 65, (408)
COX, Joe 24 (B) (437)
COX, Lin 30 (m) (B) (369)
COX, Louis 30* (405)
COX, Lyn 26 (m)* (B) (426)
COX, Margaret 18* (B) (432)
COX, Mark 50* (B) (432)
COX, Marshal 62* (501)
COX, Montgomery 23* (B) (365)
COX, Peter 43* (B) (252)
COX, Riley 20 (B) (439)
COX, Riley 20 (B) (445)
COX, Robert 32* (293)
COX, Solomon 35 (B) (368)
COX, Thomas 39* (501)
COX, Wm. 60 (B) (437)
COX?, Charles 23* (B) (224)
COYD, Green 26* (B) (389)
COZBELL, Burl 25 (m)* (B) (399)
CRABTREE, Margarett 40, (302)
CRABTREE, Mary 40, (372)
CRABTREE, Thena 70 (f)* (224)
CRAIG?, Harry? 50? (B) (203)
CRAVEN, JAmes 22* (B) (290)
CRAVER, Harriet 40* (B) (284)
CRAWFORD, A. Cas. 30 (f)* (B) (213)
CRAWFORD, Ed D. 32, (176)
CRAWFORD, Elijah 21 (B) (396)
CRAWFORD, Frank 72* (161)
CRAWFORD, Gus 19* (B) (414)
CRAWFORD, H. F. 31 (m)* (483)
CRAWFORD, J. K.? 33 (m)* (484)

CRAWFORD, J. M. 25 (m), (207)
CRAWFORD, J. M. 36 (m)* (205)
CRAWFORD, Jack 30* (B) (191)
CRAWFORD, James 75, (273)
CRAWFORD, Jas. 35, (176)
CRAWFORD, John 38 (B) (396)
CRAWFORD, John 45* (B) (476)
CRAWFORD, Julia 26* (B) (380)
CRAWFORD, M. 40 (f)* (483)
CRAWFORD, Peter 36* (183)
CRAWFORD, Philipp 32 (B) (369)
CRAWFORD, Presley 45 (m)* (280)
CRAWFORD, S. 26 (m)* (483)
CRAWFORD, Simon 38 (B) (368)
CRAWFORD, T. R. 33 (m), (324)
CRAWFORD, Thomas 72 (B) (370)
CRAWFORD, W. E. 37 (m), (161)
CRAWFORD, Washington 57 (B) (358)
CRAWFORD, _. W. 67 (m)* (211)
CRAWFORD, ____ 58 (m) (B) (326)
CRAWFORD?, Rose 6* (B) (251)
CRAYTON, Chas. 30 (B) (274)
CREDISON?, T. S. 32 (m), (406)
CRENCHAW, Lucy 40, (475)
CRENSHAW, Hennie 12 (f)* (310)
CRENSHAW, Kate 20* (B) (361)
CRENSHAW, Marsha 11* (413)
CREWDSEN, John J. 28* (364)
CREWS, Mary 45 (B) (206)
CREWS, Robert 54 (B) (219)
CREWS, Wm. 23* (230)
CRIDER, John 45* (443)
CRISP, Joe 24 (B) (183)
CRITONDON, Wash 53* (B) (380)
CRITTENDON, R. 65 (m)* (477)
CROCKET, Sam 58 (m) (B) (337)
CROCKIT, Sam 35, (450)
CROFFORD, Albert 40 (B) (454)
CROFFORD, Ella 21 (B) (462)
CROME?, Allen 29* (B) (460)
CROOK, Abner 10* (173)
CROOK, Benjamin 25, (408)
CROOK, James B. 25, (409)
CROOK, Solomon 80, (348)
CROOK, W. F. 52 (m)* (173)
CROOK, W. S. 23 (m), (409)
CROOKS, J. M. 44 (m), (409)
CROOMS, George 32 (B) (247)
CROSS, Abraham 29* (296)
CROSS, Albert 28 (B) (334)
CROSS, Delia 45* (B) (352)
CROSS, Enock 50* (B) (352)
CROSS, G. 10 (f)* (B) (495)
CROSS, Horrace 26* (B) (298)
CROSS, Isaac 30 (B) (180)
CROSS, Isham 31 (B) (354)
CROSS, JAcob 36* (B) (310)
CROSS, James 25* (283)
CROSS, Joel 46 (B) (310)
CROSS, Liza 47* (B) (236)
CROSS, Oscar 30 (B) (286)
CROSS, Richard 21* (B) (337)

CROSS, Simon 47* (B) (253)
CROSS, Thomas C. 48* (351)
CROSS, Victoria 20* (B) (352)
CROSS, Wm. 56, (293)
CROSS, Wm. 67, (370)
CROSSETT, Greer 52, (429)
CROSSETT, Irving 55* (419)
CROSSETT, John 39, (434)
CROSSETT, Sara 60* (B) (419)
CROW, M. 23 (m)* (481)
CROWDER, Amanda? 25* (B) (206)
CROWDER, Cate 26* (B) (404)
CROWDER, J. 40 (m), (207)
CROWDER, J. M. 13 (m), (477)
CROWLY, A. 53 (m)* (B) (302)
CRUMLEY, Alford 63 (B) (399)
CRUMLEY, JEssee 28 (m)* (B) (479)
CRUMLEY, Will 23 (B) (477)
CRUMLEY?, George 21 (B) (399)
CRUMP, Chockolate 75 (m)* (B) (351)
CRUSHER, Susan 6* (B) (432)
CRUTCHER, George 43 (B) (370)
CRUTCHER, Lucy 45* (B) (435)
CRUTCHER, Peater 52 (B) (368)
CRUTCHFIELD, J. 74 (m)* (205)
CRUTCHFIELD, J. P. 47 (m), (206)
CRUTCHFIELD, J. S. 36 (m), (203)
CRUTCHFIELD, Samuel 26 (B) (363)
CR___, Daniel 34, (283)
CR_____, Jerry 52 (m)* (B) (254)
CUINGHAM?, Wm. 24 (B) (377)
CULBERTH, Jas. M. 43* (165)
CULBRETH, Sallie 28, (409)
CULP, Claiborne 35* (B) (358)
CULP, Eliza 55* (334)
CULP, Lee 38 (m)* (333)
CULP, Peter 87* (469)
CULP, Robert 48* (B) (350)
CULP?, Million 22 (m)* (484)
CUMMINS, Sarah 40 (B) (396)
CUMMINS, Thomas 25 (B) (395)
CUMMINS, Wm. 24 (B) (398)
CUNNINGHAM, J. 23 (m)* (B) (315)
CUNNINGHAM, W. A. 34 (m), (306)
CUNNINGHAM, ___ 26 (m)* (B) (318)
CURK, Ann 30* (B) (481)
CURKANDOLL, J. 48 (m)* (501)
CURNEY?, H. 45 (f)* (B) (498)
CURRIE?, Henry 48?* (B) (222)
CURRIN, Alfred 57 (B) (242)
CURRIN, Dick 55 (B) (254)
CURRIN, Mary F. 21* (B) (262)
CURRY, Allen 52* (B) (183)
CURRY, Calven 24* (B) (501)
CURRY, Ike 28* (B) (497)
CURRY, J. __ (m)* (B) (486)
CURRY, Tenny 12?* (B) (174)
CURTIS, Carlton 41* (221)
CURTIS, George 32 (B) (249)
CURTIS, JAmes 21* (B) (327)
CURTLES?, Caroline 50 (B) (323)

CURY?, Adah 18* (B) (502)
C___, JOhn J. 32, (302)
C___, Tom 17* (B) (419)
C_____, ___ 21 (m)* (B) (207)
DAILY, John 40 (B) (269)
DAILY, John 50 (B) (490)
DAILY?, B. 46 (m) (B) (318)
DALY, Lewis 16* (B) (347)
DALY, Mary 35 (B) (364)
DALY, Moses 55 (B) (363)
DALY, Norah 18* (B) (347)
DANAGIE?, Alf 30 (B) (330)
DANDRIDGE, Ed __* (B) (244)
DANDRIDGE, Joe 23 (B) (243)
DANIEL, Bill W. 38 (B) (479)
DANIEL, Geo. 50* (B) (290)
DANIEL, Mack 33* (B) (347)
DANIEL, Miley 28 (m)* (495)
DANIEL, W. H. 42 (m), (487)
DANIELS, Billy 51* (B) (290)
DANIELS, Charles 21* (420)
DANIELS, Chas. 27* (284)
DANIELS, Christopher 43* (165)
DANIELS, JAmes 18* (280)
DANIELS, Jane 53, (280)
DANIELS, Miles 35 (B) (421)
DANNIEL, Dove 26 (m)* (477)
DANNIEL, James 68, (477)
DARDEN, Alfred 70* (416)
DARDEN, James 24, (430)
DARDEN?, ___ ___ (m)* (B) (418)
DASHIELDS, Andrew 26 (B) (478)
DASHIELL, Robt. 73, (176)
DAUGHERTY, Nathan 45, (369)
DAUGHETY, Wm. 74* (487)
DAUGHTY, L. 27 (m), (487)
DAVENPORT, Thomas 11?* (414)
DAVENPORT, Wm. 56, (458)
DAVID, Ann 58, (164)
DAVID, Dewitt C. 49?* (392)
DAVID, Laura 20* (376)
DAVIS, Adam 29* (B) (415)
DAVIS, Betsy 40* (B) (419)
DAVIS, Bettie 21* (B) (355)
DAVIS, Bettie 26* (332)
DAVIS, Bill 21* (B) (325)
DAVIS, Biph 54 (m), (330)
DAVIS, Charles? 23* (B) (455)
DAVIS, Davision? 68 (m), (477)
DAVIS, Edward 39* (B) (255?)
DAVIS, Ella 21* (B) (228)
DAVIS, Ellen 20* (B) (477)
DAVIS, Ellen 40* (293)
DAVIS, Fred 40 (B) (456)
DAVIS, Gus 34 (B) (388)
DAVIS, H. 30 (m) (B) (499)
DAVIS, Holland 66 (f), (487)
DAVIS, J. M. 33 (m), (486)
DAVIS, Jack 31* (469)
DAVIS, Jacob 68* (B) (354)
DAVIS, Jacob M. 28* (385)
DAVIS, James 38, (487)
DAVIS, John 32, (458)
DAVIS, Joshua 55, (293)
DAVIS, Lanson 57* (425)
DAVIS, Lawson? 25* (418)

DAVIS, Liza? 22 (B) (236)
DAVIS, Louisa 40* (B) (202)
DAVIS, Mack 45 (B) (386)
DAVIS, Martha 24 (B) (460)
DAVIS, Mary 75* (B) (251)
DAVIS, Mary 82?, (390)
DAVIS, Miles 30 (B) (251)
DAVIS, NElson 30* (B) (290)
DAVIS, Nathan 26 (B) (224)
DAVIS, Peter 24 (B) (394)
DAVIS, Pinkney 30, (458)
DAVIS, Robert 50, (441)
DAVIS, Rose 40* (232)
DAVIS, Rubin 32 (B) (256)
DAVIS, S. D. 28 (f)* (B) (335)
DAVIS, Sallie 25 (B) (472)
DAVIS, Sam 25, (293)
DAVIS, Sam 30* (B) (493)
DAVIS, Samuel __* (418)
DAVIS, Sylvester 45* (B) (420)
DAVIS, Tandy B. 80 (m), (390)
DAVIS, Thomas 22* (B) (434)
DAVIS, Thomas W. 32, (185)
DAVIS, Tom 28* (B) (472)
DAVIS, Vesta 1* (B) (434)
DAVIS, W. L. 58 (m)* (490)
DAVIS, Wes 30* (335)
DAVIS, Wm. 35* (B) (378)
DAVIS, ___ 24 (m)* (500)
DAVIS?, Parlle 14 (f)* (B) (389)
DAVITTE?, Selia 80* (B) (470)
DAWSON, David 60 (B) (354)
DAWSON, George 24 (B) (354)
DAY, Ally 45 (f)* (B) (186)
DAY, Lewis 24 (B) (174)
DAY, Morrison 35 (B) (187)
DAY, Pleasant 21* (B) (199)
DAY, Sallie 80* (B) (183)
DAY, Spencer 24* (B) (243)
DAY, Thomas 9* (B) (490)
DAY, Virginia 35? (B) (454)
DAY, Wm. 18?* (B) (190)
DAY, Wm. 19?* (B) (199)
DAY?, Daniel 78 (B) (186)
DEAN, Dennis 25* (B) (356)
DEAN, Henry 48 (B) (384)
DEAN, James 18* (B) (395)
DEAN, Marti 25 (m)* (B) (382)
DECK?, Wm. 25 (B) (428)
DEEN, Daniel 63* (B) (251)
DEENER, Shack 35* (B) (349)
DEGRAFFENRIED, Andrew 21 (B) (249)
DEGRAFFENRIED, Daniel 55 (B) (249)
DEGRAFFENRIED, Harry 34 (B) (238)
DEGRAFFENRIED, Jack 65 (B) (250)
DEGRAFFENRIED, Julia 32 (B) (229)
DEGRAFFENRIED, Nathan 28* (B) (229)
DEGRAFFINREID, Eliza 12* (B) (160)
DELAPP, Jessie 13 (m)* (B) (258)
DELK, Joe 55 (B) (249)
DELMONT, Pink 15 (m)* (B) (416)
DEMENT, Ike 27* (B) (418)

DEMONT, Fannie 20* (B) (395)
DEMPSEY, Dock 30, (287)
DEMPSEY, Nathan 26* (188)
DENA, James 23 (B) (311)
DENISON, Jane 26* (B) (392)
DENNIE, Leonard 50 (B) (457)
DENNIE, W. N. 30 (m), (341)
DENNIS, Bill 40* (B) (397)
DENNIS, Giles 50 (B) (394)
DENNIS, Oreily 55* (416)
DENSE, Dolly 23* (B) (420)
DENSON, Jennie 21* (433)
DENT, Epp 25 (m) (B) (499)
DENTON, L. C. 56 (f), (331)
DIBBLE, Geo. 35 (B) (279)
DICKENS, Allen? 40 (B) (304)
DICKENS, ___ 50 (f)* (B) (338)
DICKENSON, A. 57 (m)* (340)
DICKENSON, Dave 21 (B) (322)
DICKENSON, Dave 55* (B) (337)
DICKENSON, H. 26 (m) (B) (340)
DICKENSON, J. C. 30? (m)* (324)
DICKENSON, Leiker? 30 (m) (B) (339)
DICKENSON, Nat 23* (B) (334)
DICKENSON, Will 47* (B) (335)
DICKERSON, Alx. 27 (m), (484)
DICKERSON, Ben 50 (B) (291)
DICKERSON, Bob 23* (477)
DICKERSON, C. 30 (f)* (270)
DICKERSON, Dan 21* (B) (482)
DICKERSON, E. 19 (f)* (B) (307)
DICKERSON, Martha 19* (B) (258)
DICKERSON, Moses 57 (B) (458)
DICKERSON?, Palmira 40* (B) (460)
DICKEY, Monday 71 (m) (B) (245)
DICKINSON, A. 28 (m) (B) (330)
DICKINSON, Alfred 25 (B) (354)
DICKINSON, Asbery 55 (B) (235)
DICKINSON, Charly 24* (167)
DICKINSON, Ed 34* (167)
DICKINSON, Ed sr. 64* (177)
DICKINSON, Hellen 19* (170)
DICKINSON, Henry 28 (B) (361)
DICKINSON, Jack 50 (B) (237)
DICKINSON, James 19* (B) (234)
DICKINSON, Robt. 25, (167)
DICKINSON, Rose 16* (B) (233)
DICKINSON, Sam 40 (B) (329)
DICKINSON, Simion 56 (B) (239)
DICKINSON, Tina 24* (B) (185)
DICKINSON, Wesly 40* (B) (233)
DICKINSON, Wily 24 (B) (237)
DICKSON, Charls 16 (B) (216)
DICKSON, Henry 45 (B) (404)
DICK____, _ W. 10 (m)* (B) (177)
DIGS, J. H. 22 (m), (476)
DILLARD, A. 65 (f)* (B) (488)
DILLARD, George 54* (B) (489)
DILLARD, George? 30 (B) (245)
DILLARD, Henry? 39 (B) (245)
DILLARD, Willis 23* (B) (360)
DILLIARD, Henry 76* (415)
DILLINS, Edwin 27, (456)
DILLINS, Willie 19 (f), (456)

DINA, Daniel 54 (B) (398)
DINA, JOhn 30 (B) (398)
DINGLY?, Louis 19* (433)
DIX, Emma 25* (427)
DIX, Joseph 30 (B) (450)
DIX, Wm. 28, (450)
DIXON, E. R. 25 (m), (306)
DIXON, Henry 19* (B) (404)
DIXON, John S. 32* (223)
DOAX, Henry 33* (278)
DOBBINS, Armis 25 (f)* (B) (177)
DOBBINS, Below? 20 (m)* (B) (467)
DOBBINS, Loss 26 (m)* (B) (485)
DOBBINS, R. T. 34 (f), (483)
DOBBS, E. J. 60 (f)* (460)
DOBBS, Josh 17* (B) (440)
DOBSON, Gorge 55?* (B) (204)
DOD, Emma 30* (283)
DODD, James 45 (B) (439)
DODSON, Abagill 60* (387)
DODSON, Alen 25 (B) (216)
DODSON, Frank 53* (B) (218)
DODSON, Isaac 18* (B) (215)
DODSON, James 33 (B) (199)
DODSON, Loson 25 (m) (B) (214)
DODSON, Louis 24 (B) (245)
DODSON, Marina 25* (B) (205)
DODSON, NAncy 76* (199)
DODSON, Pilser 46 (m), (196)
DODSON, Ros? 23 (m) (B) (470)
DODSON, Sam 50 (B) (247)
DODSON, Sam 6* (B) (235)
DODSON, Thomas 16* (197)
DODSON, Tim 35? (B) (337)
DODSON, Wallace 25* (B) (268)
DODSON, Wm. 25?* (B) (170)
DODSON, Wm. 26 (B) (284)
DOFT, James 12* (B) (418)
DOLLAHIGH, Daniel 27 (B) (365)
DOLLAHIGH, Wilson 38 (B) (352)
DOLLEY?, Askew 44 (f)* (B) (302)
DONAHOE, Mary 24 (B) (405)
DONAHOE, Mose 50 (B) (405)
DONAHOO, James E. 41 (B) (405)
DONALDS, James 18* (196)
DONEGAN, Jessee 25 (m)* (B) (164)
DONELSON, Harris B. 34, (357)
DONIE, T. J. 25 (m)* (479)
DONIGAN, Wm. 30 (B) (373)
DONNELL?, Mary 42 (B) (304)
DOOLEN?, James __ (B).(172)
DORCH, Charles 45 (B) (341)
DORCH, Margaret 30 (B) (341)
DORETY?, John 38 (B) (401)
DORSE, Ella 20 (B) (436)
DORSE, Wilkes 55 (B) (438)
DORSON, Gilbert 54* (B) (453)
DORTCH, Becky 21 (B) (163)
DORTCH, Dick 26* (B) (461)
DORTCH, Eb 66 (m)* (B) (489)
DORTCH, Edmond 54 (B) (442)
DORTCH, Henry 36* (B) (187)
DORTCH, Jack 50* (B) (340)

DORTCH, John 8* (B) (171)
DORTCH, Joseph 26 (B) (176)
DORTCH, Mary 20* (B) (168)
DORTCH, Noah 55 (B) (173)
DORTCH, Polly 45 (B) (340)
DORTCH, Richard 27* (B) (413)
DORTCH, Robert 19* (B) (419)
DORTCH, Wm. 21* (B) (213)
DORTCH, Wm. B. 51* (162)
DOUGAN, John 44* (482)
DOUGGARS, Ples 65 (m), (331)
DOUGH?, Sam 40 (B) (452)
DOUGIN, John 68, (378)
DOUGLAS, Ed__ C. 37 (m), (254)
DOUGLAS, Henry 40 (B) (181)
DOUGLAS, Josiah 56* (B) (183)
DOUGLAS, Maggie 10* (B) (468)
DOUGLAS, Mary B. 52* (183)
DOUGLAS, Patiance 25* (B) (161)
DOUGLAS, Robert 54* (B) (422)
DOUGLASS, Alfred 9* (B) (231)
DOUGLASS, Burter? 30? (m) (B) (221)
DOUGLASS, Cad 60 (m)* (B) (252)
DOUGLASS, Charles 22 (B) (241)
DOUGLASS, Charles 36* (B) (253)
DOUGLASS, E. 24 (f)* (B) (312)
DOUGLASS, Jane 22* (B) (214)
DOUGLASS, John 18* (B) (251)
DOUGLASS, John 55 (B) (257)
DOUGLASS, L. 32 (m) (B) (217)
DOUGLASS, Levi 55 (B) (221)
DOUGLASS, Lin 26 (m) (B) (233)
DOUGLASS, MArcam 30 (m) (B) (217)
DOUGLASS, Margret 45 (B) (238)
DOUGLASS, Mat 33* (B) (218)
DOUGLASS, Pierce 24 (B) (290)
DOUGLASS, Silas 59* (B) (221)
DOUGLASS, Vina 57* (B) (218)
DOUGLASS, Wash 55 (B) (252)
DOUGLASS, Wes 34 (B) (232)
DOUGLASS, Wily 54 (B) (223)
DOUGLASS, Wm. 48* (221)
DOVES, Joel 66 (B) (314)
DOVEY, Joshua 13* (B) (270)
DOWD, Thomas 25 (B) (376)
DOWDEN?, Tom 27* (B) (472)
DOWDEY, Archey 32 (B) (470)
DOWDEY, Carline 31 (f) (B) (473)
DOWDY, Charly 26* (B) (469)
DOWDY, James 20? (B) (387)
DOWDY, Lisie 32? (f)* (B) (387)
DOWDY, Willis 28 (B) (469)
DOWLING, John 50, (291)
DOWNEY, Henry 25, (496)
DOWNEY, Jno. 44, (488)
DOWNEY, L. 23 (m)* (487)
DOWNS, Baltimore 45 (B) (274)
DOWNS, Wm. 45* (B) (287)
DOYL?, _____ 26 (f)* (B) (268)
DOYLE, Abe 54* (284)
DOYLE, Henry 31, (284)
DOYLE, J. W. 26 (m)* (284)
DOYLE, Syntha 53, (286)
DOYLE, Thomas 27 (B) (286)

DOYLE, Tom 23* (B) (295)
DOYLE, W. H. 55 (m), (337)
DOYLE, Wiley 22* (283)
DOYLE, Wm. 24* (274)
DOZIER, _____ 27 (f) (B) (179)
DRAKE, Clark 16* (B) (251)
DRAKE, James 40* (B) (233)
DRANE, Eliza 30* (B) (419)
DRINKS, Silas 45* (B) (425)
DRISDALE, Lucy 65* (B) (275)
DRIVER, D. H. 26 (m), (484)
DRIVER, Will 16* (280)
DRIVER, Wm. 50, (275)
DUCK, Aaron 29* (B) (345)
DUD, James 47 (B) (462)
DUDLEY, Clara 9* (B) (393)
DUDLEY, Ezekiel 35 (B) (186)
DUDNEY, John? 41, (412)
DUFFY, Pat 50* (416)
DUGAT?, Alfred 70 (B) (452)
DUGLASS, Vince 23* (B) (280)
DUKE, Dave 60 (B) (340)
DUKE, Ellis 35 (B) (402)
DUKE, Jeff 18* (B) (422)
DUKE, Lucius 39* (426)
DUKE, Sam 20 (B) (219)
DUNAWAY, Benjamin 30 (B) (358)
DUNBAR, John 50 (B) (271)
DUNCAN, Frank 25 (B) (398)
DUNCAN, John 21* (411)
DUNDAS, James 35, (330)
DUNLAP, Henry 17* (268)
DUNLAP, Ples 60 (m) (B) (453)
DUNLAP, Sallie 47* (B) (263)
DUNLAP, Wm. 25* (B) (366)
DUNSON, Bob 20 (B) (474)
DUPREE, Elizabeth 43* (B) (312)
DUPREE, G. F. 33 (m), (318)
DUPREE, P. W. 69 (m), (331)
DUPREE?, E. 48 (f)* (B) (311)
DUPREY?, A. 53 (m)* (B) (488)
DURDOLPH, Mattie 22* (424)
DURHAM, Allen 21* (B) (321)
DURHAM, Henderson 20 (B) (333)
DURHAM, Shed 25* (B) (329)
DURHAM, T. S. 57 (m), (194)
DUSCO?, Rudolph 40* (347)
DUTTEN, Mary 33, (489)
DUVAL, John W. 42* (361)
DUVAL, Lucinda 36 (B) (366)
DYER, A. C. 56 (m)* (169)
DYER, E. P. 78 (f)* (461)
DYER, John W. 60, (441)
DYER, Mary 3* (B) (441)
DYER, Mathew 43, (424)
DYER, T. M. 30 (m), (160)
D___, Winnie 10* (B) (416)
D___DANE, E. W. 70 (f)* (335)
D_____, ___dan 54 (m) (B) (178)
D_____, James A. 24, (442)
EALEY?, _. A. 50 (m), (165)
EALF, George 24* (B) (330)
EARL, George 22* (B) (313)
EARL, Turner 31 (B) (321)
EARL?, Frances __ (B) (302)
EARL?, Henderson _4* (B) (302)
EARLS, Amhers 45 (m) (B) (324)
EARLS, Fannie 65* (B) (334)

EARLY, Norman 27* (B) (387)
EARNEST?, John 48 (B) (232)
EARNHEART, Dannel 55 (m), (386)
EATON, Marinda 15* (B) (492)
EAVINS, Scott 70 (B) (381)
ECKLIN, V. R. 29 (m)* (301)
EDDINGS?, Patrick 49* (B) (174)
EDENTON, Charles 25 (B) (353)
EDENTON, Frank 9* (B) (346)
EDENTON, James C. 37, (407)
EDENTON, John 36 (B) (345)
EDENTON, John jr. 15* (B) (346)
EDENTON, M. L. M. 68 (m), (406)
EDENTON, Wm. 51 (B) (363)
EDENTON, Wm. H. 35* (406)
EDENTON, Wm. V. 8* (406)
EDGAR, Pat 34 (B) (290)
EDINGS, Benjman 28 (B) (385)
EDINGTON, Frank 52* (B) (392)
EDLEY, Junius 46 (B) (464)
EDMISTON, Richard 17* (373)
EDMONDS, Chas. 37* (190)
EDMONDSON, J. P. 30 (m)* (163)
EDMONDSON, Saml. 71* (194)
EDMONS?, Mack 40 (B) (441)
EDMONSON, Low 20 (f)* (181)
EDMONSON, Richard 50* (370)
EDMUNSON, Mattie 16* (428)
EDWARDS, A. T. 34 (m)* (294)
EDWARDS, Charles 24* (436)
EDWARDS, George 9* (307)
EDWARDS, H. 59 (m)* (489)
EDWARDS, Harry 45* (B) (420)
EDWARDS, John 70?* (B) (492)
EDWARDS, Juletta 18* (B) (270)
EDWARDS, N.? E. 22 (f)* (206)
EDWARDS, R. 50 (m) (B) (296)
EDWARDS, S. A. 36 (f)* (207)
EDWARDS, Sidny 45 (m)* (221)
EDWARDS, Simon? 7* (211)
EDWARDS, Wilkins 35* (168)
EDWARDS, Will 38 (m) (B) (287)
EHTRIDGE, T. A. 30 (m), (274)
ELAM, Wm. 41* (200)
ELCAN, Sigh? 60 (m)* (B) (287)
ELCAN?, Fibbie 21 (f)* (B) (271)
ELDER, Jeremiah 38, (353)
ELEZ?, Sam 28 (B) (320)
ELLEN, Delaware 21 (m)* (B) (255)
ELLINGTON, Petter 70 (B) (276)
ELLINGTON, Simon 24 (B) (276)
ELLIOT, James 48* (B) (429)
ELLIOTT, Ambose 39, (376)
ELLIOTT, Flanders 30 (m)* (B) (383)
ELLIS, Ellis 22 (B) (419)
ELLIS, Emmer 19 (f)* (B) (492)
ELLIS, John 27 (B) (311)
ELLIS, Mary 30* (477)
ELLIS, Rose 28 (m) (B) (307)
ELROD, W. 30 (m)* (B) (499)
EMERSON, Mollie 14* (347)
EMERSON, _ 31 (m), (276)
EMMET, JAcob 26* (181)
ENGLE____, John 25, (197)
ENGS?, Elijah 12* (B) (177)

ENZY, Ros 22 (m), (409)
EPPS, Dock 24 (B) (292)
EPPS, Ed 12?* (B) (286)
EPPS, Henry 30* (434)
EPPS, Henry 43, (449)
ERWIN, J. W. 30 (m)* (310)
ERWIN, Mattie 24 (f)* (335)
ERWIN?, John 62* (301)
ESKEW, Jerry 51 (m) (B) (452)
ETHERIDGE, Loury 25 (f)* (B) (249)
ETHRIDGE, M. 66 (m)* (274)
EUBANK, Mary 60, (241)
EVANS, Charles M. 24* (387)
EVANS, Charley 27* (B) (177)
EVANS, Elem 28 (m)* (B) (286)
EVANS, George 20* (B) (249)
EVANS, Jane 75* (B) (268)
EVANS, John 39 (B) (249)
EVANS, John H. 36* (356)
EVANS, Joseph 37, (226)
EVANS, Lizzie 56* (434)
EVANS, Plummer 45 (B) (171)
EVANS, S.? 45 (m), (302)
EVANS, Sam 35 (B) (399)
EVANS, Tom? 12* (B) (270)
EVANS, Wm. 35* (B) (458)
EWEL?, Sarah 45 (B) (448)
EWELL, Bergis 95* (B) (448)
EWELL, Charles 43 (B) (448)
EWELL, Dodridge? 50 (m), (458)
EWELL, Lavinia 42 (B) (460)
EWELL, Louis 40 (B) (459)
EWELL, Matilda 70* (B) (451)
EWELL, Ste___ 48 (m)* (B) (283)
EXUM, Edmon 28* (B) (329)
EXUM, S. 30 (m)* (B) (309)
EXUM, Tom 45* (B) (296)
EXUM, Wm. 82, (297)
E___, John 55 (B) (390)
FAIN, Dave __* (267)
FALLON, Thomas 42, (406)
FALLS, Anthony 58 (B) (493)
FALLS, Bettie 25* (434)
FALLS, Henry 24* (B) (177)
FALLS, Julius 60 (B) (454)
FALLS, Nathan 65 (B) (485)
FALLS, Thomas 27 (B) (400)
FALLS, Willis 40 (B) (454)
FANNING, Agga 55 (m)* (B) (222)
FANNING, Alford V. 29, (407)
FARABY, Walter 19* (381)
FARIS, A. J. 42 (m), (491)
FARIS, W. 17 (m)* (490)
FARIS, Wash 52* (502)
FARLEY, Jas. 31* (310)
FARLEY, Joh A. 72* (386)
FARLEY, John M. 44* (364)
FARLEY, Sterling 54, (363)
FARLEY, Thomas 28?, (409)
FARLEY, Thomas 55, (450)
FARLEY, Wm. 51, (409)
FARLEY, Wm. A. 34, (386)
FARMER, Henry M. 65, (366)
FARMER, Scot 17* (B) (473)
FARRAR, John 40, (286)
FARRAR, T.? A. 52 (f), (280)
FARRAR?, G. W. 42 (m)* (329)

FARRIS, Dan 29 (B) (484)
FARROW, Nick 70* (B) (240)
FASIER, Joe 27* (B) (216)
FASTELLE?, Abe 36 (B) (399)
FAUCETT, MArgaret 50* (168)
FA____, Willis 55* (B) (471)
FEATHERS, J. W. 28 (m), (335)
FEATHERS, Jessie 55 (m)* (335)
FEATHERS, Sam 21 (m), (341)
FEILDS, Eliza 54* (B) (289)
FENTON, Frank 30 (B) (288)
FENTRESS, Benn 27 (B) (307)
FENTRESS, Jane 50* (B) (307)
FERAR, Willie 16 (m)* (B) (426)
FERKERSON, Fill 25 (m)* (B) (466)
FERNANDERS, John 8* (B) (392)
FEROLD, Green 35 (B) (383)
FERRELL, Bryant 17* (253)
FERRELL, Perry 18?, (253)
FETHERS, J. W. 28 (m) (330)
FEUTRIL?, Josephus 41 (B) (199)
FIELD, Abram 35 (B) (420)
FIELD, Buck 25 (B) (269)
FIELDS, Ann H. 18* (B) (256)
FIELDS, Dallis 30* (B) (336)
FIELDS, David 45 (B) (439)
FIELDS, David 65 (B) (228)
FIELDS, Davy 49 (m) (B) (462)
FIELDS, Dick 35 (B) (328)
FIELDS, Ed 32 (B) (288)
FIELDS, Edmond 23* (B) (284)
FIELDS, Eliza 50* (B) (286)
FIELDS, Emily 50* (B) (305)
FIELDS, Emmet 25 (B) (402)
FIELDS, Gilbert 27 (B) (296)
FIELDS, Granerson 27* (B) (273)
FIELDS, Greer 25* (B) (276)
FIELDS, Henry 26 (B) (256)
FIELDS, JAckson 34 (B) (286)
FIELDS, John 17* (B) (167)
FIELDS, John 23* (B) (284)
FIELDS, Julia 40 (B) (288)
FIELDS, King 21* (B) (328)
FIELDS, Lucy 23* (273)
FIELDS, Luster __ (m) (B) (286)
FIELDS, Menifee 30 (m)* (B) (177)
FIELDS, Osey 44 (m) (B) (228)
FIELDS, P. O. R. 28 (m) (B) (281)
FIELDS, Phillip O. 29 (B) (284)
FIELDS, Rumsy 26 (m)* (B) (228)
FIELDS, Sallie 60* (B) (288)
FIELDS, Sally 30 (B) (211)
FIELDS, Sam 25* (B) (161)
FIELDS, Simeon 33 (B) (181)
FIELDS, Wash 47 (B) (281)
FIELDS, Wilber 30* (B) (289)
FIELDS, Wm. 22 (B) (404)
FIELDS, _____ _ (m)* B? (336)
FIELOR?, Alcy 68 (f)* (B) (170)
FIFE, J. A. 45 (m), (483)
FILE, Melvinie 27 (f)* (477)
FILLIPS, Gabe 45 (B) (338)
FILLIPS, Jim 27* (B) (339)
FILLMORE, Millard 30 (B) (355)
FINCH, Bery 40, (450)
FINCH, Lenah 19* (407)
FINDLEY, J. J. 25 (m), (338)
FINDLEY, S. R. 52 (m)* (338)

FINDLEY, W. J. 23 (m)* (338)
FINE?, Warner 30* (369)
FINLEY, Jas. 57 (B) (162)
FINLEY, John 4* (B) (382)
FINLEY, Lazinka 6/12 (f)* (B) (163)
FINLY, George 5* (B) (172)
FINLY, Louis 30* (B) (402)
FINNEY, Abraham 32* (B) (170)
FINNEY, Albert 79 (B) (163)
FINNEY, Armsted 30 (B) (338)
FINNEY, H. W. 42 (f)* (280)
FINNEY, James 66* (B) (172)
FINNEY, Manda 3* (B) (336)
FINNEY?, Robt. 29* (B) (338)
FINNIE, Beng. 23 (B) (289)
FINNY, JAmes 32?* (B) (181)
FINNY, John 26 (B) (171)
FINNY, Moses 33* (B) (166)
FIRTH, ____ 37 (m), (442)
FISHER, Berta 34* (335)
FISHER, Henry 38 (B) (477)
FISHER, John 27 (B) (456)
FISHER, John 7* (B) (176)
FISHER, Mandy 52 (m) (B) (248)
FISHER, Robert 27* (B) (305)
FISHER, Sandy 40 (m) (B) (336)
FISHER, Scot 20* (B) (340)
FISHER, __ __ (m), (180)
FITTS, Lucy 18* (B) (257)
FITZ, Jas. 55* (B) (318)
FITZ, Richard 27* (B) (183)
FITZGERALD, Ben 40 (B) (331)
FITZGERALD, Sam 69, (292)
FITZGERALD, Wm. 48, (408)
FITZHUE, Wash. 41 (m)* (B) (167)
FLANIGAN, Robert 30 (B) (289)
FLANIGAN, Wm. 32 (B) (283)
FLANNIGAN, Robt. 25* (B) (269)
FLEET, Mary 25 (B) (363)
FLEMING, A. A. 30 (m), (278)
FLEMING, Henry 26* (B) (315)
FLEMING, Spencer 22 (B) (346)
FLEMING, Spencer 53 (B) (357)
FLEMING, Wm. 46 (B) (356)
FLEMMING, Amy 35* (B) (386)
FLEMMINS, Robert 48, (411)
FLEMMON?, Jack 50 (B) (404)
FLETCHER, Abe 31, (420)
FLETCHER, Addison 10* (B) (255?)
FLETCHER, Asbury 47, (425)
FLETCHER, G. 29 (m) (B) (457)
FLETCHER, George 70 (B) (175)
FLETCHER, Liza 40* (B) (331)
FLETCHER, Vinie 75 (f)* (B) (378)
FLINT, Matilda 67 (B) (446)
FLINT?, Goleston 37 (m) (B) (446)
FLIPPIN, Ed 30* (B) (323)
FLIPPIN, James 50, (331)
FLIPPIN, Sintha? 29* (B) (241)
FLIPPIN, Thos. J. 47* (169)
FLORENCE?, James T. 51* (411)
FLOURNOY, George M. 25 (B) (255?)

FLOURNOY, Hercules 57* (B) (257)
FLOURNOY, Oscar 32* (415)
FLOURNOY, Walter 31* (269)
FLOYD, J. C. 54 (m), (288)
FLOYD, JAmes 23* (288)
FLYNN, Ann 40* (287)
FOLWELL, Fayette 30 (B) (395)
FORBES, Fanny G. 46, (196)
FORBES, R. C. 72 (m), (286)
FORBES, ____* (195)
FORBS, Jim 18* (B) (225)
FORD, Elizabeth 59* (160)
FORD, John 54* (B) (263)
FORD, Nellie 20* (B) (387)
FORD, Wm. 19, (481)
FORD?, J. C. 41 (m), (314)
FOREST, _. 49 (m) (B) (499)
FORT, Silas 25 (B) (418)
FORTNER, Marthia 40* (468)
FORTNUE?, P. D. 23 (m), (475)
FORTUNE, Mary 58, (409)
FORTUNE, Rufus W. 35, (411)
FOSHEE, Andy 28 (B) (464)
FOSTER, A. G. 56 (m), (203)
FOSTER, Alburt 50 (B) (478)
FOSTER, John L. 23* (388)
FOSTER, Julius 55 (B) (464)
FOSTER, Robert 36* (B) (390)
FOSTER, Viney 64* (B) (390)
FOSTON, George 80* (B) (479)
FOUCE, Anderson 25* (B) (222)
FOUST, Walter 26 (B) (211)
FOWLER, J. 21 (m)* (211)
FOWLER, Lena 20* (222)
FOWLER, Lindsay 9 (m)* (B) (366)
FOWLER, Nicie 21, (410)
FRANK, Cha___ 27 (m)* (B) (244)
FRANK, Thomas 14* (B) (417)
FRANKEY, Wryley 19 (m)* (388)
FRANKIN, W. E. 46 (Dr.)* (443)
FRANKLIN, Champ 31 (B) (435)
FRANKLIN, Elizabeth 40* (B) (355)
FRANKLIN, Hed? 50 (m)* (B) (321)
FRANKLIN, Henry 37* (B) (433)
FRANKLIN, Jane 29* (433)
FRANKLIN, Perry 46 (B) (435)
FRANKLIN, Perry 55* (B) (477)
FRANKLIN, Sina 28 (f)* (B) (426)
FRANKLIN, Tobe 20* (B) (437)
FRANKLIN, W. 5 (m)* (B) (498)
FRANKS, Gabreal 18* (B) (490)
FRASER, Edward 45 (B) (270)
FRASER, Robert 34, (190)
FRASIER, D. N.? 68 (m), (186)
FRASIER, Jinny 23?* (B) (165)
FRAZER, Albert 62* (B) (307)
FRAZER, Lindsy 23 (m)* (201)
FRAZIER, Charles 25 (B) (236)
FRAZIER, Emily E. 46* (283)
FRAZIER, Henry 23* (B) (275)
FRAZIER, Mary 52* (225)
FREELAND, J. J. 37? (m), (209)
FREELING, J. R. 29 (m), (207)
FREEMAN, Daniel 35 (B) (243)

FREEMAN, H. F. 54 (m)* (204)
FREEMAN, Leathy 30 (B) (281)
FREEMAN, Mary 50* (B) (422)
FREEMAN, Naomy 50, (164)
FREEMAN, Robert 28* (B) (420)
FREEMAN, W. 38 (m)* (306)
FREEMAN, W. H. 39 (m), (277)
FREEMAN, Weastor 21 (m)* (B) (422)
FREEMON, Alen 102* (206)
FREY?, J. G. 46 (m), (339)
FRIDELL, Alex 20* (195)
FRIER, Eaton 53, (406)
FRIERSON, Ben 24* (B) (285)
FRINSTER?, Hunter? 4* (B) (415)
FRISBY, Albert 34, (184)
FRYASON, Wash 15* (B) (397)
FR__, Lucinda 65 (B) (461)
FULLER, E. F. 20 (m)* (170)
FULLER, J. B. 53 (m), (169)
FULLER, J. H. 53 (m)* (213)
FULTON, W. F. 40 (m)* (289)
FUMER?, George 12* (B) (309)
FURERON, Carles 30 (m)* (414)
FUTRELL, Peter 53 (B) (245)
FUTRELL?, Mollie 22* (B) (246)
F____, Mary 60* (291)
GAINES, Henry 50* (B) (183)
GAINES, Jack 38* (B) (258)
GAINOR, Thomas 16* (B) (357)
GAITHER, Andrew 18* (B) (478)
GAITHER, Berry 24* (B) (175)
GAITHER, DAve 39* (476)
GAITHER, Emma 55* (480)
GAITHER, Fielden 19* (B) (480)
GAITHER, Harriss? 40 (B) (476)
GAITHER, Henry? 27 (B) (481)
GAITHER, Henry? 50 (B) (476)
GAITHER, J. B. 52 (m)* (482)
GAITHER, J. G. 28 (m)* (482)
GAITHER, J. P. 50 (m)* (482)
GAITHER, Miles 42 (B) (479)
GAITHER, S. E. 35 (m), (483)
GAITHER, Wile? 18 (m)* (476)
GAITHER, Wm. 43* (480)
GALE, L. 40 (f)* (B) (311)
GALE?, ___ 35 (m) (B) (211)
GALLAGHER, James 58, (191)
GALLAHA, John 55, (451)
GALLAWAY, Cuff 45 (B) (279)
GALLAWAY, N. W. 38 (m)* (279)
GALLAWAY, Simon 60* (B) (279)
GALLAWAY, T. S. 39 (m)* (169)
GAMER, JAckson 9* (B) (296)
GAMMON, Henry 28 (B) (449)
GAMMON, Jane? 50, (261)
GANT, Edd 30 (B) (339)
GANT, Henry 44* (171)
GANT, Margrett 60* (B) (280)
GANT, Martha 70* (488)
GARDENER, Frank 20* (B) (369)
GARDENER, _. 36 (m) (B) (304)
GARDER, Frank 22* (B) (426)
GARDNER, Edward 28 (B) (352)
GARDNER, Mose 55 (B) (402)
GARDNER, ____ 45 (m)* (B) (228)
GARISON, Elln 43?* (393)

GARMON, Mary 15* (B) (206)
GARMON, Moses 57* (B) (354)
GARNER, George? 15* (B) (296)
GARNETT, Frank 25* (B) (236)
GARRETT, Bennet? 47 (m) (B) (288)
GARRETT, John 45* (250)
GARRISON, Caleb 70* (B) (342)
GARRISON, J. T. 42 (m)* (332)
GARRISON, ____ 32 (f)* (319)
GARRISON?, Ann 50* (315)
GARVIN, Hillery 82 (m), (327)
GARVIN, J. A. 40 (m)* (327)
GARVIN, Oliver 28* (B) (171)
GASTON, Jane 60* (B) (258)
GATES, A. C. 47, (203)
GATES, John 23* (168)
GATES, Lottie 4 (f)* (329)
GATEWOOD, Allen 25* (433)
GATEWOOD, Kesiah 53* (183)
GATEWOOD, Wm. M. 44, (408)
GATHER, Mary J. 50* (440)
GATHRIGHT?, Wm. 30* (B) (258)
GATHWRIGHT, Phillis 21* (B) (239)
GATLEY, MArtha 85* (488)
GATLEY, R. 50 (m), (490)
GAVAN, Lee 16 (m)* (B) (498)
GAVAN, Mary 75* (499)
GAVAN?, P. 45 (m)* (B) (497)
GAYTON, Harrison 37, (365)
GEATER?, Albert 37 (B) (471)
GENTER?, Bettie S. 2* (B) (483)
GEORGE, Evan 72, (170)
GERALD, John 22* (230)
GEREALD, Andrew 60, (250)
GERMAN, Crockett 49* (181)
GERMAN?, John 39 (B) (384)
GIBSON, Matt 29* (B) (389)
GIBSON, Wm. 50 (B) (387)
GIBSON, Wm. 53 (B) (387)
GIDEON?, Dick 22 (B) (270)
GIFFORD, Robert 55, (361)
GILBERT, Margaret 50* (B) (386)
GILCHRIST, Steve 39 (B) (466)
GILES, Cicero __* (B?) (199)
GILES, Ned 36 (B) (214)
GILFORD, Elias 47* (B) (288)
GILL, Beckey 23 (B) (477)
GILL, Edward T. 42* (357)
GILL, S. S. 49 (m)* (314)
GILLAM, Charley 23* (466)
GILLASPIE, Ike 24 (B) (184)
GILLASPIE, Richard 53 (B) (184)
GILLERNSTER?, James 25* (B) (425)
GILLESPIE, E. 29 (m)* (316)
GILLESPIE, E. A. 23 (m)* (344)
GILLIAM, Hugh 21 (B) (389)
GILLIAM?, Julia 45* (B) (389)
GILLIAN, Ann 10* (B) (482)
GILLIAN, James 55* (230)
GILLIS, Silas 50 (B) (462)
GILLISPA, Virgia 50 (f) (B) (491)
GIMERSON, July 17* (B) (236)
GLASCOCK, Bettie 26* (162)
GLASGOW, Isaac 65 (B) (349)
GLASS, Margret 7* (B) (261)
GLASS, Minty 65? (f), (393)

GLASS, Wm. 10?* (B) (197)
GLASS?, Trusty 26 (m)* (B) (190)
GLASTOR, Stephen 21 (B) (251)
GLAVES?, J. G. 26 (m), (317)
GLEN, Alace 17* (B) (222)
GLENN, Allen 52 (B) (288)
GLENN, Charlotte 50* (B) (348)
GLENN, Jack 60 (B) (294)
GLENN, Martha 56* (B) (314)
GLOSTER, Davy 50 (B) (457)
GLOSTER, Fred 32 (B) (445)
GLOVER, A. D. 35 (m), (323)
GLOVER, Ann 30 (B) (434)
GLOVER, James 36, (342)
GLOVER, Jno. W. 34, (199)
GLOVER, Julie 30 (B) (479)
GLOVER, Manuel? 26 (B) (448)
GLOVER, W. _. 40 (m), (205)
GLOVER, Wm. 59 (B) (460)
GOBER, Benjamin 38* (B) (429)
GOBER?, Wm. 19* (B) (416)
GOBERT, Asbury 40* (429)
GODBY, Ann 63* (299)
GODSEY, Daniel 26, (359)
GODSEY, Jerry 70 (m)* (332)
GODSEY, John 28* (332)
GODSEY, Wm. 40, (412)
GOEN, L. 52 (m)* (324)
GOEN, W. A. 28 (m), (324)
GOEN, Wm. 40 (B) (488)
GOFF, John 24* (277)
GOLDEN, _. W. 24 (m)* (B) (168)
GOLDING, George 51 (B) (349)
GOLMON, Pink 22 (m)* (B) (494)
GOOD, J. V. 48 (m), (329)
GOOD, Joseph 22* (B) (452)
GOOD, Olly 17 (m)* (B) (500)
GOOD, W. J. 25 (m), (329)
GOODE, Alex 30 (B) (277)
GOODE, Andrew 72 (B) (349)
GOODE, D. A. C. 5_ (m)* (284)
GOODE, Ella 10* (B) (460)
GOODE, Henry 58 (B) (348)
GOODE, James 56 (B) (348)
GOODE, Plummer 35 (B) (348)
GOODE, Rebecca 60 (B) (460)
GOODEN, Abram 50 (B) (267)
GOODEN, Ches 28 (m) (B) (272)
GOODEN, Henry 2* (B) (473)
GOODEN, Monroe 31* (B) (264)
GOODEN, Susan 35* (B) (466)
GOODLOE, Frank 24* (B) (265)
GOODMAN, Edmond 30 (B) (273)
GOODMAN, Isom? 49 (B) (276)
GOODMAN, Jim 30 (B) (294)
GOODMAN?, A. 30 (m) (B) (313)
GOODWIN, Hana 38* (B) (229)
GOODWIN, Patsy 14* (B) (262)
GOODWIN, Sandy 45 (B) (435)
GOODWIN, Willie 6 (f)* (B) (263)
GOODY, Egby? 43 (m) (473)
GOODY?, Frank 24* (B) (167)
GOOSMANN, Fred 28, (166)
GORAN, Anne 40 (B) (416)
GORMON, Peter 25* (B) (355)
GORVIN, M. T. 38 (f)* (477)

GOSER?, Caesar 73* (B) (361)
GOSS, H. 23 (m) (B) (186)
GOSSER, Isidore 29* (166)
GOSSETT, Martin 30, (385)
GOSSETT, Taylor 35, (385)
GOSSETT, Thomas 40, (383)
GOSSETT, Wm. H. 38, (385)
GOWERS, _. 28 (m), (494)
GRAEBY?, A. 50 (f) (B) (310)
GRAHAM, Chas. __ (B) (434)
GRAHAM, H. C. 66 (m), (182)
GRAHAM, Ike 28? (B) (161)
GRAHAM, James 4_ (B) (405)
GRAHAM, Robert 38* (429)
GRAHAM, Thomas 16* (B) (170)
GRAHAM, Walter 36, (331)
GRAHAM?, Edmond 5* (381)
GRANBERRY, A. 18 (m)* (B) (308)
GRANBERRY, Albert 22 (B) (401)
GRANBERRY, Alonzo 41 (B) (396)
GRANBERRY, Arry? 52 (f) (B) (309)
GRANBERRY, Dudney? 27 (m) (B) (397)
GRANBERRY, Everette 60 (B) (400)
GRANBERRY, Geo. __ (B) (290)
GRANBERRY, Henry 48 (B) (398)
GRANBERRY, James 36 (B) (330)
GRANBERRY, John 35 (B) (398)
GRANBERRY, John 65 (B) (356)
GRANBERRY, R. 21 (m) (B) (309)
GRANBERRY, Rose 55* (B) (346)
GRANBERRY, Susan 26* (B) (402)
GRANBERRY, Wash 52* (B) (397)
GRANBERRY, Wesley 27 (B) (399)
GRANBERRY, Willie 23? (m) (B) (398)
GRANBERRY, Wm. B. 45, (407)
GRANBERRY, Wooton? 37 (m) (B) (401)
GRANBERY, Grandison 25* (B) (351)
GRANBERY, Henderson 27* (B) (351)
GRANBERY, James H. 52* (349)
GRANBERY, John 21* (B) (184)
GRANBERY, Milton 35 (B) (349)
GRANBERY, Peter 44 (B) (359)
GRANBURY, Cary 50 (m) (B) (401)
GRANBURY, James 24 (B) (401)
GRANDBERRY, Jackson 35* (B) (397)
GRANT, Jack 31 (B) (284)
GRANT, Joseph C. 49* (392)
GRANT, Thom 38 (m)* (B) (498)
GRANTHAM, Sue H. __ (cook)* (B) (445)
GRAVES, Adaline 25 (B) (457)
GRAVES, Anthony 22 (B) (457)
GRAVES, Ben 44 (B) (438)
GRAVES, Elizabeth 50* (444)
GRAVES, Ellen 62* (415)
GRAVES, Frank 26 (B) (467)

11

GRAVES, James 54* (376)
GRAVES, James H. 25 (B) (362)
GRAVES, John 30* (389)
GRAVES, Mary 41, (438)
GRAVES, Mary 45 (B) (445)
GRAVES, Nancy 19* (B) (376)
GRAVES, rank 28* (B) (370)
GRAY, Alexander 24* (B) (419)
GRAY, Bob 30 (B) (470)
GRAY, Cater? 35 (m) (B) (466)
GRAY, Cato 50 (B) (185)
GRAY, Eliga 25* (B) (208)
GRAY, George 24* (B) (493)
GRAY, Harriet 50* (322)
GRAY, Israel 24* (B) (419)
GRAY, James 55* (B) (225)
GRAY, John J. 24* (346)
GRAY, Sarah 21 (B) (184)
GRAY?, James 30* (B) (267)
GRAYHAM, Jack 60, (373)
GREAN, Moses 32 (B) (459)
GREEN, Alphonso 12* (202)
GREEN, Amber 33 (m), (450)
GREEN, Annie 22* (221)
GREEN, Bud 20 (f)* (B) (229)
GREEN, Carter 40 (B) (379)
GREEN, Edward 44, (197)
GREEN, George 26 (B) (175)
GREEN, George 28* (B) (167)
GREEN, Gilbert 60* (B) (201)
GREEN, H. M. 52 (m)* (208)
GREEN, H. S. 18 (m)* (203)
GREEN, Hampton 47* (B) (360)
GREEN, Hanna 80* (B) (286)
GREEN, Harry 70 (B) (195)
GREEN, Isaac 60* (B) (273)
GREEN, Jesse 26, (191)
GREEN, John 45 (B) (173)
GREEN, Joseph 32, (224)
GREEN, Lucind 35 (f) (B) (453)
GREEN, Mary 22* (B) (205)
GREEN, Mary A. 70* (370)
GREEN, Miles 45* (B) (384)
GREEN, Rosa 28* (B) (284)
GREEN, Rosa 45 (B) (377)
GREEN, S. 75 (f)* (B) (489)
GREEN, Sandy 45 (m) (B) (455)
GREEN, Susan 80* (B) (392)
GREEN, Sylva 75* (B) (479)
GREEN, Thomas 56 (B) (360)
GREEN, Tinnie 22 (f) (B) (401)
GREEN, W. 28? (m) (B) (267)
GREEN, Wilbert 24 (B) (277)
GREEN, Wm. 30* (B) (420)
GREEN, _____ 24? (m) (B) (193)
GREEN, _____ __ (B) (193)
GREEN?, George 45, (169)
GREEN?, Patrick 55 (B) (451)
GREEN?, Virginia 52, (442)
GREEN?, William 27, (442)
GREENLAW, Jack 40 (B) (396)
GREENLEA, John 14* (B) (229)
GREENLEE, Abraham 38 (B) (298)
GREENLEE, J. 12? (m)* (B) (304)
GREENLEE, Jane 43* (B) (304)
GREENWAY, Ama 28* (198)
GREENWAY, Orange 60 (B) (171)
GREENWAY, Sug 47 (f), (161)

GREER, Eugenia 3* (B) (429)
GREER, James J. 47, (201)
GREER, Nora 30 (B) (282)
GREGGEN, Andrew 18* (B) (255?)
GREGOR, Thomas 52 (B) (424)
GREGORY, Geo. T. 22* (280)
GREGORY, JOhn 37, (408)
GRIFFIN, Allen 35, (408)
GRIFFIN, Charles 25* (B) (391)
GRIFFIN, David 45* (B) (495)
GRIFFIN, E. 50 (m), (299)
GRIFFIN, H. S. 24 (m)* (298)
GRIFFIN, J. E. 30 (m)* (279)
GRIFFIN, JOhn 39 (B) (307)
GRIFFIN, Larkin 29 (B) (446)
GRIFFIN, Margaret 42* (425)
GRIFFIN, Samuel 20* (424)
GRIFFIN, Thomas 21, (425)
GRIFFIN, Thomas 35, (408)
GRIFFIN, W. F. 36 (m)* (321)
GRIFFIN, _____ __ (f)* (192)
GRIGG, Archie 50* (B) (265)
GRIGG, Winnie 80* (B) (265)
GRIGGIN?, John 15* (B) (257)
GRIGGS, Elizabeth 46* (184)
GRIGGS, Jordan 52* (B) (177)
GRIGGS, Payton 50 (B) (245)
GRIGGS, Rose 17* (B) (184)
GRIGSBY, Jerry 20* (B) (267)
GRIMES, W. M. 4 (m)* (274)
GRIMES, Walter 18* (B) (315)
GRIMM?, Lou 44 (m), (443)
GRISSOM, Isaac 53, (274)
GRISSOM, Wylie 63* (B) (361)
GRIZLE, Isrel? 37 (m) (B) (206)
GROVES, Lewis? 22* (B) (271)
GRUDGER, Nancy 60* (214)
GUDGER, Wm. 43 (B) (184)
GUINN?, Eligah 30* (B) (391)
GUNN, Albert 35 (B) (413)
GUNN, Joe 10* (B) (420)
GUY, C. J. 25 (m), (480)
GUY, Hiram 50* (414)
GUYN, Cain 34 (B) (415)
GUYN, Hugh 38, (423)
GUYN, James 49* (414)
GWYN, James 35, (423)
GWYN, James 42 (B) (429)
GWYN, James 8* (B) (365)
G____, Green 23, (414)
G____, Thomas 22* (305)
G____S, JOhn 20* (465)
HACK, Wm. 45* (B) (337)
HAHN, Ben 60* (443)
HAHN?, John 30 (B) (456)
HAILEY, _. S. 57* (203)
HAIR, Ceasar 60 (B) (294)
HAIR, James 23, (324)
HAIR, John S. 50, (406)
HAIRE?, Precilla 80* (B) (229)
HAKINS, Pleas 24, (194)
HALE, Bernard 40 (B) (261)
HALE, Malinda 59* (B) (270)
HALEY, Salie 30 (B) (210)
HALL, Alfred 54 (B) (272)
HALL, Ann 45 (B) (205)
HALL, Antemey? 22 (m) (B) (482)
HALL, Dennise? 35 (m) (B) (330)

HALL, Easter 32 (B) (208)
HALL, Edmon B. 77* (478)
HALL, George 46* (B) (422)
HALL, Hariet 18* (B) (211)
HALL, James 35 (B) (336)
HALL, Jennie 15* (317)
HALL, Jennie 15* (342)
HALL, John 34* (B) (254)
HALL, John 35* (B) (262)
HALL, Louis 29 (B) (375)
HALL, MAggie 34* (324)
HALL, Mariah 17* (B) (329)
HALL, Mariah 65* (B) (337)
HALL, Martha 20* (B) (205)
HALL, Mike 60 (B) (206)
HALL, W. C. 50 (m), (316)
HALL, W. C. 50 (m), (344)
HALL, Wm. 67 (B) (255?)
HALLEY, Allice 18* (B) (175)
HALLEY, Bill 70 (B) (326)
HALLEY, Oppy? 30 (m), (326)
HALLEY, Wm. 75* (B) (175)
HALLS, George 19* (B) (501)
HAMBLET, W. T. 31 (m)* (344)
HAMBLETON, F. M. 57 (m), (291)
HAMBLETT, J. G. 32 (m), (275)
HAMBLETT, W. T. 51 (m)* (316)
HAMBRIC, Mary 37, (408)
HAMBROUGH, James 40 (B) (384)
HAMELL, Candiss 21 (m) (B) (354)
HAMELL, Cherry 48 (f) (B) (356)
HAMER, Alfred 24* (B) (284)
HAMER, Bettie 30* (B) (501)
HAMETT?, Monroe 32 (B) (450)
HAMILTON, Lucinda 32, (334)
HAMLETT, Wm. 7* (B) (309)
HAMLIN, Louis 49* (B) (241)
HAMMER, J. H. 41 (m)* (280)
HAMMOCK, E. 16 (f)* (488)
HAMMOND, Frank 55* (B) (353)
HAMMOND, Jerry 58? (m) (B) (200)
HAMMOND, Lewis 27* (B) (191)
HAMNER, Austin M. 48, (345)
HAMNER, L. D. 34 (m)* (284)
HAMNER, Laura 9* (280)
HAMON, Alax 20* (B) (250)
HAMPSTON, Edd 25 (B) (394)
HAMPTON, Armisted 50, (427)
HAMPTON, Bettie 65* (B) (427)
HAMPTON, Frank 37, (427)
HAMPTON, John 58* (427)
HAMPTON, M.? 30 (m) (B) (389)
HAMPTON, Martha 17* (B) (359)
HANCOCK, L. 14 (m)* (B) (447)
HANCOCK, Wm. 50, (447)
HANCOCK, _____ 61 (f)* (187)
HANERFORD, Ned 28 (B) (393)
HANES, J. 25 (m)* (B) (206)
HANES, Smithie 40 (f)* (375)
HANES?, Jim 45 (B) (267)
HANNER, Isabella 30* (B) (242)
HARBER, Hettie 50* (B) (332)

HARBERD, Chany 32 (m)* (B) (215)
HARDEN, G. M. 30 (m)* (168)
HARDEN, M. L. 64 (m)* (205)
HARDEN, Sarah 61* (194)
HARDIN, Jim 46* (B) (206)
HARDY, Dave 59 (B) (479)
HARDY, George 57 (B) (301)
HARDY, HEnry 46 (B) (224)
HARDY, Tandy 32 (m) (B) (208)
HARE, Alexander? 38* (B) (164)
HARE, Ross 55 (B) (232)
HARE?, Mollie 18* (B) (348)
HARGIS, J. M. 27 (m)* (488)
HARGROVE, Mary 35 (B) (405)
HARIS, E. E. 78 (f)* (205)
HARIS, M. 26 (f) (B) (205)
HARIS, Thomas 46 (B) (384)
HARISON, Lela 37* (B) (418)
HARPER, Lucey 17* (B) (267)
HARPER?, Cornelious 30 (B) (392)
HARPER?, Joe 19* (B) (265)
HARR, Larance 20 (m) (B) (381)
HARR, Nelson 40 (B) (382)
HARREL, Bryant 24 (B) (209)
HARREL, L. C. 30 (m)* (317)
HARREL, M. A. 60 (f)* (317)
HARREL, Petter 60* (B) (288)
HARRELL, James C. 40, (367)
HARRELL, M. C. 60 (f)* (342)
HARRELL, Wm. R. 30* (360)
HARRELL, _. C. 30 (m)* (342)
HARRELS, Asberry 45 (B) (395)
HARRIS, Abe 24* (B) (262)
HARRIS, Abram 46 (B) (457)
HARRIS, Agnes 60* (B) (349)
HARRIS, Andrew 60 (B) (307)
HARRIS, Berry 40 (B) (177)
HARRIS, Bert 45* (468)
HARRIS, C. B. 28 (m)* (295)
HARRIS, Caleb 78* (268)
HARRIS, Calvin C. 50, (162)
HARRIS, Chas. 19* (277)
HARRIS, Daniel 32* (273)
HARRIS, David 37 (B) (431)
HARRIS, Dorse 22 (m)* (B) (456)
HARRIS, Edd 30 (B) (477)
HARRIS, Eliza 58 (B) (285)
HARRIS, Eliza 58 (B) (285)
HARRIS, Elizabeth 23 (B) (314)
HARRIS, Elizabeth 61, (289)
HARRIS, Ellen 50 (B) (499)
HARRIS, Gill 40 (m)* (B) (285)
HARRIS, HEnderson 25* (B) (292)
HARRIS, HEnry 25 (B) (294)
HARRIS, Henry 34* (295)
HARRIS, Henry 37 (B) (288)
HARRIS, Henry 46 (B) (178)
HARRIS, Hudson 52, (427)
HARRIS, Isaac 30 (B) (400)
HARRIS, Isaac 50 (B) (402)
HARRIS, J. 35 (m) (B) (171)
HARRIS, Jacob 60* (B) (234)
HARRIS, James 51 (B) (289)
HARRIS, Joe 21* (B) (340)
HARRIS, John 23* (B) (167)
HARRIS, John 27, (433)
HARRIS, John 27 (B) (290)

HARRIS, John 37* (B) (474)
HARRIS, Joseph 31* (B) (384)
HARRIS, Juda 18* (B) (498)
HARRIS, Kate 14* (B) (161)
HARRIS, Littleton 30 (B) (465)
HARRIS, Lucy A. 35?* (297)
HARRIS, Mary 50 (B) (280)
HARRIS, Moses 17* (B) (390)
HARRIS, Moses 60* (B) (262)
HARRIS, N. 62 (m)* (501)
HARRIS, NAnnie 17* (B) (169)
HARRIS, Nelson 23* (B) (484)
HARRIS, Nelson 32* (B) (234)
HARRIS, Orange 50 (m) (B) (292)
HARRIS, Rece? 60 (m) (B) (260)
HARRIS, Robert 40, (417)
HARRIS, Rody 40 (f) (B) (376)
HARRIS, Scott 24* (B) (192)
HARRIS, T. 69 (m), (486)
HARRIS, Thomas 42, (196)
HARRIS, Tildy 21* (B) (206)
HARRIS, Tucker 26* (348)
HARRIS, Ump? 26 (m) (B) (262)
HARRIS, Virginia 7?* (B) (262)
HARRIS, W. O. 24 (m)* (280)
HARRIS, Whit. A. 55 (m)* (163)
HARRIS, Wilks? __ (B) (190)
HARRIS, Willson 30 (B) (397)
HARRIS, Wilson 55 (B) (162)
HARRIS, Wm. 25 (B) (383)
HARRIS, Wm. 26 (B) (436)
HARRIS, Wm. 42* (428)
HARRIS, Wm. 50 (B) (259)
IIARRIS, ____ __* (B) (190)
HARRIS?, John 25 (B) (485)
HARRISON, Bart 76 (B) (328)
HARRISON, D. W. 53 (m), (328)
HARRISON, Eliza 74, (328)
HARRISON, Henry 39 (B) (457)
HARRISON, Joe 35 (B) (328)
HARRISON, Miles 24, (328)
HARRISON, Milly 20* (322)
HARRISON, R. 50 (m)* (255?)
HARRISON?, D. W. 55 (m), (327)
HARRISS, Charlette 70* (B) (335)
HARRY, Tidda 16 (f)* (B) (244)
HART, MAry __* (259)
HARTRIDGE, Mary 25* (164)
HARVELL, W. F. 38 (m), (293)
HARVEY, G.? E. 26 (m), (163)
HARVEY, Henry 48 (B) (428)
HARVEY, J. 21 (m) (B) (498)
HARVEY, Martha 41* (466)
HARVEY, Nancy 77* (424)
HARVEY, R. F. 29 (m), (267)
HARVEY, Richard 64, (230)
HARVEY, Sarah 65, (201)
HARVEY, Simon 36, (245)
HARVEY, Willis H. 30, (239)
HARVEY?, David 30* (192)
HARVGY, Henry 37 (B) (385)
HARVILL?, Basil? 50 (m) (B) (270)
HARVY, Granvil 66 (m) (B) (203)
HARVY, James 47 (B) (384)
HARVY, Jef 30 (B) (499)
HARVY?, Louis 40 (B) (454)
HARWELL, Abe 50? (B) (253)

HARWELL, Columbus 68 (B) (265)
HARWELL, Fisher 12* (287)
HARWELL, Hannah 65* (B) (261)
HARWELL, Harry 50? (B) (266)
HARWELL, Jane 23 (B) (266)
HARWELL, Joe 42 (B) (261)
HARWELL, Joe jr. 19?* (B) (261)
HARWELL, Lucy 45, (445)
HARWELL, Napoleon? _2, (265)
HARWELL, Phil 15* (B) (253)
HARWELL, West 40* (B) (264)
HARWELL, ____ 20 (m) (B) (266)
HARWELL, ____ 32 (m)* (B) (266)
HARWELL?, Lou 20 (f)* (B) (264)
HASKINS, Calvin 27* (168)
HASKINS, Clora 22* (B) (235)
HASKINS, John 21 (B) (258)
HASKINS, John 57 (B) (165)
HASKINS, Martha 48* (B) (164)
HASLER, James 39, (423)
HASLETT, Jobe 50 (B) (394)
HASLETT, ____ 64 (f) (B) (300)
HASLETTE?, Ann E. 22* (411)
HASLETTE?, Haywood 45 (B) (404)
HASLETTE?, James A. 76, (411)
HASLETTE?, Jessie 30 (m) (B) (402)
HASLETTE?, John C. 45, (410)
HASLETTE?, Millie 50 (B) (403)
HASLETTE?, Robert 27 (B) (403)
HASLETTE?, Zeke 24 (m) (B) (403)
HASSLER, Daniel 53* (421)
HASTELLE?, Albert 21 (B) (403)
HASTELLE?, Allen 30 (B) (400)
HASTELLE?, Fielden 25 (B) (400)
HASTELLE?, James 25* (B) (400)
HASTELLE?, Leander 25 (B) (400)
HASTINGS, Mary 26* (B) (443)
HASTINGS, Tucker 28 (B) (423)
HASTLET, Alsie 65 (f) (B) (162)
HATCH, Manie 25 (f) (B) (389)
HATCHER, Jas. A. 37* (B) (270)
HATLEY, Turner? 14* (B) (496)
HATTON, Analiza 51, (441)
HATTON, James 27* (440)
HATTON, James 35, (441)
HATTON, Lula 24* (441)
HAULWOOD, George 23 (B) (450)
HAVELCAMP?, L. 11 (f)* (489)
HAVERCAMP?, H. 50 (m)* (490)
HAWKINS, Frances 20* (B) (343)
HAWKINS, John 25, (201)
HAWKINS, W. K. 26 (m)* (168)
HAWLEY, Henry H. 50, (385)
HAYES, Adeline 36 (B) (347)
HAYES, John 30* (B) (355)
HAYES, MArgaret 31 (B) (162)
HAYS, Aron 50, (278)

HAYS, Carrie 6* (B) (226)
HAYS, J. 65 (m) (B) (252)
HAYS, JOhn T. 24* (168)
HAYS, James 54 (B) (187)
HAYS, Parish 36 (m) (B) (299)
HAYS, Reuben 25* (B) (305)
HAYS, Reuben 62* (B) (305)
HAYS, Samuel 55 (B) (305)
HAYS, ____ 22 (m) (B) (235)
HAYSE, ____ 45 (f)* (B) (185)
HAYWOOD, L. F.? 54 (m), (309)
HAZELETT, Betsy 56* (B) (417)
HAZELETT?, Jerome 50 (B) (402)
HAZELWOOD, J.? L. 40 (m), (204)
HAZLETTE, Bucker 24 (m)* (B) (468)
HAZLETTE, Frank 50* (B) (193)
HAZLEWOOD, Anston 69 (m) (B) (207)
HAZLEWOOD, John 59* (422)
HAZLEWOOD, M. F. 62 (f)* (213)
HAZLEWOOD, _. E. 33 (m)* (204)
HA__LER, J. R. 22 (f)* (179)
HA____LL, ____ 18 (f) (B) (264)
HEAD, James 28, (426)
HEAD, Jane 72* (430)
HEAD, Munsey 30 (m), (426)
HEART, Eliza 42 (B) (491)
HEART, James 40 (B) (467)
HEART, Jane 45 (B) (489)
HEART, Matilda 19* (B) (200)
HEART, Scott 25* (B) (489)
HEART?, Clabe 25 (m) (B) (467)
HEASLETT, Lewis 60 (B) (359)
HEATHCOCK, Jas. 24, (200)
HEATHCOCK, Mahaley 49, (191)
HEATHROE, Betsy 40* (190)
HECHT?, Ike 34* (434)
HEIFLIN, George 58* (225)
HEINRICH, John B. 38, (167)
HEINSUCKER?, Arch 60, (429)
HELM, Bill 52* (B) (339)
HEMMAUGH?, C. 52 (m), (493)
HENCELY, Jake 26, (490)
HENDERSON, Caroline 50 (B) (346)
HENDERSON, Fannie 35 (B) (243)
HENDERSON, Fletcher? 19* (B) (231)
HENDERSON, Green 27 (B) (249)
HENDERSON, JAck 19* (B) (239)
HENDERSON, Joshua 78 (B) (247)
HENDERSON, Kerry? 25 (m) (B) (243)
HENDERSON, Moss 63 (m) (B) (239)
HENDERSON, Peter 30 (B) (399)
HENDERSON, Puss 29* (B) (243)
HENDERSON, Rebecca __* (B) (243)

HENDERSON, Richmon 73 (B) (239)
HENDERSON, Smith 27* (B) (168)
HENDERSON, Winnie 45* (B) (432)
HENDERSON, Wm. 14* (B) (239)
HENDERSON, Wm. 25 (B) (244)
HENDERSON, Wyatt 55* (B) (246)
HENDON, John R. 75* (165)
HENDRICK, _. G. 70 (m)* (269)
HENDRICKS, Ellie 63 (m) (B) (472)
HENDRIX, Polly 26* (B) (285)
HENDRIX, Will 10* (B) (321)
HENLEY, Elijah 58* (190)
HENLEY, V. 26 (m), (190)
HENLEY, Wm. 29, (385)
HENLY, Mark 42, (332)
HENLY, Ninie 37 (f)* (406)
HENN, Betsey 50* (B) (295)
HENNON, Dudney? 15 (m)* (372)
HENRURY?, Walker 9* (B) (375)
HENRY, Ann 4/12?* (B) (259)
HENRY, Benjamin 42, (376)
HENRY, John 29, (376)
HENRY, John 80, (417)
HENRY, Thomas 85* (391)
HENSON, A. 31 (m), (321)
HENSON, Elizabeth 21* (384)
HENSON, Henry 18* (B) (163)
HERALD?, Orange 25 (B) (390)
HEREFORD, Anderson 27* (B) (422)
HERGASON?, Peter 23?* (B) (162)
HERNDON, Dora 22* (199)
HERNDON, E. E. 32 (m)* (182)
HERNDON, H. E. 66 (m), (162)
HERNDON, John 30* (370)
HERNDON, Martha 46* (441)
HERNDON, Rena 60 (B) (166)
HERRON, Eliza 60, (295)
HERRON, Emma 30, (279)
HERRON, George 22* (B) (273)
HERRON, HArrison 37* (284)
HERRON, J. R. 33 (m)* (295)
HERRON, John 26 (B) (221)
HERRON, John T. 20* (284)
HERRON, Mealy 20 (f)* (B) (279)
HERRON, P. 60 (f)* (B) (289)
HERRON, Polly 60* (B) (274)
HERRON, T. 27 (m), (279)
HERRON?, Bill 21* (B) (251)
HERSTON, Joshaway 35 (m) (B) (456)
HESSY, Green 25 (B) (398)
HESTER, Alace 25 (B) (454)
HESTER, Ann 38 (B) (177)
HESTER, David 21 (B) (177)
HESTER, Henry 26* (167)
HESTER, James 44? (B) (313)
HESTER, Lizzie 22* (348)
HESTER, Mollie 10* (B) (426)
HESTER, Willis 26 (B) (177)
HESTER?, George _* (338)

HESTER?, John 30* (426)

HEVENTON?, Tom? 70* (B) (382)

HEWETT?, Minkle 10 (m)* (221)

HICK, George 22* (236)

HICKMAN, Fannie 20* (B) (356)

HICKMAN, Leanna 34 (B) (351)

HICKS, G. 32 (m)* (B) (341)

HICKS, Jobe 30* (205)

HICKS, Landon 23, (234)

HICKS, W. A. 13 (f)* (206)

HICKS, Wm. 28, (207)

HICKS, Wm. 38 (B) (273)

HIGGASON, C. 7 (f)* (B) (161)

HIGGASON, Elizabeth 67* (164)

HIGGASON, John 23* (B) (418)

HIGGASON, Violet 58* (B) (162)

HIGGINS, James 50 (B) (397)

HIGGS, Louis 35 (B) (438)

HIGH, Eader? 11 (f)* (389)

HILL, A. 27 (m)* (B) (494)

HILL, Albert 40 (B) (346)

HILL, Bettie 41* (433)

HILL, C. C. 47 (m), (207)

HILL, Citt 41 (m) (B) (476)

HILL, D. 36 (m) (B) (498)

HILL, Emma 6* (B) (196)

HILL, Ferguson 17* (B) (361)

HILL, George 30* (B) (449)

HILL, Green 63 (B) (248)

HILL, HArrison 20* (476)

HILL, Henry 20* (B) (415)

HILL, Henry N. 45* (478)

HILL, Houston 12* (B) (263)

HILL, J. W. 25 (m) (B) (497)

HILL, Jacob 35 (B) (383)

HILL, James 18* (B) (372)

HILL, James 18* (B) (383)

HILL, Jessie 40 (m) (B) (378)

HILL, Jim 40 (B) (328)

HILL, John 23 (B) (326)

HILL, John 23 (B) (441)

HILL, Jordan 51?* (B) (432)

HILL, Joseph A. 55, (258)

HILL, Jule? 45 (m) (B) (476)

HILL, Lue 19 (f)* (B) (498)

HILL, Marshall 25* (B) (367)

HILL, Mary 26* (B) (327)

HILL, Patience 60* (B) (277)

HILL, Ranklin 44 (B) (308)

HILL, Richard S. 43, (478)

HILL, Samuel 2* (389)

HILL, Seth H. 24, (389)

HILL, Stella 30* (B) (431)

HILL, Thomas 22 (B) (361)

HILL, Thomas 23* (B) (362)

HILL, Wilborn T. 38, (230)

HILL, Wm. 54 (B) (446)

HILL, Wm. 55 (B) (217)

HILL, ___ 56 (m) (B) (496)

HILLIARD, Daniel 56 (B) (262)

HILLIARD, Dina 8* (B) (344)

HILLIARD, Dixy 18 (m)* (290)

HILLIARD, Donnie 8 (f)* (B) (316)

HILLIARD, Drew 5* (B) (344)

HILLIARD, Finis 29 (m) (B) (299)

HILLIARD, Frank 19* (B) (317)

HILLIARD, Frank 19* (B) (342)

HILLIARD, J. B. 35 (m), (212)

HILLIARD, J. _. 33 (m), (220)

HILLIARD, Lytle 35 (B) (283)

HILLIARD, Matilda 65, (162)

HILLIARD, Mittie 25 (f)* (B) (316)

HILLIARD, Mittie 25 (f)* (B) (344)

HILLIARD, Mockee? 49 (f)* (271)

HILLIARD, Nicholas? 44, (195)

HILLIARD, Rufus 14* (B) (277)

HILLIARD, Sallie 13* (B) (305)

HILLIARD, Spencer 32* (B) (262)

HILLIARD, Thomas 64, (212)

HILLIARD, W. A. 74 (m)* (253)

HILLIARD, W. C. 41 (m), (306)

HILLIARD, _. 65 (m) (B) (309)

HILLIARD, _. H. 43 (m), (203)

HILLIARD, ____ 51 (m) (B) (325)

HILLIARD, ____ 14 (m)* (B) (287)

HILLIARD?, John 57* (307)

HILLIDRD?, _. B. 31 (m)* (220)

HILLMAN, James 32, (275)

HILLMAN, Lena 4* (275)

HILLOWELL, Marion 39?* (389)

HIMES, Bell 3/12* (B) (188)

HIMES, Lula 21* B? (188)

HINEMAN, Daniel 50 (B) (465)

HINEMAN, Mary 50 (B) (465)

HINES, Alexander 19* (B) (217)

HINES, Seab 50 (m)* (B) (368)

HINES, Thompson 49* (B) (217)

HINKLE, George W. 70?* (221)

HINSON, J. C. 24 (m), (289)

HINSON, M. 42 (m)* (208)

HINTON, Jacob 48 (B) (303)

HIRSH, Julius 27* (162)

HISSER, F. __ (f)* (324)

HOBSON, Auster 25 (m)* (B) (244)

HOBSON, Dennis __ (B) (338)

HOBSON, Dock 55 (B) (243)

HOBSON, E. 18 (m)* (B) (339)

HOBSON, E. H. L. 2 (m)* (B) (340)

HOBSON, Merit 50 (B) (338)

HOBSON, Randal 70* (B) (330)

HOBSON, Simpson 60* (B) (203)

HOBSON, T. J. 52 (f)* (160)

HOBSON, Travis 56 (B) (246)

HOBSON, ___ 18 (m) (B) (245)

HOB__, C. H. 36 (m), (315)

HODGE, Jerry 55 (m), (277)

HODGE, Robert 50 (B) (395)

HODGE, Squire? 30 (B) (269)

HODGE, Tom 34* (B) (269)

HODGE, Will 24* (B) (340)

HODGES, Andrew 29, (242)

HODGES, Jeff 23 (B) (261)

HODGES, Jennie 32* (279)

HODGES, Loucinda 37 (B) (380)

HODGES, Martha 58, (293)

HODGES, Thomas 21* (254)

HODGES, Wm. J. 38?* (254)

HODSON, James 46* (B) (443)

HOG, Dock 35 (B) (203)

HOGAN, Anna 36* (B) (291)

HOGAN, Ellen 47* (183)

HOGAN, Rebecca 35, (411)

HOGAN, Wm. 33* (432)

HOGLE, Alfred 37 (B) (421)

HOGSETT, Pack 22 (m)* (B) (375)

HOGUE, S. A. 50 (m)* (182)

HOGUE, W.? T. 24 (m)* (182)

HOLCOMB, Wm. 76* (B) (437)

HOLDEN, Joseph 26* (348)

HOLDEN, M. 42 (f), (302)

HOLKUM, Catherine 66* (B) (467)

HOLKUM, ____y 44 (B) (470)

HOLLAND, Andrew 30? (B) (449)

HOLLAND, Dock 53 (B) (282)

HOLLAND, J. T. 27 (m), (279)

HOLLAND, Jack 24* (B) (455)

HOLLAND, John 26 (B) (337)

HOLLAND, Margaret _4* (386)

HOLLEY, Emma 48* (B) (304)

HOLLIDA, Dick 22, (482)

HOLLIDAY, Harden 45* (B) (269)

HOLLINGSWORTH, John 26* (275)

HOLLINGSWORTH?, Will 18* (280)

HOLLMON, Jo 37 (m)* (B) (500)

HOLLOWAY, Louisa 2* (169)

HOLLOWAY, Mack 45 (B) (339)

HOLLOWAY, Phill 53* (B) (165)

HOLLOWAY, Roann 30* (B) (163)

HOLLOWAY, S. 57 (m)* (B) (502)

HOLLOWAY, Thomas 34* (B) (172)

HOLLOWAY, Tillman 45* (B) (191)

HOLLOWAY, Wm. 14* (B) (180)

HOLLOWAY, Wm. 36 (B) (186)

HOLLOWAY, Wm. 40 (B) (184)

HOLLOWAY, Wm. H. 36 (B) (171)

HOLLY, Michell 40 (B) (300)

HOLMES, Angia 20* (B) (485)

HOLMES, Cary 50 (f) (B) (473)

HOLMES, Geo. W. 20* (483)

HOLMES, Nancy 70* (502)

HOLMES, Sam 16 (m)* (B) (485)

HOLMES, Thomjas 52, (413)

HOLMES, Tildy 20* (B) (468)

HOLMES?, Dick 27* (B) (172)

HOLMON, Newton 44, (411)

HOLSON, Jack? J. N. 33, (410)

HOLT, Albert 23 (B) (192)

HOLT, Amelia 1* (B) (191)

HOLT, Carter 39 (B) (439)

HOLT, Claban 54 (m) (B) (193)

HOLT, Dan 14* (B) (487)

HOLT, David 56 (B) (197)

HOLT, Isaac 30* (B) (447)

HOLT, Jas. G. 63 (B) (202)

HOLT, Moses 54* (B) (190)

HOLT, Richard 39 (B) (192)

HOMAN, Henry 40 (B) (224)

HOMER, Ben 22* (B) (451)

HOMER, Jerry 35 (B) (459)

HOMER, Mary 80, (451)

HOMER?, Jane 40 (B) (444)

HOMES, Charles 52 (B) (249)

HOMES, Charly jr.? 23* (B) (249)

HOMES, Felix 25* (B) (223)

HOMES, Henry 25* (B) (249)

HOMES, Ike 30 (B) (224)

HOMES, John 24* (440)

HOMES, Levy 38* (B) (242)

HOMES, Lucinda 27* (B) (223)

HOMES, Mary 20* (B) (234)

HOMES, Wm. 23* (B) (239)

HONEL, Mary 36* (420)

HON__ENT, Frank 65, (420)

HOOD, Adron 40 (B) (403)

HOOEY?, Dannel 40 (m), (375)

HOOKS, John H. 5_* (383)

HOOKS, Major 53* (B) (386)

HOOKS, Peedy 21 (m) (B) (375)

HOOKS, Sarah 72* (388)

HOOKS, Warren 25 (B) (385)

HOPE, Louis 18, (433)

HOPE, W. 21 (m)* (433)

HORACE, Eliza 6* (B) (419)

HORDAMAN, Thos. 40 (B) (455)

HORN, Simon 45 (B) (422)

HORNE, Wiley 9* (281)

HORSHAW, MEeda 13 (f)* (B) (232)

HOSKINS, Mary 32* (B) (184)

HOSLETT, Dee 25 (m) (B) (478)

HOUP?, Steven 50, (478)

HOUSE, Ben 55* (B) (162)

HOUSE, Caroline 40* (B) (181)

HOUSE, Laurence 32* (427)

HOUSE, Pink 30 (m) (B) (276)

HOUSE, Wm. 18* (B) (181)

HOUSE?, Elzira 55* (B) (255?)

HOUSE?, Taylor 22* (B) (270)

HOUSTON, Bettie 60* (316)

HOUSTON, Daniel 36 (B) (420)

HOUSTON, Elick 60* (B) (164)

HOUSTON, Henry 58 (B) (413)

HOUSTON, James 35 (B) (442)

HOUSTON, John 51 (B) (440)

HOUSTON, Mike 24?* (B) (413)

HOUSTON, Robert 100?* (B) (420)

HOUSTON, Sallie 70* (B) (173)

HOUSTON, ____ 80 (m)* (B) (420)

HOWARD, Alex 22* (B) (291)

HOWARD, Dennis 20* (B) (221)

HOWARD, Fred 40* (282)

HOWARD, J. W. 45 (m) (B) (291)

HOWARD, P. 20 (m)* (B) (472)

HOWARD, Rebecca 45* (461)

HOWARD, Rosa 16* (277)

HOWEL, Charles 56, (370)

HOWEL, Samuel 15* (393)

HOWEL?, Samuel 24, (426)

HOWELL, Hiram 53* (392)

HOWELL, Jack H. 30, (368)

HOWELL, Mary 24* (277)

HUDDLE, Frank 33* (B) (329)

HUDGINS, Geo. 33* (B) (281)

HUDGINS, Jett? 25 (m) (B) (281)

HUDGINS, MArtha 32 (B) (275)

HUDGINS, Sigh? 60 (m), (281)

14

HUDGINS, Wilks 20 (m) (B) (275)
HUDSON, Celess 35 (f)* (B) (184)
HUDSON, Cora 18* (B) (171)
HUDSON, Edmonia 16?* (B) (201)
HUDSON, J.? 35 (m) (B) (499)
HUDSON, Joe 22, (275)
HUDSON, John 30 (B) (173)
HUDSON, Martha 27?, (436)
HUDSON, Roland 29* (B) (417)
HUDSON, Sucky 63 (f)* (B) (181)
HUES, S. A. 18 (m)* (330)
HUFF, George 27 (B) (358)
HUGHES, Francis M. 28, (359)
HUGHES, Hercules 10* (B) (258)
HUGHES, J. W. 33 (m), (330)
HUGHES, JAmes 49* (235)
HUGHES, James 57, (353)
HUGHES, Jim 25 (B) (225)
HUGHES, John 40* (B) (173)
HUGHES, Marshall 25* (B) (350)
HUGHES, Occie 7 (m)* (280)
HUGHES, Susan 44* (286)
HUGHES, Willie 3 (m)* (286)
HUGHLETT, John 33* (B) (287)
HUGHS, Caleb 12* (B) (415)
HUGHS, Fred 21, (445)
HUGHS, Jordan 28 (B) (398)
HUGHS, Robert 57, (411)
HULL, Alice 19* (B) (194)
HULL, Ginnie 27* (B) (251)
HULL, H. 40 (f)* (B) (488)
HULL, H. _* (160)
HULLEM, Thos. 45 (B) (439)
HULLIAM?, Robert 21* (B) (432)
HULLUM, Wash 50 (m) (B) (436)
HULLUNN, Daniel 56* (B) (429)
HULSEY, Wm. 46, (449)
HUMPHREIS, T. T. 27 (m)* (167)
HUMPHREY, Elias 53 (B) (191)
HUMPHREY, Mary 46 (B) (202)
HUMPHREY, Sid 33 (m)* (B) (192)
HUMPHREYS, Collin 34* (B) (175)
HUMPHREYS, F. 49 (m), (479)
HUMPHREYS, Gabe 46* (B) (242)
HUMPHREYS, MArgaret 45* (171)
HUMPHREYS, ____ 18 (f)* (163)
HUMPHRY, Elijah 39 (B) (174)
HUNGSUCKER?, Buck 17* (334)
HUNT, Adam 36* (B) (467)
HUNT, Armstead 23 (B) (467)
HUNT, Dennis 60 (B) (465)
HUNT, Frank 21 (B) (465)
HUNT, George 3* (B) (179)
HUNT, Henry 35 (B) (453)
HUNT, Holland 37* (B) (448)
HUNT, J. 45 (m) (B) (466)
HUNT, John G. 42* (B) (406)
HUNT, Jordin 24 (B) (455)
HUNT, Peter 32 (B) (178)
HUNT, Wm. 30 (B) (464)
HUNT?, N.? 25 (m) (B) (181)
HUNT?, ____ 64 (m) (B) (501)

HUNTER, Alf 25 (B) (479)
HUNTER, Anderson 40 (B) (399)
HUNTER, Andrew 34 (B) (347)
HUNTER, Andrew J. 52, (359)
HUNTER, Bryant 23 (B) (359)
HUNTER, Caesar 29 (B) (350)
HUNTER, Charley 58* (B) (479)
HUNTER, Charly 20* (B) (248)
HUNTER, Cherry 30 (f) (B) (345)
HUNTER, Clarissa 40 (B) (355)
HUNTER, Frank 30* (B) (405)
HUNTER, George A. 31? (m), (406)
HUNTER, George T. 55, (412)
HUNTER, Hardy 34* (B) (347)
HUNTER, Henrey 28 (B) (215)
HUNTER, J. L. 29 (m)* (440)
HUNTER, JAck 38 (B) (400)
HUNTER, James 27* (B) (346)
HUNTER, Jesse 45 (m) (B) (347)
HUNTER, John 52, (215)
HUNTER, John D. 33, (346)
HUNTER, Lewis 20 (B) (359)
HUNTER, Mary 46* (B) (354)
HUNTER, Pennie 22 (f)* (B) (339)
HUNTER, Phillip 54* (B) (374)
HUNTER, Rena? 22* (B) (405)
HUNTER, Right? 40 (m)* (B) (327)
HUNTER, Robert 75* (B) (352)
HUNTER, Wesley 30* (B) (405)
HUNTER, ____ 26 (m) (B) (398)
HURDLE, Charles 25* (B) (435)
HURDLE, John 18* (342)
HURDLES, John 18* (317)
HURLEY, Jas. 33* (200)
HURST, Jas. H. 27, (198)
HURST, T. P. 34 (m), (478)
HUSE?, Fred 39 (B) (447)
HUSTEN, Wm. 12* (B) (263)
HUSTON, Bettie 60* (344)
HUSTON, James 35* (B) (482)
HUTCHENS, Stephen 53* (B) (171)
HUTCHINGS, Juli M. 2 (f)* (171)
HUTCHINS, Eldridge 21 (B) (171)
HUTCHINSON, Light 54 (m) (B) (387)
HUTCHINSON, Mose 35 (m) (B) (387)
H__, George 45* (B) (461)
H__, Martha 40, (441)
H____ING, Wm. 20* (B) (388)
H____TT, Gill 52 (B) (393)
H____, John 24* (427)
ING, Wade 22* (279)
INGRAHAM, John 35 (B) (200)
INGRAM, Allice 32* (228)
INGRAM, M. C. 22 (m)* (207)
INGRAM, Rome? 15 (m)* (209)
INGRAM, Wash 35 (B) (289)
INGRUM, Ollen 24 (m) (B) (496)
IRBY, Mat 20 (f)* (B) (204)
IRBY, Robt. Lee 5* (B) (196)
IRISH, Wm. 10* (B) (496)
IRVIN, Davie 45 (B) (404)
IRVIN, E. H. 38 (m), (323)
IRVIN, James 30 (B) (404)

IRVING, Robert 29, (430)
IRWIN, Clay 31* (316)
IRWIN, Clay 31* (344)
IRWIN, J. L. 38 (m), (344)
IRWIN, R. W. 43 (m)* (326)
IRWIN, T. L. 38? (m), (316)
IRWIN, U.? G. 31 (m)* (316)
IRWIN, V. A. 31 (m)* (344)
IRWIN, W. S. 34 (m)* (333)
ISAACS, Isom 50 (B) (394)
ISBELL, Andrew 25 (B) (354)
ISBELL, Beverly 40 (m)* (B) (162)
ISBELL, Eliza J. 67* (392)
ISBELL, John 30* (B) (173)
ISBELL, R. 50 (m) (B) (499)
ISBELL, Thomas 30 (B) (170)
ISBELL, Wm. 46* (221)
ISHELL, Robt. 27? (B) (338)
ISHELTON?, ____ 35 (m) (B) (452)
ISSOM, Carrol 48, (277)
IVENS, Scott Z. 24 (B) (498)
IVENS, Squire? 53 (B) (498)
IVIE, Wash 74?* (483)
IVINS, Elvira 6* (332)
IVY, A. J. 43 (m)* (315)
IVY, Asa V. 65, (374)
IVY, Benjamin 23* (B) (310)
IVY, Ephrim 25* (334)
IVY, J. V. 29 (m)* (315)
IVY, James 55, (314)
IVY, Jane 17* (B) (306)
IVY, Nellie 22* (B) (343)
IVY, R. 38 (m), (305)
IVY, Richard 19 (40?)* (B?) (340)
IVY, Samuel 30* (B) (306)
IVY, Thomas 19* (334)
IVY, W. 28 (m)* (B) (340)
IVY?, Henry 28 (307)
IVY?, John E. 21* (315)
JACK, Daniel B. 37* (411)
JACK, Wm. 54, (411)
JACKAM, Wm. 58* (B) (425)
JACKS, Eliza 30 (B) (399)
JACKSON, A. 32 (m)* (B) (499)
JACKSON, Adair 53* (B) (459)
JACKSON, Albert 25* (280)
JACKSON, Albert S. 26, (361)
JACKSON, Andrew 20* (B) (292)
JACKSON, Andrew 30 (B) (426)
JACKSON, Andrew 38 (B) (248)
JACKSON, Andrew 9* (B) (354)
JACKSON, Annie 70 (B) (444)
JACKSON, C. A. 17 (m)* (407)
JACKSON, Charlie 18?* (238)
JACKSON, D. A. 394* (277)
JACKSON, Dennis 30* (B) (273)
JACKSON, E. 5 (m)* (B) (336)
JACKSON, Ed? 30 (B) (277)
JACKSON, Edmond S. 39, (278)
JACKSON, Elisha 32, (288)
JACKSON, Ely 23* (B) (374)
JACKSON, Frank 23 (B) (451)
JACKSON, G.? 52 (m) (B) (494)
JACKSON, George 50 (B) (374)
JACKSON, H. 31 (m)* (B) (218)
JACKSON, Henry 30* (B) (184)
JACKSON, Henry 40 (B) (165)
JACKSON, Henry 45 (B) (451)

JACKSON, Isaac 35 (B) (456)
JACKSON, Jennie 60 (277)
JACKSON, Jerry 21 (m)* (B) (485)
JACKSON, John 35* (B) (278)
JACKSON, John 37 (B) (413)
JACKSON, John 50 (B) (454)
JACKSON, Junius 26* (B) (288)
JACKSON, L. 64 (m) (B) (303)
JACKSON, Lizzie 55* (B) (276)
JACKSON, M. J. 22 (f)* (445)
JACKSON, MArquis 55* (250)
JACKSON, Mitchell 35* (B) (292)
JACKSON, Mollie 25* (B) (473)
JACKSON, Monroe 30* (B) (368)
JACKSON, Pompy 40 (m) (B) (444)
JACKSON, Robert 36 (B) (370)
JACKSON, Sam 26* (B) (473)
JACKSON, Sam 42 (B) (243)
JACKSON, Samuel? F. 17* (406)
JACKSON, Sousen? 50* (B) (380)
JACKSON, Stephen 60 (B) (232)
JACKSON, Wily 60 (B) (264)
JACKSON, Wm. 23* (B) (264)
JACKSON, Wm. 35* (B) (284)
JACKSON, Wm. H. 33* (368)
JACKSON?, Henry 21* (B) (433)
JAMES, Caroline 40 (B) (240)
JAMES, Ellen 45 (B) (385)
JAMES, Ida 18* (B) (500)
JAMES, Jenkins 35, (456)
JAMES, John 26* (332)
JAMES, John 42* (261)
JAMES, John 45* (B) (251)
JAMES, LEwis 50* (B) (308)
JAMES, Levy 30* (B) (309)
JAMES, Lucy 40* (B) (379)
JAMES, Robt. 28 (B) (329)
JAMES, Willis 24* (B) (370)
JAMES?, Mat 46 (B) (333)
JAMISON, Leonard 17* (B) (359)
JAMISON, Scott 28 (B) (430)
JAMISON, Wm. S. 22, (359)
JARMAN, John 35 (B) (390)
JARMAN, Sigh 25 (m) (B) (204)
JARMON, Albert 20 (B) (206)
JARMON, Charles 22 (B) (208)
JARMON, Dick 23 (B) (211)
JARMON, Ed 38 (B) (211)
JARMON, Green 25 (B) (207)
JARMON, Henry 45 (B) (211)
JARMON, Jim 30* (B) (204)
JARMON, Robert __* (B) (210)
JARMON, Will 48 (B) (209)
JARMON, Zen 20 (m) (B) (209)
JARMON, ____ 46 (m) (B) (208)
JASON, Wm. 33* (B) (228)
JASON?, F. W. 16 (m)* (338)
JASONS?, Matilda 40* (B) (338)
JEFERSON?, Tom 25 (B) (258)
JEFFERSON, G.? 60 (m)* (B) (499)
JEFFERSON, Miles 53 (B) (284)
JEFFERSON, Primus? 29 (m) (B) (299)
JEFFERSON, Thomas 26* (B) (187)
JEFFERSON, Wm. 30* (B) (227)

JEFFERSON?, Elizabeth? 55 (B) (260)
JEFFISON, Ather 40 (m) (B) (373)
JEMMERSON, Lillie 16* (B) (265)
JENAS?, Shelton 22* (B) (304)
JENKINS, James L. 38, (360)
JENKINS, Jennie 25* (B) (471)
JENKINS, Robert 39* (353)
JENKINS, Sam 24?* (B) (175)
JENKINS, Sam 27 (B) (326)
JENKINS, Thomas 34* (445)
JENKINS, Wm. C. jr. 36, (359)
JENKINS, Wm. C. sr. 68* (357)
JENNING?, John 25* (271)
JENSEN, Charles 34, (196)
JERRY, Tempy 9 (f)* (B) (186)
JESTER, James 50, (433)
JETER, John 25* (B) (167)
JEWEL, Peter 48 (B) (206)
JIMISSON, Sam 18 (B) (255)
JOHNS, Alex 17* (B) (435)
JOHNS, Edna 23* (B) (420)
JOHNS, Jerry 65 (m)* (B) (302)
JOHNSON, Albert 2* (B) (254)
JOHNSON, Alf 21* (B) (475)
JOHNSON, Alf 45 (B) (471)
JOHNSON, Allen 50* (B) (255?)
JOHNSON, Amanda 30, (191)
JOHNSON, Amos 42 (B) (305)
JOHNSON, Andrew 30 (B) (230)
JOHNSON, Andrew 30 (B) (493)
JOHNSON, Annanias 31* (B) (353)
JOHNSON, Annie 8?* (B) (249)
JOHNSON, Anthony 63 (B) (417)
JOHNSON, Anthony? 20 (B) (270)
JOHNSON, Ather 25 (m), (220)
JOHNSON, Baltimore 20 (m)* (B) (345)
JOHNSON, Bean? 27 (m) (B) (260)
JOHNSON, Benjamin 26 (B) (355)
JOHNSON, Betsy 37 (B) (405)
JOHNSON, Bettie 18* (B) (484)
JOHNSON, Bill 23 (B) (395)
JOHNSON, Bill 33 (B) (287)
JOHNSON, Bill 50 (B) (472)
JOHNSON, Boswell 80* (B) (190)
JOHNSON, Catherine 50 (B) (264)
JOHNSON, David 45* (424)
JOHNSON, Denis 6* (B) (315)
JOHNSON, Doctor 14* (B) (345)
JOHNSON, Dora 10* (B) (173)
JOHNSON, Easter 16* (B) (395)
JOHNSON, Edmon 40 (B) (403)
JOHNSON, Eliza 53* (427)
JOHNSON, F. 29? (m) (B) (302)
JOHNSON, Farel 50 (m)* (B) (213)
JOHNSON, Fed 40 (B) (228)
JOHNSON, Ferry? 4 (m)* (B) (421)
JOHNSON, Frank 28* (B) (413)
JOHNSON, George 16* (B) (425)
JOHNSON, George 22 (B) (362)
JOHNSON, George 50* (B) (261)
JOHNSON, George 55* (B) (301)

JOHNSON, Grant 30 (B) (450)
JOHNSON, H. W. 26 (m), (220)
JOHNSON, Henry 35 (B) (312)
JOHNSON, J. 22 (m)* (B) (297)
JOHNSON, J. H. 60 (m), (220)
JOHNSON, Jacob 32 (B) (417)
JOHNSON, James 47 (B) (390)
JOHNSON, James 55 (B) (367)
JOHNSON, Jefferson 34* (B) (313)
JOHNSON, Jennie 60* (279)
JOHNSON, John 18 (B) (474)
JOHNSON, John 20* (B) (485)
JOHNSON, John 25 (B) (205)
JOHNSON, John 27 (B) (362)
JOHNSON, John 45 (B) (314)
JOHNSON, John 55 (B) (434)
JOHNSON, Krup 30 (m) (B) (469)
JOHNSON, Leanna T. 11/12 (B) (356)
JOHNSON, Lewis 20 (B) (359)
JOHNSON, Liddie? 7 (f)* (B) (270)
JOHNSON, Louis? 15* (B) (425)
JOHNSON, Lucy 60 (B) (405)
JOHNSON, Lula 8* (B) (428)
JOHNSON, M. 45 (f)* (302)
JOHNSON, M. 8 (m)* (B) (496)
JOHNSON, MAtt 62 (m)* (B) (473)
JOHNSON, Mack 37* (B) (308)
JOHNSON, Manerva J. 30* (375)
JOHNSON, Manuel 20* (B) (347)
JOHNSON, Margaret? 55?* (B) (300)
JOHNSON, Mariah 38* (B) (170)
JOHNSON, Mary 23* (B) (301)
JOHNSON, Mary 84* (477)
JOHNSON, Mathew 25 (B) (270)
JOHNSON, Matilda 47* (B) (345)
JOHNSON, Mollie 12* (433)
JOHNSON, Monroe 35* (B) (366)
JOHNSON, Nannie 11* (B) (214)
JOHNSON, Nick 64* (B) (475)
JOHNSON, Pat 50 (m) (B) (274)
JOHNSON, Pattie 75* (269)
JOHNSON, Paul 22 (B) (301)
JOHNSON, Pearce 34 (B) (390)
JOHNSON, Peter 28* (B) (257)
JOHNSON, Phillip 25* (187)
JOHNSON, Robert 40 (B) (391)
JOHNSON, Robert 56* (B) (422)
JOHNSON, Rolin 31, (195)
JOHNSON, Sallie 19* (B) (366)
JOHNSON, Sam 37 (B) (207)
JOHNSON, Samuel 24 (B) (358)
JOHNSON, Scott 38 (B) (268)
JOHNSON, Smith 47 (B) (375)
JOHNSON, V. B. 56 (m), (275)
JOHNSON, V. B. 56 (m) (B) (285)
JOHNSON, Vinie 22* (B) (405)
JOHNSON, W. C. 44 (m), (255)
JOHNSON, Wash 57* (477)
JOHNSON, Wm. 17* (B) (204)
JOHNSON, Wm. 18* (B) (363)
JOHNSON, Wm. 21* (B) (229)
JOHNSON, Wm. 28 (B) (178)
JOHNSON, Wm. 38 (B) (363)
JOHNSON, Wm. 55, (410)
JOHNSON, Wm. 60* (190)

JOHNSON, Wm. H. 31, (362)
JOHNSON, Wylee 10 (m)* (B) (389)
JOHNSON, ____ 22? (m) (B) (254)
JOHNSON?, Robert 35 (B) (260)
JOHNSTON, Alexander 6_, (188)
JOHNSTON, Armstead 26* (B) (186)
JOHNSTON, Eliza 58* (B) (275)
JOHNSTON, Ellen 33 (B) (186)
JOHNSTON, Fanny 18* (B) (281)
JOHNSTON, G. T. 30 (m), (209)
JOHNSTON, G. T. 39 (m), (209)
JOHNSTON, J. D. 19 (m) (B) (341)
JOHNSTON, J. H. 36 (m)* (206)
JOHNSTON, J. R. 57 (m)* (306)
JOHNSTON, J. T. 61 (m), (209)
JOHNSTON, James 38, (183)
JOHNSTON, Joe 35, (322)
JOHNSTON, M. B. 70 (f), (183)
JOHNSTON, Ned 45 (B) (341)
JOHNSTON, Robt. 20* (B) (173)
JOHNSTON, Robt. 40 (B) (341)
JOHNSTON, Steven 60 (B) (280)
JOHNSTON, Thos. 50 (B) (278)
JOHNSTON, Thos. D. 57* (280)
JOHNSTON, W. A. J. 28 (m), (330)
JOHNSTON, Wm. 29* (332)
JOHNSTON, ____ 28 (m) (B) (341)
JOHNSTON?, Andrew 28 (B) (321)
JOINER, James A. 52, (472)
JOLLEY, Wm. 35 (B) (376)
JOLLY, L. 22 (m)* (334)
JOMER, H. 32 (m), (471)
JONAS, Sam 17* (B) (328)
JONES, A. 55 (f) (B) (496)
JONES, Alfred 18* (B) (168)
JONES, Allen 27* (268)
JONES, Ambrose 60* (B) (172)
JONES, Ambrose J. 22* (B) (172)
JONES, Anderson 27* (B) (420)
JONES, Anderson 30* (B) (321)
JONES, Anderson 37, (281)
JONES, Anderson 37 (B) (173)
JONES, Andrew 30 (B) (270)
JONES, Archer 23* (B) (226)
JONES, Asbury 56* (B) (391)
JONES, B. 27 (m)* (498)
JONES, Blake 52 (B) (499)
JONES, Bob? 25* (B) (264)
JONES, Calvin 22* (B) (413)
JONES, Carles 47* (434)
JONES, Carrie? 22 (B) (449)
JONES, Catherin 49* (B) (173)
JONES, Charl. 37 (m) (B) (397)
JONES, Charley 45* (B) (271)
JONES, Charlot 55* (B) (174)
JONES, Chas. 23* (B) (284)
JONES, Cinda 12 (f)* (B) (265)
JONES, Claxton 19* (B) (413)
JONES, Daniel 20* (B) (258)
JONES, Daniel 22 (B) (260)
JONES, Darby 27 (f) (B) (265)
JONES, Darlin 50 (m), (407)
JONES, Dennis 1* (B) (174)

JONES, Dick 25 (B) (369)
JONES, E. 30 (m) (B) (299)
JONES, Edmon 40 (B) (317)
JONES, Edmond? 50 (B) (208)
JONES, Eli 20* (B) (174)
JONES, Eliza 42* (498)
JONES, Elizabeth 26 (B) (167)
JONES, Elizabeth 35 (B) (454)
JONES, Ely 34* (B) (313)
JONES, F. 10 (f)* (B) (488)
JONES, Fannie 10* (B) (251)
JONES, Fed 35? (m) (B) (226)
JONES, Fed R. 24 (m), (222)
JONES, Fennel 55* (B) (378)
JONES, Forest 17* (B) (217)
JONES, Fran___ 45 (f)* (240)
JONES, Frances __* (B) (256)
JONES, Frank 17* (B) (429)
JONES, Frank 21* (B) (239)
JONES, George 13* (B) (255)
JONES, Hanna 35 (B) (476)
JONES, Hannible? 55 (B) (421)
JONES, Henderson 25 (B) (248)
JONES, Henry 17* (B) (429)
JONES, Henry 25 (B) (347)
JONES, Henry 33 (B) (263)
JONES, Henry 70* (B) (164)
JONES, Hilliard 51* (B) (258)
JONES, Irving 54 (B) (363)
JONES, Isah 38 (m) (B) (211)
JONES, Isaha? 22 (m) (B) (175)
JONES, J. C. 56 (m), (275)
JONES, J. S. 19 (m)* (332)
JONES, JAck 20* (B) (224)
JONES, Jack 50* (B) (264)
JONES, Jacob 40 (B) (174)
JONES, James 20* (B) (363)
JONES, James 30 (B) (391)
JONES, James 54 (B) (337)
JONES, Jasper 22* (B) (223)
JONES, Jim 25 (B) (251)
JONES, Joe? 12* (291)
JONES, John 22* (164)
JONES, John 27 (B) (224)
JONES, John 28 (B) (214)
JONES, John 32* (B) (177)
JONES, John 63* (B) (275)
JONES, John J. R. 25 (B) (228)
JONES, John L. 29* (B) (193)
JONES, Jonas 38 (B) (313)
JONES, Julious 32 (B) (339)
JONES, Katie 25* (B) (478)
JONES, King 28 (B) (263)
JONES, Laura 30* (B) (339)
JONES, Lee 20 (m)* (B) (347)
JONES, Levy 35* (B) (165)
JONES, Lewis 70 (B) (193)
JONES, Lijah 20* (B) (267)
JONES, Lot 55 (B) (339)
JONES, Lou 24 (f)* (B) (310)
JONES, Lou 30 (m) (B) (237)
JONES, Louis 40 (B) (337)
JONES, Louis 44 (B) (291)
JONES, Lovick 65 (m)* (B) (213)
JONES, Lucinda 32 (B) (444)
JONES, M. E. 48 (f)* (316)
JONES, M. E. 48 (f)* (344)
JONES, MAtthew 50* (B) (172)
JONES, Mariah 24* (B) (163)

16

JONES, Martha Ellen 2/30* (B) (265)
JONES, Mary 18 (B) (188)
JONES, Mary 30* (B) (180)
JONES, Mary 40* (B) (330)
JONES, Mary 5* (B) (416)
JONES, Mary R. _/12* (B) (270)
JONES, Milly 38, (497)
JONES, Morgan 42 (B) (330)
JONES, NEd 38 (B) (214)
JONES, Nance 31* (253)
JONES, Nathan 65 (B) (256)
JONES, Nelson 25* (B) (387)
JONES, Nelson 52* (B) (492)
JONES, Nice 20 (f)* (B) (212)
JONES, Oston 25 (m) (B) (383)
JONES, P. T. 28 (m)* (161)
JONES, Parthena 40* (B) (499)
JONES, Paswell? 26 (m)* (B) (453)
JONES, Percy 8 (m)* (392)
JONES, Peter 18 (B) (398)
JONES, Peter 55? (B) (448)
JONES, Peter 61* (B) (269)
JONES, Peter 61 (B) (353)
JONES, Phoeba 19* (B) (239)
JONES, Pinkney 36* (B) (385)
JONES, Price 30* (B) (404)
JONES, Prince 20 (B) (180)
JONES, Priscilla 10* (B) (282)
JONES, R. A. 32 (m)* (344)
JONES, R. G. 32 (m)* (316)
JONES, Raphf? 48 (m) (B) (214)
JONES, Richard? 56* (B) (498)
JONES, Robert 22* (B) (385)
JONES, Rose 18* (B) (352)
JONES, Ruggin 24 (m)* (B) (258)
JONES, Russel 37 (B) (330)
JONES, STephen 43* (B) (175)
JONES, Sam 18* (B) (468)
JONES, Sam 37 (B) (268)
JONES, Samuel 38 (B) (182)
JONES, Samuel 52, (409)
JONES, Sarah 33* (B) (313)
JONES, Sena 9 (f)* (B) (489)
JONES, Solomon 30* (B) (232)
JONES, Susan 16* (B) (364)
JONES, Sylvester 50 (B) (245)
JONES, Thomas 26* (B) (494)
JONES, Thos. W. 36* (187)
JONES, Tom 24 (B) (337)
JONES, Venus? 38* (B) (174)
JONES, Vick 25 (f)* (B) (166)
JONES, Wash 50* (B) (265)
JONES, West _ (B) (190)
JONES, Wiley B. 67, (453)
JONES, Willie 22 (m)* (B) (208)
JONES, Wily 31 (B) (306)
JONES, Wm. 21* (B) (162)
JONES, Wm. 21* (B) (356)
JONES, Wm. 23* (B) (456)
JONES, Wm. 23 (B) (266)
JONES, Wm. 24 (B) (327)
JONES, Wm. 35 (B) (454)
JONES, Wm. 47 (B) (350)
JONES, Wm. 5* (B) (214)
JONES, Wm. 52* (B) (185)
JONES, Wm. 55* (B) (187)
JONES, Wm. 56, (347)
JONES, Wm. jr. 22 (B) (347)

JONES, _. B. 50 (m)* (216)
JONES, ____ 45 (m)* (B) (492)
JONES, ____ 69 (m), (177)
JONES, ____ 39 (m), (318)
JONES?, Elizabeth 40 (B) (448)
JONES?, George 25 (B) (396)
JONES?, J. W. 47 (m), (447)
JONES?, JAck 60* (B) (416)
JONES?, Jennie 13* (B) (422)
JONES?, Lincoln 16?* (B) (311)
JONES?, Stephen 45* (B) (163)
JORDAN, Anderson 40 (B) (267)
JORDAN, Anthony 32* (B) (360)
JORDAN, Apson? 65* (B) (195)
JORDAN, Burrell 25, (421)
JORDAN, Charles 25 (B) (365)
JORDAN, Edward 24 (B) (366)
JORDAN, Eveline 18* (B) (366)
JORDAN, Frances 26 (B) (270)
JORDAN, Green D. 74* (350)
JORDAN, Henry 42 (B) (366)
JORDAN, John 29* (B) (253)
JORDAN, John 50* (314)
JORDAN, Julius 22* (B) (366)
JORDAN, Lewis 47 (B) (267)
JORDAN, Lucy 60* (B) (360)
JORDAN, Mark 28* (B) (359)
JORDAN, Mary 50 (B) (359)
JORDAN, Mattie 7 (f)* (B) (360)
JORDAN, Nathaniel 32* (B) (359)
JORDAN, Peter 37* (B) (181)
JORDAN, Sam? 60 (m)* (290)
JORDAN, Seaborn 57 (B) (181)
JORDAN, Tom 45 (B) (268)
JORDAN?, Charley 47, (318)
JORDEN, J. J. 30 (m), (483)
JORDEN, J. W. 35 (m), (470)
JORDEN, M. C. 50 (f), (470)
JORDON, Candy 18 (B) (330)
JOURDAN, Harvy 30* (B) (375)
JOURDAN, Jery 55 (m)* (B) (370)
JOY, Anderson 14* (B) (296)
JOY, Claiborne 50* (B) (297)
JOY, J. C. _3 (m)* (298)
JOY, Margaret 37* (424)
JOY, Robert 60 (B) (298)
JOYNER, Gainer 27 (m) (B) (387)
JOYNER, John 42, (386)
JOYNER, Wesley 43 (B) (386)
JOYNER, Wm. 28* (B) (361)
JUDAH, Jane 4* (B) (398)
JUSTISS, Charity 18* (B) (354)
JUSTISS, Lizzie 9* (B) (355)
J___DER, Wes 30 (B) (343)
J____, Frances 34* (B) (392)
J____, John 30* (B) (302)
J____, Orange 25 (B) (336)
J____S, Edmon 40 (B) (342)
KALE, Liddie 6* (253)
KANIP, Willie 12 (m)* (469)
KARR, Fed 50 (m) (B) (307)
KARR, J. W.? 54 (m)* (315)
KEAMEY?, Bob 42* (334)
KEE, J. L.? 32 (m)* (181)
KEE, Mollie 21* (B) (471)
KEE, Wm. 24* (B) (479)
KEE, Wm. 25* (B) (483)
KEENER?, Henry 25 (B) (473)
KEER, Arthur D. 26?, (222)

KEER, Francis B. 79* (222)
KEER, John 56 (B) (222)
KEER, MAriah 670* (B) (222)
KELLEY, John 26 (B) (482)
KELLY, J. G. 7 (m)* (323)
KELLY, Small 22* (B) (435)
KELLY, Warren 45 (B) (404)
KENDRICK, Irvin 50 (B) (402)
KENIP?, F. 44 (m)* (498)
KENNEDAY, ____ 52 (m), (450)
KENNEDY, Anderson 63 (B) (365)
KENNEDY, Mark 27 (B) (395)
KENNON, Blunt 23* (B) (368)
KENNON, Elijah 63* (368)
KENNON, Evie 6 (f)* (B) (368)
KENNON?, Bettie 23* (370)
KEOUGH, Peter 53, (409)
KERBY, Dick 42 (B) (334)
KERR, Samuel 56* (424)
KERR?, Alace 20* (B) (213)
KETCHNER?, Rosa 55* (B) (318)
KETCHUM, And___* (326)
KETCHUM, Ella 23* (253)
KETCHUM, Eph 35 (B) (340)
KETCHUM, George 25* (B) (327)
KETCHUM, Georgia 50* (341)
KETCHUM, James 22 (B) (324)
KETCHUM, Jane 46, (238)
KETCHUM, L. 45 (m)* (B) (399)
KETCHUM, Nelson 53* (B) (396)
KETCHUM, Wash 48 (B) (397)
KETCHUM, Will 30* (323)
KETCHUM, Wm. 20 (B) (396)
KEY, Frances 22* (B) (382)
KEY, Henry 45 (B) (382)
KEY, Mary 60* (B) (381)
KEY, Prater ___ (m)* (B) (382)
KEY, Tobe 36 (B) (386)
KEY, Wm. 21 (B) (382)
KEY, _. F. 33 (m)* (160)
KEY?, Thary 1* (B) (381)
KE_, George 35 (B) (178)
KILEY, Mat 28 (m) (B) (230)
KILGORE?, Perry 25, (447)
KILPATRIC, W. 65 (m)* (B) (436)
KIMBEL, Joe 48 (B) (429)
KIMBROUGH, Allen 33 (B) (370)
KINDER, Ealom 28* (481)
KINDRICK, Thomas 24* (330)
KING, Andrew 17* (370)
KING, Anjaline 45 (B) (380)
KING, George 47* (412)
KING, H.? 27 (m)* (495)
KING, J. L. 46 (m), (487)
KING, Jenni 23* (B) (241)
KING, Lindsy 33 (m) (B) (227)
KING, Margret 40 (B) (210)
KING, Peter 30* (495)
KING, R. B. 23 (m)* (479)
KING, Richard 31* (B) (172)
KING, Smith 25* (B) (308)
KING, Tom? 24 (B) (426)
KING, W. A. 38 (m)* (477)
KING, Willis 21 (f)* (B) (323)
KING, ____ 46 (m), (449)
KINNIE?, Billie 24 (B) (485)
KIRK, Allen 40* (B) (355)
KIRK, John 43, (362)

KIRKMAN, Shadrack 41 (B) (365)
KIRTLAND, Julia 10* (425)
KISER, Frances 16* (B) (418)
KISER, M. J. 24 (f)* (328)
KITCH, Matilda 45 (B) (442)
KITCHENS, Livy 18 (m), (304)
KITTREL, Ed 28 (B) (257)
KIZER, Philip 60 (B) (450)
KLEN?, Henry 30 (B) (413)
KNIGHT, Haywood 30* (B) (365)
KNIGHT, Wm. 28* (B) (314)
KNOX, Caroll 22* (B) (391)
KNOX, Emly 50* (369)
KNOX, George? 25 (B) (391)
KNOX, James 26* (167)
KNOX, Jule? 28 (m)* (167)
KNOX, Mat 18 (f)* (B) (398)
KNOX, Milton J. 50, (380)
KNOX, Robert 46* (433)
KNOX, Wash 25* (B) (377)
KNOX?, John 22* (B) (395)
KOONCE, James 47* (471)
KOONCE, Mollie 6* (471)
KOONCE, Wm. A. 40* (162)
KURTZ, Ama 44* (392)
KUSBEL?, Henry 25 (B) (388)
KYLE, Alabama 22 (f)* (334)
KYLE, B. 70 (m)* (334)
KYLE, Charles 35 (B) (307)
KYLE, J. B. 29 (m)* (316)
KYLE, J. B. 29 (m)* (344)
KYLE, S. B. 34 (m), (328)
K___, Lizzie 35* (483)
LACK, Elijah 23 (B) (363)
LACK, Elisha 26* (B) (395)
LACK, George 23 (B) (395)
LACK, Laura 31* (B) (194)
LACY, Alfred 37 (B) (262)
LACY, Beverly 28 (m) (B) (255)
LACY, Elizabeth 25? (B) (270)
LACY, Fanny 50* (B) (260)
LACY, George 33* (B) (262)
LACY, J. H. 67 (m)* (487)
LACY, James 78* (170)
LACY, Victoria 35* (B) (194)
LACY, Wilber 6* (B) (329)
LACY?, Robert 40 (B) (253)
LACY?, Wilbert 5* (B) (301)
LAMB, L. Berry 38 (m), (256)
LAMBERT, John 40* (466)
LAMBERT, W. 51 (m)* (B) (499)
LAND, Labern 37, (442)
LAND?, Rufus 33, (422)
LANDERS, Amos 19 (B) (358)
LANDERS, Enoch 30* (440)
LANDERS, Jefferson 20 (B) (358)
LANDERS, John 46 (B) (358)
LANDROM, L. E. 30 (m)* (440)
LANDRUM?, Enus 30, (440)
LANE, Daniel 40* (B) (355)
LANE, George 35 (B) (464)
LANE, Ida 16* (B) (347)
LANE, Ira 28 (B) (438)
LANE, Ira 28 (B) (445)
LANE, Ivin? 23 (B) (337)
LANE, JEssee 52 (m)* (189)
LANE, Moses 50 (B) (243)
LANEAR, Don 54 (B) (485)
LANEAR, Millard 23 (B) (468)
LANGDON, James J. 40, (370)

LANGE, Zack 40 (B) (444)
LANGLEY, P. 90 (f)* (B) (307)
LANIEN, A. W. 65 (m), (442)
LANKSTON, Wm. 38 (B) (459)
LANSDELL, Sam? 37 (m), (489)
LAP?, R. 53 (m)* (497)
LARGENT, JAmes 44* (201)
LARGENT, Silas 22* (B) (423)
LARGENT, Wm. 45, (200)
LASANE, Archey 25 (B) (377)
LASANE, Thomas 28 (B) (375)
LASANE, Thomas 55 (B) (368)
LASLEY, James 56, (195)
LATTAMER, Guy 30 (B) (223)
LATTIN, MArgarett 57, (167)
LAUENA?, Maggie 8* (B) (436)
LAURENCE, Jessie 6 (m)* (B) (437)
LAURENCE, Unnia? 58 (f), (425)
LAWSON, Wm. 50* (B) (443)
LAY, Abe 23? (B) (393)
LAY, Champ 22* (B) (374)
LAY, Fank 54 (m)* (B) (206)
LAY, G. A. 41 (f)* (206)
LAY, Wm. 19* (B) (393)
LAYTON, F. S. 60 (m)* (279)
LAZENBY, A. J. 29 (m), (304)
LAZENBY, J. F. 51 (m)* (476)
LAZENBY, W. C. 32 (m)* (482)
LEACH, Salley 31* (195)
LEAK, Thomas 37 (B) (456)
LEAK, Wade 27 (B) (362)
LEARY, George 50?* (416)
LEARY, John 21* (365)
LEATH, Lafayett 39* (224)
LEDFORD, Bill 25* (411)
LEDFORD?, Andrew 60 (B) (428)
LEE, Henry 13* (443)
LEE, Jack 30 (B) (270)
LEE, Juba 30 (m) (B) (397)
LEE, Julia 13* (362)
LEE, Liddie 35* (B) (266)
LEE, Solomon 28* (B) (387)
LEE, Wm. 41 (B) (239)
LEECH, Floid 25* (325)
LEEK, Hamp 60 (m)* (B) (340)
LEERY, Green 35 (B) (245)
LEFTWICH, C. L. 28 (m)* (333)
LEGGAT, Joe 30* (B) (432)
LEGGETT, D. 35 (m), (275)
LEGGITT, Margaret 30* (196)
LEMONS, Henry 50 (B) (169)
LEMONS, Lewis 33 (B) (177)
LEMPKIN, Wilson 42, (193)
LENARD, Mat 28 (m)* (B) (251)
LENDERMAN, Sam 29 (B) (385)
LENIN?, G.? 38 (m) (B) (501)
LENIX?, Edd 50 (B) (394)
LENON, Mary 6* (B) (415)
LEWIS, Ann 55* (269)
LEWIS, Armisted 30* (B) (420)
LEWIS, B. T. 47 (m)* (481)
LEWIS, E. 35 (m) (B) (170)
LEWIS, Elizabeth 31* (B) (181)
LEWIS, F. J. 71 (f)* (481)
LEWIS, Frank 25 (B) (402)
LEWIS, Jacob 22 (B) (421)
LEWIS, John 24* (B) (356)
LEWIS, John 54 (B) (396)

LEWIS, Lack 28 (m)* (B) (194)
LEWIS, Mark 30* (B) (346)
LEWIS, Mary 30* (B) (459)
LEWIS, Nathan 50* (B) (202)
LEWIS, Patrick H. 72 (B) (181)
LEWIS, Peyton 30 (B) (178)
LEWIS, Phill 38 (B) (187)
LEWIS, Ransom 31 (B) (201)
LEWIS, Richard 22* (460)
LEWIS, Sindy 25* (B) (372)
LEWIS?, Coleman? 47 (B) (445)
LIGHTLE?, J. C. 58 (f)* (477)
LIGON, Benj. H. 76* (260)
LIGON, MArtha S. 55* (266)
LIGON, Wm. 30 (B) (263)
LILE, Henry 80* (B) (392)
LILE, Jack 25* (B) (392)
LILE, Orange 57?* (B) (393)
LILE, ____ 36 (m) (B) (393)
LILL, M. 10 (f)* (B) (392)
LIMING?, W. H. 38 (m), (301)
LINCK, George 65 (B) (271)
LIND, MArtha 69* (301)
LINDOP?, John 35, (328)
LINDSEY, W. 48 (m), (332)
LINDSEY?, Burrel 29* (B) (416)
LINEBARGAR, Mary 51, (208)
LINEBARGAR?, _. F. 5_ (m), (205)
LINSEY, Daniel 42 (B) (175)
LINTON, J. E. 37 (m), (486)
LINZY, James 25* (B) (403)
LINZY, Thomas 23 (B) (380)
LIPSCOMB, G. R. 45 (m)* (440)
LIPSCOMB, George 67, (461)
LIPSCOMB, Joseph __* (392)
LIPSCOMB, W. 40 (m)* (461)
LIPSCOMBE, R. H. 26 (m), (440)
LISLE, Joe 16* (B) (425)
LITTLE, Gabriel 44 (B) (357)
LITTLE, W. M. 48 (m), (277)
LITTLEJOHN, C. 26 (m) (B) (259)
LITTLEJOHN, Essex 26 (B) (227)
LITTLEJOHN, John 61 (B) (259)
LLOYD, Andrew? 56 (B) (465)
LLOYD, Thos.? P. 65, (452)
LOCK?, ____ 36 (m)* (167)
LOCKE, Robert 42* (413)
LOCKE, Wm. _9?* (256)
LOCKETT, L. 14 (m)* (B) (496)
LOCKETT, Phelix 22* (B) (498)
LOCKETT, Walter? 19* (B) (498)
LOCKHEART, M. 10 (f)* (B) (499)
LOFTIN, Nelson 37* (B) (357)
LOFTIS, John 45 (B) (372)
LOFTIS, Mary 37* (B) (370)
LOFTIS, Wm. 52* (B) (426)
LOLLAND?, Cicero 22, (335)
LONDY?, John 35 (B) (323)
LONE, Robert E. 3* (440)
LONG, Henry 18* (B) (365)
LONG, James 28 (B) (444)
LONG, Jery 45 (m) (B) (379)
LONG, Mary 26* (375)
LONGHAM?, Mollie? 17* (250)
LOTHARPE, C. A. 25 (m), (294)
LOUIS, D. A. 28 (m)* (497)

LOUIS, Ellen 50* (B) (424)
LOUIS, Enous? 30 (m)* (B) (372)
LOUIS, George 47 (B) (481)
LOUIS, J. C. 20 (m)* (487)
LOUIS, Joe 24 (B) (240)
LOUIS, Leanders 50? (B) (401)
LOUIS, Richard 55 (B) (240)
LOUIS, Wilson 38* (B) (388)
LOUIS, Wyly 19 (B) (237)
LOVE, Dora 12* (B) (340)
LOVE, Edward 4* (B) (305)
LOVE, George 20* (B) (405)
LOVE, James 33* (202)
LOVE, James 55 (B) (350)
LOVE, Joseph 25 (B) (314)
LOVE, Mollie? 33* (B) (340)
LOVE, Rebeca J. 38, (162)
LOVE, Sallie 24* (B) (306)
LOVE, Wash 50 (B) (275)
LOVELACE, Aaron 45* (B) (257)
LOVELACE, Aron 16* (B) (226)
LOVELACE, Ed 19 (B) (259)
LOVELACE, Littie 14* (B) (257)
LOVELACE, MAggie 26* (B) (231)
LOVELACE, Minerva 6* (B) (259)
LOVELACE, Pinkny 24* (B) (257)
LOVELACE, Robert 72 (B) (257)
LOVELACE?, Ed L. __* (261)
LOVELACE?, Henry 43, (416)
LOVELESS, Julia 50 (B) (335)
LOVERTON, J. P. 35 (m)* (168)
LOVING, Lucy 8* (B) (360)
LOWERY, John 21* (466)
LOWREY, James 58, (181)
LOWREY, Saml. 23* (181)
LOYD, Eliza 37* (183)
LOYD, James 30* (292)
LOYD, Lou 40 (f)* (B) (474)
LOYD, Lucy __* (161)
LUCADO?, Griss__ 65 (f)* (198)
LUCAS, J. Y. 64 (m)* (178)
LUCAS, Mike 35* (292)
LUCK, E. J. 6 (f)* (316)
LUCK, E. J. 6 (f)* (344)
LUCK, V. B. 32 (m)* (314)
LUCUS, George 19* (B) (235)
LUCUS, Ike 18* (B) (489)
LUCUS, Joseph 45 (B) (386)
LUCUS, Tom 50 (B) (450)
LULLINGER?, J. E. 53 (m), (473)
LUMLY, _. Owen 18* (278)
LUMPKIN, Peter 19 (B) (448)
LUNDY, Eliza 27* (B) (178)
LUNDY?, Wm. 35?, (188)
LUTTA?, W. S. 40 (m)* (163)
LYNCH, John 60* (244)
LYNCH, John 68* (183)
LYNCH, W. M. 31 (m), (483)
LYNN, Thomas 56 (298)
LYNN?, Frank 55 (299)
LYNTZ, Joe 33* (162)
LYON, May 5* (364)
LYTTLE, F. 24 (m), (311)
MABEN, Baker 52 (B) (311)
MABEN, Fannie 20* (B) (309)
MABEN, James 25* (B) (310)
MABEN, King 55 (B) (304)

MABEN, Lewis 60 (B) (304)
MABEN, Thomas 19* (B) (305)
MABER, J. 56 (m)* (B) (312)
MABIN, Harris 20* (B) (389)
MABIN, Nick 23 (B) (221)
MABINE, Marshall 21* (B) (395)
MABINE, Mary 65 (B) (399)
MABINS, Edmon 52 (B) (223)
MACENTOSH, Saml. 18* (175)
MACKILIN, Joseph 23 (B) (289)
MACKINTOSH?, Margaret 59* (188)
MACKLIIN, _. H. 39 (m) (B) (287)
MACKLIN, George 6* (B) (231)
MACKLIN, Henderson 56 (B) (286)
MACKLIN, Joe 30 (B) (286)
MACKLIN, John 30 (B) (282)
MACKLIN, Martha __* (B) (226)
MACKLIN, Missouri 35 (f)* (B) (228)
MACKLIN, Nellie 25* (289)
MACKLIN, Richmond 25 (B) (294)
MACKLIN, Ruben 30* (B) (232)
MACKLIN, Tennessee 17 (f)* (373)
MACLIN, Horace 49 (B) (265)
MACLIN, James 19 (B) (267)
MACLIN, R. 45 (m)* (B) (309)
MACLIN, Ross 28* (B) (265)
MACLIN, Simon 50 (B) (257)
MACLIN, Telie? 36 (f)* (B) (261)
MACLIN, V. D. 15 (f)* (440)
MACLIN?, Allen 35 (B) (260)
MACLIN?, Beverly 43 (m) (B) (264)
MACLIN?, Bud 30 (B) (260)
MACLIN?, Money 26 (m) (B) (261)
MACON, Adolphus 27 (B) (186)
MACON, Alfred 58 (B) (187)
MACON, Alfred 62 (B) (252)
MACON, George 54* (B) (256)
MACON, Hattie 19* (B) (187)
MACON, John 24 (B) (231)
MACON, Judy 26? (B) (283)
MACON, NAncy 20* (B) (260)
MACON, Robert 12* (B) (188)
MACON, Simon 12* (B) (254)
MACON, Wilson 52 (B) (231)
MACON, Wm. 40* (B) (233)
MACON?, Allen 20* (B) (160)
MACON?, Leilla 65* (B) (421)
MACON?, Sallie 26?* (B) (259)
MADDEN, __ 70 (m)* (B) (297)
MADDINS?, Ben 30, (442)
MADOX, Frank L. 37* (165)
MAGAHA, Cain 24* (B) (455)
MAGGOT, Hardy 65 (B) (426)
MAGHEE, Charly 24 (B) (335)
MAGHEE, John 38, (344)
MAGINNIS?, Denis 39 (B) (385)
MAHAN, Frank 42 (B) (421)
MAHON, Felix G. 28* (367)
MAIDEN, D.? W. 26 (m)* (478)
MAJOR, John 30?* (165)
MALONE, Andrew 23* (B) (223)
MALONE, Benn 22 (B) (403)

MALONE, Bertie 22* (B) (264)
MALONE, Frank 38* (B) (281)
MALONE, Gus 5* (B) (232)
MALONE, Lou 21 (f) (B) (247)
MALONE, Many? 35 (f)* (484)
MALONE, Tank 32 (m) (B) (365)
MALONE, Thomas 54 (B) (377)
MALONE, Tom 25 (B) (403)
MALONE, Vick 39 (m) (B) (281)
MAN?, Melvina 60* (441)
MANLEY, F. C. 35 (m), (183)
MANLEY, Stanton 24 (B) (309)
MANLEY?, Haily 15 (f)* (B) (310)
MANLY, Rachal 65* (B) (235)
MANLY, _____ 22 (f)* (B) (325)
MANN, Elisabeth 42* (361)
MANSFIELD, Curly 21, (304)
MANSON, Johnson 44 (B) (217)
MAPLES, Mikel? 31 (m)* (392)
MAPOLES?, Mary A. 39* (381)
MARABLE, Bil 26 (B) (208)
MARION, Wm. 35 (B) (444)
MARK, Ben 53 (B) (494)
MARKES, Major 30 (B) (431)
MARKS, J. B. 68 (m)* (218)
MARLIN, T. N. 59 (m), (296)
MARLOW, MArtha 20* (356)
MARMAN, Man? 75 (m) (B) (499)
MARR, Nathaniel C. 50* (310)
MARSH, _. 30 (f) (B) (334)
MARSHAL, Bry 19 (B) (381)
MARSHAL, Eliza N. 77* (381)
MARSHAL, Laura 12* (B) (381)
MARSHAL, Law 45 (m) (B) (377)
MARSHAL, Lis 28 (m) (B) (380)
MARSHAL, Mary J. 22* (376)
MARSHAL, Nute 50 (m) (381)
MARSHAL, Tennessee 22 (f)* (B) (381)
MARSHAL, Tite 50 (m) (B) (382)
MARSHAL, Toney 45 (B) (381)
MARSHAL, Wallis 38 (B) (381)
MARTIN, A. M. 38 (m)* (B) (480)
MARTIN, Allen 39* (B) (480)
MARTIN, Andrew 21 (B) (369)
MARTIN, Araminda 33* (175)
MARTIN, Edd 23 (B) (480)
MARTIN, Ollie 30 (f)* (341)
MARTIN, Rebecca 26* (B) (174)
MARTIN?, M. 28 (m)* (495)
MARTON, Wash 25 (B) (440)
MARUM, Thomas 30* (375)
MARX, Frank 36* (168)
MARYWETHER, Ben 60* (B) (448)
MARYWETHER, Bill 60 (B) (444)
MARYWETHER, John 27* (B) (459)
MASK, F. 60 (m) (B) (488)
MASK, H. _ (m)* (B) (486)
MASON, Abraham? 65 (B) (322)
MASON, Agnes? 22* (B) (271)
MASON, Albert 21* (B) (260)
MASON, Bob 33* (B) (263)

MASON, Branch 25 (m)* (B) (451)
MASON, Charley 16* (B) (266)
MASON, Dilly A. 30 (f)* (297)
MASON, HArrison 53 (B) (260)
MASON, Hank? 40* (B) (496)
MASON, Harriet 15* (B) (263)
MASON, Henry 28?* (B) (258)
MASON, Jamie? 21 (m)* (259)
MASON, Laura 27* (B) (262)
MASON, Lewis 40* (B) (428)
MASON, Mary 39 (B) (261)
MASON, Pat 24 (m) (B) (283)
MASON, R. E. 49 (m)* (263)
MASON, Sallie 6* (B) (267)
MASON, Sue 37* (433)
MASON, Tom 30 (B) (257)
MASON, W. F. 22 (m)* (326)
MASON, Wm. 38 (B) (258)
MASON, Wm. 40 (B) (294)
MASON, Wm. 43, (430)
MASON?, Mollie 25* (444)
MASSEY, Jackson A. 30* (373)
MASSEY, Milton 26, (423)
MASSEY, Richard 63* (477)
MASSEY, Thomas 34, (414)
MASTON, Clarrie? 47 (f) (B) (457)
MATEHWS, Charlie 28* (228)
MATHAS, MAck 26* (B) (211)
MATHES, Sarah 65* (381)
MATHEWS, Aaron 50 (B) (396)
MATHEWS, Bob 55 (B) (283)
MATHEWS, Chaney 29 (f) (B) (286)
MATHEWS, D. 25 (m), (487)
MATHEWS, Emma 27* (386)
MATHEWS, J. S. 44 (m)* (300)
MATHEWS, London 65* (B) (228)
MATHEWS, MAriah 55* (B) (323)
MATHEWS, Magie 25, (410)
MATHEWS, Mary 54, (407)
MATHEWS, Polly 68* (324)
MATHEWS, Sam 35, (277)
MATHEWS, Susan 50, (410)
MATHEWS, Tom 25, (407)
MATHEWS, Tom 26 (B) (401)
MATHEWS, ___ 20 (m)* (B) (323)
MATHIS, Anna 25 (B) (450)
MATHIS, Emma 40* (B) (461)
MATHIS, Frank 46 (B) (391)
MATHIS, Sam 39 (B) (464)
MATHUS, Bob 25 (B) (480)
MATTHEWS, Alfred 46 (B) (190)
MATTHEWS, Billey 32 (B) (332)
MATTHEWS, F. 18 (f)* (324)
MATTHEWS, George 45 (B) (175)
MAURY, Branch 48* (B) (164)
MAURY, JAmes M. 37* (187)
MAURY?, Richd. 23* (B) (168)
MAXWEL, C. 24 (m) (B) (500)
MAXWELL, Joe 25* (B) (422)
MAXWELL, MArtha 50, (228)
MAXWELL, Mollie 40* (B) (440)
MAXWELL, Monica 35* (B) (461)

MAXWELL, Nancy 17* (B) (461)
MAXWELL, Sophia 52, (228)
MAXWELL, Tenmon? 32 (m), (228)
MAX__, Albert 34* (B) (197)
MAY, Amelia 16* (B) (496)
MAY, Chabe 47 (m) (B) (469)
MAY, Frank 15* (B) (469)
MAY, W. A. 18 (m)* (497)
MAY?, Brown 45 (B) (496)
MAYBERRY, Susan 40 (B) (474)
MAYBERY, Ben 23 (B) (475)
MAYFIELD, Bob 35 (B) (459)
MAYFIELD, Mollie 23* (437)
MAYHEM, A. J. 53 (m), (274)
MAYOWE, Hastey? 40 (f)* (B) (468)
MAYOWE, Ike 30 (B) (476)
MAYOWE, Wm. 12* (B) (468)
MAYS, Clarah 60* (B) (242)
MAYS, D. D. 45 (m), (217)
MAYS, Fredrick 34* (169)
MAYS, Mary 72* (241)
MAYS, W. 38 (m)* (B) (500)
MAYSEUR?, Charles 58, (425)
MA_____, Joe 68, (320)
MCABEN?, John 37 (B) (312)
MCADAMS, J. T. 28 (m)* (167)
MCAELROY, Rosett 28* (B) (377)
MCBRIDE, David 36, (433)
MCBRIDE, MAggie 48* (176)
MCCALLY, Jake 24 (B) (380)
MCCARLEY, J. C. 52 (m), (502)
MCCARLY, Peter 53 (B) (495)
MCCARVER, James W. 50, (366)
MCCASKILL, W. 47 (m), (469)
MCCASLEY, Henry 26 (B) (468)
MCCAWLEY, Eligah 19* (B) (393)
MCCLAIN, Salle? 22 (f) (B) (453)
MCCLANAHAN, Henry 38* (B) (291)
MCCLANAHAN, Wm. 38, (291)
MCCLANAN, Z. A. 45 (m), (483)
MCCLELAN, Judy 75* (B) (168)
MCCLELLAN, John 32 (B) (199)
MCCLELLAN, T. G. 55 (m), (161)
MCCLELLEN, J. 52 (m) (B) (479)
MCCLERAN, Adline 60* (B) (396)
MCCLERAN, Thomas 40* (B) (177)
MCCLOUD, Sarah 81* (235)
MCCL_____, George? 26 (B) (485)
MCCL_____, Sandy 53 (m)* (B) (485)
MCCON, John 48?, (173)
MCCONNELL, Chas. 40, (433)
MCCORD, Lucinda 45, (408)
MCCOY, Ann 45 (B) (164)
MCCRAW, J. D. 32 (m)* (287)
MCCRAW, J. H. 60 (m)* (294)
MCCRAW, Jane 60* (B) (281)
MCCRAW, Smith 40 (B) (280)
MCCREA, Lithea 32 (f)* (B) (259)
MCCROSKY, A. B. 25 (m)* (335)

MCCULLEY, Dick 43 (B) (318)
MCCULLEY, F. 46 (f)* (B) (310)
MCCULLEY, Henry 40 (B) (334)
MCCULLEY, J. M. 45 (m)* (342)
MCCULLEY, Jake 35* (B) (321)
MCCULLEY, R. J. 49 (m), (327)
MCCULLEY, Samuel 38* (B) (307)
MCCULLEY, Silas 29 (B) (321)
MCCULLEY, Tom 34 (B) (322)
MCCULLEY, Tom 53 (B) (324)
MCCULLEY, _____ 40 (m) (B) (301)
MCCULLEY, _____ 60 (m) (B) (322)
MCCULLEY, _____ 22 (m) (B) (322)
MCCULLIE, Mag 45 (f)* (333)
MCCULLY, Alfred 44 (B) (320)
MCCULLY, W. C. 47 (m), (334)
MCCURREL, Robert 35 (B) (463)
MCDANIEL, Julia 25* (B) (186)
MCDONA, Martha 30 (B) (188)
MCDONALD, David 43, (411)
MCDONALL, Bettie 11* (B) (433)
MCDONNAL, Isaac 50 (B) (458)
MCDOWE, Sol 26 (B) (377)
MCDOWEL, Abe 35 (B) (374)
MCDOWEL, Alec 45 (B) (377)
MCDOWEL, Charles 22* (B) (377)
MCDOWEL, David 22 (B) (377)
MCDOWEL, Ike 29* (B) (490)
MCDOWEL, John R. 31* (378)
MCDOWEL, Joseph 46 (B) (381)
MCDOWEL, LEwis 36 (B) (178)
MCDOWEL, Malissa 40 (B) (376)
MCDOWEL, Samuel 50 (B) (377)
MCDOWEL, Thomas 29 (B) (375)
MCDOWEL, W.? 1 (m)* (493)
MCDOWELL, Billey 45 (B) (323)
MCDOWELL, C.? P. 38 (m), (180)
MCDOWELL, Henry 35 (B) (178)
MCDOWELL, Henry 48* (B) (305)
MCDOWELL, R. 27 (m), (303)
MCDOWELL, Samuel 29 (B) (365)
MCDOWELL, _. 14 (m)* (296)
MCFADDEN, Cass 45 (m) (B) (336)
MCFADDEN, Green 45* (B) (327)
MCFADDEN, J. 55 (m), (502)
MCFADDEN, Robt. 35* (B) (270)
MCFADDEN, W. S. 49 (m), (331)
MCFADDEN, Wm. 28* (492)
MCFADEN, Thomas 25* (B) (369)
MCFARLAND, H. 40 (m)* (B) (270)
MCFARLIN, Docha? 24 (f)* (B) (263)
MCFARLIN, MArtin 12* (B) (254)
MCFARLING, Isac 50 (B) (378)

MCFARLING, Margret 23 (B) (219)

MCFERRIN, Addison 35* (B) (345)

MCFERRIN, E. 60 (m) (B) (308)

MCFERRIN, George 21 (B) (325)

MCFERRIN, Virgil 55, (326)

MCFERRIN, _ 28 (f) (B) (308)

MCGAHEE, Lue 50 (f) (444)

MCGEE, JEssie 24 (m)* (485)

MCGEE, James 20, (433)

MCGEE, Nannie 18* (B) (423)

MCGEE, Torie 25 (m) (B) (412)

MCGEE, Wm. 22 (B) (405)

MCGHEE, John 38, (316)

MCGILL, Wash 35, (476)

MCGOWAN, Allen 22* (B) (200)

MCGOWAN, Ann 20* (B) (193)

MCGOWAN, Billy 60 (B) (229)

MCGOWAN, Lige 40 (m) (B) (245)

MCGRAW, C. T. 24 (m), (273)

MCGRIME, Geo. 22?* (B) (200)

MCGUIRE, Fillis 21* (B) (279)

MCGUIRE, George 47 (B) (191)

MCGUIRE, Jim 6* (B) (239)

MCGUIRE, Joe 27 (B) (294)

MCGUIRE, M. 60 (m) (B) (245)

MCGUIRE, Sopha 35* (B) (238)

MCGWIRE, Julia 30* (B) (199)

MCGWIRE, Peter 45, (167)

MCILWEE?, Dave 22* (B) (333)

MCINEY, Lillie __* (B) (383)

MCINTURF, Vina 35 (B) (337)

MCIN___, Goerge 31* (326)

MCKAE?, Sam 27 (m) (B) (473)

MCKEE, JAmes H. 65* (253)

MCKENSIE, Gilbert 29* (B) (353)

MCKENSIE, Wm. 50* (B) (350)

MCKENZE?, Sallie 30* (B) (461)

MCKENZIE, Alex 44* (166)

MCKENZIE, Ann 30* (B) (453)

MCKENZIE, Ben 50 (B) (453)

MCKENZIE, Chas.? 46, (447)

MCKENZIE, George 30 (B) (438)

MCKENZIE, George 30 (B) (445)

MCKENZIE, Peter 19* (B) (459)

MCKENZIE, Will? 22* (B) (283)

MCKINLEY, Andy 38, (431)

MCKINLEY, Sara 55, (431)

MCKINNAY, H. 31 (m)* (301)

MCKINNEY, A. H. 37 (m), (204)

MCKINNEY, Solomon 20* (365)

MCKINNEY, __ 40 (m)* (487)

MCKINNY, D. 32 (m) (B) (486)

MCKINSSIE, J. W. 33 (m), (331)

MCKINSTRY, W. F. 29 (m), (411)

MCKINZY, C. 29 (f)* (B) (500)

MCKINZZIE, Henry 24 (B) (455)

MCKNIGHT, A. L. 26 (m), (282)

MCKNIGHT, J. W. 25 (m)* (291)

MCKNIGHT, T. R. 51 (m), (278)

MCKNIGHT, Virgil 21* (292)

MCKOUL?, _____ 47 (f), (258)

MCLAIN, Henry 53* (B) (286)

MCLANE, Bob 20* (B) (282)

MCLANE, Curn 45 (m) (B) (376)

MCLANTER, John 40* (443)

MCLARTY, Wm. 40, (478)

MCLAWAINE, Joe 26 (B) (275)

MCLEAN, Vinitia 10 (f)* (B) (364)

MCLEMORE, James 24* (B) (436)

MCLOUIS, James 24?* (B) (472)

MCLREE, Alex 55 (B) (276)

MCMAYON?, Ather 50 (m)* (294)

MCMICHEL, Wm. 26* (B) (164)

MCMILLAN, Miles 53 (B) (418)

MCMULLINS, Wallis 30, (452)

MCNABB, John 23* (250)

MCNAMEE?, Thos. 24* (B) (461)

MCNARY, George 33 (B) (370)

MCNEAL, Green 40 (B) (482)

MCNEAL, Joe 25 (B) (468)

MCNEAL, John 30 (B) (449)

MCNEAL, Sam? 22 (m) (B) (458)

MCNEAL, Wm. 17* (B) (378)

MCNEEL, Austin 35 (B) (229)

MCNEEL, Benjman 30 (B) (379)

MCNEEL, Frank? __* (B) (259)

MCNEEL, H. 32 (m) (B) (501)

MCNEEL, JOhn C. 41, (440)

MCNEEL, Lutha 60 (f)* (B) (492)

MCNEEL, Mae 67* (500)

MCNEER, Frank __* (B) (258)

MCNEIL, Buck 35 (B) (493)

MCNEIL, George 48* (B) (179)

MCNEIL, Henry 37 (B) (493)

MCNEIL, J. 12 (m)* (B) (298)

MCNEIL, Leandus 23 (m) (B) (372)

MCNEIL, Lucy 60 (B) (493)

MCNEIL, MAggie 40* (208)

MCNEIL, Marshal 18 (B) (179)

MCNEIL, Osburn 48 (B) (492)

MCNEIL, Sarah 8* (B) (489)

MCNEIL, Thos. 40 (B) (178)

MCNEIL, Washington 35 (B) (180)

MCNEILL, John 40 (B) (500)

MCNELI_, Hugh 42* (368)

MCRAVAN, George _2* (B) (382)

MCREE, C. W. 39 (m), (410)

MCREE, R. A. 36 (m), (410)

MCROW, John 15* (B) (233)

MCSEIL?, Martha 27* (B) (183)

MCTEWE?, W. 25 (m)* (501)

MCTHOMAS?, Thos. 23* (B) (440)

MCVANCE?, _____ 70 (m), (447)

MCVANNA?, Walter 21* (440)

MC_NLOCK, Wash 21 (B) (376)

MC___, Luella 49?* (300)

MC___, Maggie 26, (442)

MC___, Mary 56, (448)

MC___, Sas? 63 (f) (B) (300)

MC___, _____ 39 (m), (447)

MEACHEM, Richard? 65* (B) (259)

MEAD, Morgan 8* (B) (429)

MEADOW, Carlos? 31, (430)

MEBANE, Amos 31 (B) (356)

MEBANE, Archer 46 (B) (352)

MEBANE, Collin 25 (B) (347)

MEBANE, David 42* (B) (354)

MEBANE, Edward 9* (B) (367)

MEBANE, Freeman 38* (B) (360)

MEBANE, Green 16* (B) (345)

MEBANE, Isaac 65 (B) (360)

MEBANE, Isaiah 21* (B) (349)

MEBANE, James 45* (B) (352)

MEBANE, Larry 25 (B) (366)

MEBANE, Laura 29 (B) (350)

MEBANE, Lemuel 16* (B) (352)

MEBANE, Lewis 12* (B) (360)

MEBANE, Lilly A. 12* (B) (352)

MEBANE, Lydia 76* (B) (351)

MEBANE, Mark 52 (B) (349)

MEBANE, Monroe 25 (B) (367)

MEBANE, Moses 30 (B) (358)

MEBANE, Robert 21* (B) (349)

MEBANE, Thomas 54 (B) (352)

MEBANE, Tony 15* (B) (359)

MEBANE, Wm. 51* (B) (345)

MEBANE, Wm. G. 41* (B) (345)

MEDOWS, Thomas 25* (372)

MELLS, James 40* (B) (344)

MELTON, Cathrine 50* (B) (284)

MELTON, Geo. 30 (B) (287)

MELTON, Harry 35 (B) (294)

MELTON, Hulbert? 14* (269)

MELTON, MArtin 52* (B) (288)

MELTON, O. 30 (f)* (287)

MENEFEE, Judy 20* (B) (171)

MENEFER, Anna 28* (B) (181)

MERCER, J. F. 71 (m)* (322)

MERCER, J. L. 24 (m), (279)

MERIMAN, Jesse 79 (m)* (432)

MERIWEATHER, JAck 48* (B) (186)

MERRIWEATHER, Aron 39 (B) (225)

MERRIWEATHER, Edmon 22 (B) (248)

MERRIWEATHER, George 35 (B) (249)

MERRIWEATHER, Jesse 52 (m) (B) (248)

MERRIWEATHER, Mattie 8 (f)* (B) (249)

MERRIWEATHER, Mollie 53? (B) (224)

MERRIWEATHER, Rand? 58 (m) (B) (224)

MERRIWEATHER, Sandy 47* (B) (225)

METCALF, George 19* (407)

METZLER?, J. F. 28 (m)* (168)

MEWBORN, Jas. C. 40, (406)

MEWBORN, Mary J. 59, (406)

MEWBORN?, Frank 23 (B) (323)

MEWBORN?, Joe 20* (B) (325)

MEWBORN?, M. 22 (m) (B) (311)

MEWBORN?, W. 35 (m)* (B) (311)

MEYER, Peter 24* (447)

MEYERS, Emma 10* (309)

MICHAEL, John 50, (441)

MICHIE?, John 54 (B) (417)

MICHON, John 30 (B) (233)

MIDDLEBROOK, A. J. 41 (m), (205)

MIDDLEBROOK, C. 19 (f), (218)

MIDDLEBROOK, Wes 45 (B) (225)

MIDDLEBROOKE, SAllie 23* (B) (482)

MIKINEY?, James 52 (B) (385)

MILLER, Ann 18* (B) (389)

MILLER, Ann? 17* (377)

MILLER, Becky 23* (B) (161)

MILLER, Charity 12* (B) (360)

MILLER, Commodore 31* (B) (426)

MILLER, Ella 60 (B) (489)

MILLER, Gorge 24* (B) (211)

MILLER, Harey 60 (B) (214)

MILLER, Harie 67 (B) (216)

MILLER, Hary 26* (B) (213)

MILLER, Haywood 34 (B) (345)

MILLER, Henry 26 (B) (355)

MILLER, Henry24* (B) (419)

MILLER, Henry? 18?* (B) (266)

MILLER, Jack 54* (B) (426)

MILLER, Jane 50 (B) (381)

MILLER, John 26 (B) (275)

MILLER, John S. 30* (367)

MILLER, Jose 30 (f)* (407)

MILLER, Josey 11 (m)* (B) (206)

MILLER, Larkin 52* (B) (206)

MILLER, Lee 27 (m) (B) (288)

MILLER, Lewis 35 (B) (215)

MILLER, Peter 40 (B) (356)

MILLER, Rachel? 50* (B) (217)

MILLER, Rhoda 45* (B) (198)

MILLER, Rolly 45 (m) (B) (215)

MILLER, Sallie 39* (B) (215)

MILLER, Sarah 30* (B) (228)

MILLER, Sarah 43* (384)

MILLER, Thomas 73* (B) (195)

MILLER, Wiley 24* (B) (280)

MILLER, Will 14* (B) (484)

MILLER, Zilk 60 (m) (B) (215)

MILLER, _. 38 (m)* (B) (497)

MILLER, _. A. 57 (m), (214)

MILLER, _____ 21 (m)* (B) (213)

MILLS, Harriet 35* (B) (323)

MILLS, Rufus 18* (B) (342)

MILLY, Anderson 53 (B) (492)

MILSON, George 30* (B) (322)

MILTON, Edmond 55* (B) (268)

MILTON, Finis 22* (B) (261)

MILTON, Moses 55 (B) (261)

MILTON, Polk 30, (477)

MINER, Harvy 50* (B) (383)

MINER, James 54* (B) (458)

MINER, John 25* (B) (418)

MINER, Wm. 22 (B) (382)

MINER, Wm. 50 (B) (454)

MINON, Charley 24? (B) (214)

MINOS, Thos. 40 (B) (453)

MINTER, M. 32 (m)* (B) (494)

MIRE?, Lee 30 (m), (335)

MIRES, Alexander 25* (332)

MIRES, George 50 (B) (331)

MIRT, G. A. 14 (f)* (B) (317)

MIRT?, J. H. 42 (m)* (335)

MITCHEL, Catherin 30* (B) (254)

MITCHEL, Donell? _9 (B) (267)

MITCHEL, Easter 22 (f)* (B) (214)

MITCHEL, HArriett 60* (183)
MITCHEL, Jessey 57 (m) (B) (209)
MITCHEL, John 10* (B) (254)
MITCHEL, John 28?* (B) (257)
MITCHEL, Lewis 25 (B) (209)
MITCHEL, R. D. 5 (m)* (B) (204)
MITCHEL, Thee 47 (m) (B) (210)
MITCHEL, Tilda 46 (B) (215)
MITCHEL, Z. T. 33 (m)* (211)
MITCHEL, _. H. 40 (m)* (211)
MITCHELL, Abraham 60 (B) (361)
MITCHELL, Benjamin 76 (B) (353)
MITCHELL, Bettie 37, (410)
MITCHELL, Dann 27 (B) (394)
MITCHELL, Dave 19 (B) (403)
MITCHELL, Dave 60 (B) (398)
MITCHELL, David 49 (B) (354)
MITCHELL, Esther 65* (B) (364)
MITCHELL, Florence 20* (361)
MITCHELL, Henry 30 (B) (398)
MITCHELL, J. H. 40 (m)* (292)
MITCHELL, John 24* (B) (274)
MITCHELL, Sarah 22* (283)
MITCHELL, Tom 12* (B) (275)
MITCHELL, _____ 12 (m), (285)
MITCHEM, Wm. 27? (B) (296)
MOBY, Minta 31 (B) (444)
MOCK, Warner 35 (B) (254)
MODDEN, _____ 26 (m) (B) (296)
MOELIN?, HArriet 27* (B) (253)
MOLLOY, Pat 25* (413)
MOMAN, Gabe 17* (B) (469)
MOMAN, Julious 25 (B) (472)
MONCRIEF, Wm. 74, (353)
MONROE, Henry 33* (293)
MONROE, Henry 35 (B) (372)
MONROE, Jesse 14 (m)* (B) (353)
MONROE, Mag 20 (B) (404)
MONROE, W. 49 (m)* (315)
MONROE, Wm. 7* (B) (357)
MONTAGUE, A. J. 22 (m) (B) (328)
MONTAGUE, Alferd 22* (B) (254)
MONTAGUE, Alfred 40 (B) (330)
MONTAGUE, Ann 60* (B) (329)
MONTAGUE, Dock 26* (B) (256)
MONTAGUE, George 23* (254)
MONTAGUE, Henry 53* (B) (328)
MONTAGUE, J. R. 38 (m)* (B) (328)
MONTAGUE, M. 37 (f)* (254)
MONTAGUE, R. 18 (m)* (B) (254)
MONTAGUE, Shev__ 20 (m) (B) (254)
MONTAGUE, Wm. 50 (B) (254)
MONTGOMERY, J. 38 (m), (493)
MONTGOMERY, J. 52 (f)* (490)
MONTGOMERY, J. D. 35 (m), (213)

MONTGOMERY, Manda 31* (B) (197)
MONTGOMERY, Owen 30* (B) (369)
MONTGOMERY, Robt. 23* (168)
MONTGOMERY, Wm. 79* (489)
MONTGOMERY, _____ 12 (f)* (B) (199)
MOODEY, Alf 40* (B) (473)
MOODEY, J. M. 42 (m)* (473)
MOODY, Cooper 25* (B) (414)
MOODY, Edmund 71 (B) (391)
MOODY, Guy 76* (B) (423)
MOODY, J. H. 29 (m)* (303)
MOODY, Lissa 85* (B) (473)
MOODY, Louis 30* (B) (382)
MOODY, Louisa 5/12* (B) (429)
MOODY, Richard 54, (441)
MOODY, _____ J. 23 (m)* (392)
MOODY, _____ 25 (f)* (B) (429)
MOOR, James L. 52* (392)
MOORE, Allen 60 (B) (358)
MOORE, Anny? 25 (B) (419)
MOORE, Bumpass 25* (B) (173)
MOORE, George 46* (168)
MOORE, J.? A. 43, (306)
MOORE, JAmes A. 27* (369)
MOORE, JAmes K. 30* (408)
MOORE, James 50* (B) (368)
MOORE, John H. 17* (B) (258)
MOORE, John T. 28, (279)
MOORE, Joseph 50 (B) (465)
MOORE, Laura 20* (B) (186)
MOORE, Lorena 12* (279)
MOORE, Lotta 4* (201)
MOORE, Luke 23* (B) (481)
MOORE, Malcolm J. M. 46, (367)
MOORE, Martin 34* (B) (303)
MOORE, Mary 12* (B) (303)
MOORE, Minnie 14* (412)
MOORE, Moses 72, (409)
MOORE, Obey 20 (m) (B) (405)
MOORE, Oliver 24* (B) (199)
MOORE, P. 60? (m), (199)
MOORE, Patrick 44?* (B) (171)
MOORE, Rebecca __, (414)
MOORE, Robert 22 (B) (352)
MOORE, Robert 62 (B) (176)
MOORE, Russell 9* (274)
MOORE, Samuel 22* (B) (353)
MOORE, Sewell 42 (B) (350)
MOORE, T. R. 46 (m), (306)
MOORE, W. S. 28 (m)* (289)
MOORE, Warren 32 (B) (400)
MOORE, Wm. 35 (B) (350)
MOORE, Wm. H. 48* (222)
MOORE, Zed 18 (m)* (188)
MOORE, _____ 25 (m) (B) (400)
MOORFIELD, John 26* (201)
MOORFIELD, SElena 31* (200)
MOORFIELD?, Charles 24* (198)
MOORING, George 18* (B) (405)
MOORMAN, Buck? 27 (B) (425)
MOORMAN, H. C. 38 (m)* (163)
MOORMAN, Lou 50 (f)* (B) (421)
MOOTRIE, Samuel? 36* (B) (309)
MORA, C. A. 28 (m)* (324)

MORE, George 19* (B) (321)
MORE, Isreal 27* (B) (337)
MORE, Judge 28 (B) (340)
MORE, Wm. 24 (B) (339)
MORE?, Edmon 35* (B) (340)
MORE?, R. R. 36 (m), (340)
MORELAND, George W. 44* (365)
MORGAN, Harriet 38* (B) (160)
MORGAN, JAmes 26 (B) (255?)
MORGAN, Jack 68 (B) (380)
MORGAN, James 33, (376)
MORGAN, Joe 51* (B) (280)
MORGAN, John 30* (B) (325)
MORGAN, Lucy 53* (B) (280)
MORGAN, Richard 35 (B) (193)
MORGAN, Victoria 11* (B) (433)
MORGAN, Viney 1/12* (B) (362)
MORGAN, W. 22 (m) (B) (484)
MORGAN, Wylie 23* (B) (362)
MORIS, Abby 55 (B) (241)
MORIS, Alen 28* (206)
MORIS, J. M. 34 (m), (204)
MORIS, Ned 50 (m)* (B) (241)
MORIS?, Cresy 25 (f)* (B) (270)
MORMAN, Fred 50 (B) (473)
MORMAN, M. 20 (m)* (B) (498)
MORMON, Lou 75 (f)* (B) (454)
MORRIS, A. 19 (m)* (B) (311)
MORRIS, Albert 16* (B) (356)
MORRIS, Allen 50, (191)
MORRIS, Anna 12* (B) (405)
MORRIS, Anna 9* (B) (405)
MORRIS, Ben 14* (B) (307)
MORRIS, Benton 62* (201)
MORRIS, Burton 24* (B) (426)
MORRIS, Caroline 50 (B) (367)
MORRIS, Edd 24* (472)
MORRIS, Eddie _* (198)
MORRIS, Edmund 68 (B) (355)
MORRIS, Edward 21 (B) (418)
MORRIS, Fannie 13* (230)
MORRIS, Frazier 20 (B) (398)
MORRIS, G. W. 48 (m)* (482)
MORRIS, Henry 20, (199)
MORRIS, Hiram 69, (472)
MORRIS, Isaac 48 (B) (404)
MORRIS, JEb 29 (B) (242)
MORRIS, James 30, (220)
MORRIS, James S. 33, (356)
MORRIS, John 45* (488)
MORRIS, Joshua 36* (430)
MORRIS, Laura 16* (B) (366)
MORRIS, Lewis 22, (356)
MORRIS, Martha 35* (488)
MORRIS, Mary 45 (B) (404)
MORRIS, May E. 8* (167)
MORRIS, Morison 24* (223)
MORRIS, Nancy 36?* (198)
MORRIS, Parthenia 65 (B) (356)
MORRIS, Rebecca 51* (424)
MORRIS, Rena 70* (B) (243)
MORRIS, Sam 31 (m)* (486)
MORRIS, Susan 15* (B) (359)
MORRIS, Thomas W. 17* (407)
MORRIS, Wm. 10* (218)
MORRIS, Wm. 33 (B) (304)
MORRIS, Wm. 37, (192)
MORRIS, Wm. 61* (241)
MORRISON, D. Z. 51 (m)* (186)

MORRISON, J. M. 42 (m)* (492)
MORRISON, _. 37 (m)* (492)
MORRISS, Albert 7* (B) (323)
MORROW, Ad? 8/12 (f)* (B) (494)
MORROW, Alac 18* (B) (493)
MORROW, Ch__ 50 (f)* (201)
MORROW, Chany 43 (f) (B) (491)
MORROW, D. M. 34 (m), (219)
MORROW, Daniel? 11* (B) (201)
MORROW, Eliza 22* (B) (487)
MORROW, G. W. 60 (m), (493)
MORROW, G.? 53 (m) (B) (493)
MORROW, G.? D. 27 (m), (180)
MORROW, George 32* (B) (488)
MORROW, H. 37 (m)* (B) (491)
MORROW, H. 47 (m) (B) (493)
MORROW, Isaac 33 (B) (201)
MORROW, J. M. 53 (m)* (493)
MORROW, Julia 20 (B) (491)
MORROW, Levi 25* (B) (495)
MORROW, P. 24 (B) (495)
MORROW, Petter 43 (B) (288)
MORROW, R. 68 (m), (493)
MORROW, Ransom 60 (B) (491)
MORROW, Rebeca 55 (B) (493)
MORROW, Rose 22* (B) (491)
MORROW, S. _* (B) (486)
MORROW, Sam 70, (491)
MORROW, Simon 29* (B) (200)
MORROW, Terrill 25 (B) (200)
MORROW, Thomas 31 (B) (491)
MORROW, Thomas 50 (B) (192)
MORROW?, _____ 26 (m) (B) (494)
MORTON, Adam 51 (B) (457)
MORTON, Adeline 20* (B) (374)
MORTON, Fanny 38* (B) (162)
MORTON, Frank 23?* (B) (423)
MORTON, John 22* (253)
MORTON, Nancy 30 (B) (383)
MORTON, Preston 24* (B) (381)
MORTON, Robert 29* (415)
MORTON, S. H. 39 (m)* (167)
MORTON, Sarah E. 51, (370)
MORTON, W. H. 56; (m), (477)
MORTON, Wm. 24* (B) (374)
MORTON, Wm. 40 (B) (373)
MOSBEY, Griffin 24 (B) (476)
MOSBEY, James 62 (B) (467)
MOSBEY, Jorden 25 (B) (220)
MOSBEY, M. D. 25 (m) (B) (482)
MOSBEY, Townsley 53* (B) (471)
MOSBY, Adline? 10 (f)* (B) (494)
MOSBY, App 23 (m)* (B) (243)
MOSBY, Clara 60* (B) (246)
MOSBY, Cornelia 50, (244)
MOSBY, Edmond 45 (B) (378)
MOSBY, Frank 19* (B) (428)
MOSBY, George? 38 (B) (446)
MOSBY, Harrison 51 (B) (199)
MOSBY, Joe 18* (B) (240)
MOSBY, Mary 4* (B) (202)
MOSBY, Mary A. 28* (B) (353)
MOSBY, Phelix 18* (B) (489)
MOSBY, Sela 52 (f)* (B) (244)
MOSBY, Spencer 27* (440)
MOSBY, Tom 25 (B) (223)
MOSBY, Wash 51* (B) (244)

21

MOSBY, Wm. 52* (B) (238)
MOSBY, _____ 75? (m) (B) (245)
MOSBY?, James 21* (B) (187)
MOSE, Duglas 30 (B) (378)
MOSER?, George 23* (B) (421)
MOSLEY, John N. 34* (255)
MOSLEY, Mall 5 (f)* (B) (402)
MOSLEY, Turner 40 (B) (402)
MOSS, C. C. 24 (m) (B) (187)
MOSS, David 19 (B) (400)
MOSS, Henry 31, (434)
MOSS, J. B. F. 38 (m), (483)
MOSS, Nick 25 (B) (399)
MOSS, Wm. 27, (385)
MOSSES, George 55 (B) (481)
MOTLEY, Anderson 52 (B) (194)
MOTLEY, J. J. 46 (m), (203)
MOTLEY, JOel S. 41, (196)
MOTLEY, Sam 25 (B) (276)
MOWRY?, John 29, (450)
MUIER, Emmit A. 25, (406)
MULLER, James 51, (305)
MULLINS, Wm. 24, (304)
MUNDON, West 24 (B) (276)
MUNFORD, Jones 23* (B) (267)
MUNICA?, Robert 70* (B) (424)
MUNICE, Henry 21 (B) (424)
MUNROE, John 39, (315)
MUNTICA?, Jack 21* (B) (424)
MURCHESON, D. P. 38 (m), (283)
MURELL?, Emma 32* (B) (301)
MURPHEY, Boman? 47 (m), (408)
MURPHEY, Willie 9 (m)* (B) (199)
MURPHEY?, Wm. 35* (194)
MURPHY, Ada T. 49* (184)
MURPHY, Ben 25 (B) (237)
MURPHY, Ben? 22?* (B) (200)
MURPHY, Burel 50 (B) (368)
MURPHY, Green 44 (B) (205)
MURPHY, James 37, (321)
MURPHY, Judy 26* (B) (205)
MURPHY, M. 35 (f) (B) (196)
MURPHY, Monroe 19* (B) (417)
MURPHY, Rachal 18* (B) (239)
MURPHY, Roland 30 (B) (175)
MURPHY, Washington 4_? (B) (196)
MURPHY, Wiley 45 (B) (196)
MURPHY, Wm. 70* (320)
MURRAY, R. L. 35 (m), (296)
MURRAY, Taylor 39 (B) (297)
MURREL, Lafayette 45* (B) (374)
MURRELL, Amos R. 45, (407)
MURRELL, Benjamin 27* (311)
MURRELL, Celia 21* (B) (297)
MURRELL, Charlie 24 (B) (296)
MURRELL, Edward 24 (B) (347)
MURRELL, F.? 30 (m)* (B) (313)
MURRELL, Henry 13* (322)
MURRELL, Huse 35 (m) (B) (322)
MURRELL, James 21* (B) (344)
MURRELL, Joel 55 (B) (308)
MURRELL, John 10* (B) (366)
MURRELL, John 23 (B) (311)
MURRELL, Jonas? 21* (B) (316)

MURRELL, Marion 23* (B) (302)
MURRELL, Matt 26 (f)* (B) (312)
MURRELL, Neat? 6 (f)* (B) (312)
MURRELL, Parlee 24* (B) (404)
MURRELL, Quincy 54, (407)
MURRELL, R. E. 32 (m)* (344)
MURRELL, R. E. 32? (m)* (316)
MURRELL, Robert 40 (B) (313)
MURRELL, Robt. 21* (B) (318)
MURRELL, Romp 63 (m) (B) (334)
MURRELL, S. 64 (f)* (B) (313)
MURRELL, Steven 65 (B) (308)
MURRELL, W. J. 30 (m), (296)
MURRELL, Wm. 34 (B) (310)
MURRELL, ___ 26 (m)* (B) (297)
MURRILL, D. 23 (m)* (B) (325)
MURRILL, Lan? 18 (m)* (B) (321)
MURTA, Joseph 40* (423)
MURY, Elleck 17* (B) (413)
MURY, Richard 9* (B) (375)
MUSTGROVE, J. A. 25 (m), (342)
MYER, Frank 30, (268)
MYERS, B. H. 25 (m)* (261)
MYERS?, Geo. 50 (B) (317)
MYRES, James 27* (B) (311)
MYRICK, Edward 59* (441)
M__, Lenard 67, (441)
M____, Alfred 40?, (301)
M_____, Fred _ * (B) (436)
NABIE, Edd 50 (B) (400)
NALLEY, MArtha 39* (307)
NANFIT?, S. 33 (m)* (B) (389)
NARRAMORE, W. E. 33 (m)* (167)
NASH, I.? 66 (m)* (195)
NASH, John 31, (428)
NASH, Sarah 38 (B) (175)
NATHANIEL, Henry 25 (B) (322)
NCNEIL, S.? 21 (m)* (B) (492)
NEAL, Abraham 24* (B) (235)
NEAL, Albert 28 (B) (349)
NEAL, Callie 4* (B) (418)
NEAL, R. B. 41 (m), (301)
NEAL, R. K. 37 (m)* (467)
NEAL, Samuel 25* (B) (369)
NEAL, Wm. H. 23* (B) (361)
NEBHERT?, John 54* (436)
NEBLETT, J. D. 50 (m)* (215)
NEBLETT?, Frank 24, (440)
NEEL, Anderson 55 (B) (327)
NEEL, Austin 45 (B) (404)
NEEL, Benn 48 (B) (397)
NEEL, Burt 46 (B) (401)
NEEL, Caroline 22* (B) (401)
NEEL, Dock 30 (B) (396)
NEEL, Dora 17* (B) (325)
NEEL, Frank 60 (B) (396)
NEEL, Jordan 28 (B) (396)
NEEL, Richard 21* (B) (340)
NEEL, Richard 24 (B) (400)
NEEL, Rosa 25 (B) (334)
NEEL, Shepherd 22 (B) (401)
NEEL, Thomas G. 75, (406)
NEEL, Thomas S. 35, (406)

NEEL, York 42 (B) (173)
NEELEY, C. F. 44 (m), (209)
NEELEY, Handy 54* (B) (206)
NEELEY, N. B. 52 (f) (B) (210)
NEELLY, W. F. 36 (m), (336)
NEELY, J. J. 33 (m)* (334)
NEIL, Drew 28 (B) (184)
NEIL, James 23* (B) (430)
NEIL, John F. 64* (185)
NEIL, Johnson 25* (B) (188)
NELL, Bobb 37 (B) (396)
NELL, Rice 42 (B) (396)
NELLY, Thomas 23 (B) (340)
NELMS?, S. J. 44 (m)* (313)
NELSON, Edmond 28 (B) (225)
NELSON, H. 60 (m) (B) (496)
NELSON, Henry? 24 (B) (310)
NELSON, Jack 67 (B) (171)
NELSON, James 28 (B) (364)
NELSON, Jane 30* (B) (311)
NELSON, Martha 42 (B) (309)
NELSON, Martin 57 (B) (366)
NELSON, Moses 21 (B) (366)
NELSON, Robert 45* (B) (347)
NELSON, Ros 23 (m)* (B) (162)
NELSON, Tom 25 (B) (247)
NELSON, Wm. 32* (B) (171)
NESBIT, Minter 24 (B) (167)
NESBITT, ____ 40 (m) (B) (300)
NETHERLAND?, James 45 (B) (312)
NETHERTON, James 45, (458)
NETTLES, Ike 20* (B) (212)
NETTLES, Milleyan 10 (f)* (B) (213)
NEVILLE, Albert 48* (379)
NEVILLE, Jane 60* (B) (383)
NEVILLE, Mike 33 (B) (390)
NEW, Wiley 8* (B) (460)
NEW?, Ben 33 (B) (446)
NEWBERRY, Mary 52* (B) (309)
NEWBORN, Clay 26 (B) (404)
NEWBORN, Sela 23 (f)* (B) (236)
NEWBY, Georgia 28 (f)* (419)
NEWBY, Henry 47 (B) (471)
NEWBY, John 28 (B) (451)
NEWBY, Jordan 50 (B) (481)
NEWBY, M. M. 44 (m), (471)
NEWBY, Sarah 41 (B) (376)
NEWBY, Thomas 20* (B) (377)
NEWBY, Wm. 18* (183)
NEWE, Esquire __* (B) (204)
NEWMAN, Wm. 52* (183)
NEWSOM, Annika? 23 (f)* (B) (194)
NEWSOM, Ike 28 (B) (211)
NEWSOM, J. W. 48 (m)* (313)
NEWSOM, John 20 (B) (210)
NEWSOM, John 30* (B) (337)
NEWSOM, John 30 (B) (337)
NEWSOM, M. O. 37 (m)* (207)
NEWSOM, May _* (B) (205)
NEWSON, Bettie B. 45, (367)
NEWSON, J. T. 30 (m), (206)
NEWTON, Joel 49 (B) (309)
NEWTON, John 60 (B) (257)
NICKERSON, Alex 24* (B) (200)
NIX, Nervie 50 (f), (409)
NIXON, Eliza 18* (293)

NOAH, James 33, (428)
NOELL, Jefferson 33 (B) (360)
NOLES, Bill 19* (332)
NOLLEY?, Isaac 28 (B) (315)
NORMAN, Bristo 18 (m)* (B) (183)
NORMAN, Gorge 23* (B) (204)
NORMAN, Henry 44 (B) (470)
NORMAN, Robert 29 (B) (388)
NORMAN, Simon 22* (B) (342)
NORMAN, Simon? 22* (317)
NORMONT, Sam 25 (B) (212)
NORRIS, David 49, (226)
NORRIS, Hiram 40 (B) (427)
NORRIS, Jane 70, (456)
NORRIS, John 49, (456)
NORWOOD, George 50 (B) (405)
NOWEL, E. __ (B) (199)
NOWEL, Samuel 54* (B) (198)
NOWELL, Willie 21 (m)* (269)
NUCKOLS, Charles E. 26* (350)
OATES, L. K. 33 (m), (485)
OATS?, John 52, (309)
OBANION, C. 45 (f)* (296)
OBEY, Thomas __, (278)
OBEY, Wm. 26* (B) (349)
OBRIEN, Mike 35* (416)
OBRIENT, Riley 40* (B) (273)
OB__Y, Tom 42* (B) (315)
OCONNER, Michel 60* (164)
OCONNOR, James 25, (375)
OCONNOR, Wm. 32, (375)
ODOM, Polly 55, (407)
OGLESWORTH, Darcus 60 (B) (402)
OKELLEY, Alex 27* (279)
OKELLEY, J.? P. 58 (m)* (292)
OKELLEY, Llesie? 43 (m)* (290)
OKELLEY, Louis 46* (292)
OKELLEY, W. S. 51 (m), (284)
OLD, George 52* (B) (235)
OLD, Wm. E. 40, (161)
OLDMOND, Wm. 25* (282)
OLDS, Andrew __* (B) (262)
OLDS, Daniel? 68* (B) (263)
OLDS, Harriet 6* (B) (262)
OLDS, Mat 36 (B) (285)
OLDS, Zack 32* (B) (254)
OLIVER, Bidsdie 27 (f) (B) (162)
OLIVER, Edward 20* (B) (177)
OLIVER, James 38 (B) (303)
OLIVER, Julia 63* (444)
OLIVER, Rachel 8* (B) (181)
OLIVER, Thomas 48, (200)
OLIVER, Wm. 28, (201)
ONEEL, Marion 18* (B) (327)
ONEILL, Patrick J. 32?* (376)
OORMSBY?, Lucy 27* (426)
ORGAM, Louesa 45* (B) (238)
ORR, Allen 40* (B) (296)
ORR, Henry 16* (306)
ORR, Susan J. 66 (f)* (315)
OSBERN, James 76, (447)
OSBERN, Wm. 45, (456)
OSBORNE, J. R. 35 (m)* (329)
OSBURN, George 17* (B) (492)
OSIER, Elizabeth 45, (470)
OSIER, Lou 37 (f), (470)
OSUR, George 30 (B) (466)

OTTOWAY, Peryear? 24 (m) (B) (475)
OTTOWAY, R__ 80 (m) (B) (475)
OURSLER, John A. 24* (380)
OURSLER, Martin 23* (B) (388)
OUTBREATH?, Wm. 11* (408)
OVERTON, James 30? (B) (448)
OWEN, Edward M. 49* (374)
OWEN, F. H. 38 (m)* (300)
OWEN, George 4 (B) (381)
OWEN, Nash L. 53* (356)
OWEN, Rubin 45 (B) (380)
OWEN, Thornton 27* (424)
OWEN?, Alaxander 55* (B) (416)
OWEN?, Samuel 20* (B) (420)
OWENS, Bill 22 (B) (394)
OWENS, Charly 25? (B) (188)
OWENS, Granderson 36 (B) (164)
OWENS, Jack? 60 (B) (394)
OWENS, Peter 17* (B) (402)
OWINGS, Thomas B. 57, (406)
OZIER, Hill 33 (B) (180)
OZIER?, M. 64 (f)* (489)
PADERSON, Jurdan 35 (B) (340)
PAGE, John 29* (487)
PAGE, Joseph 14* (205)
PAIN, Charley 20* (B) (217)
PAIN, Julia 38 (B) (405)
PAIN, Julia 42* (B) (405)
PAINE?, H. N. 45 (m)* (335)
PAINE?, Joseph 52* (192)
PALMER, Lee 20 (m) (B) (377)
PALMER, MAry 19* (B) (250)
PALMER, Mike 57 (B) (174)
PALMER, Sarah 45* (B) (165)
PALMER, Stephen 28 (B) (445)
PANKEY?, Wm. 31* (445)
PARER, Fannie 16* (B) (429)
PARHAM, Ben 30* (B) (443)
PARHAM, Ben M. 55, (441)
PARHAM, Dan 45 (B) (462)
PARHAM, Daniel 52 (B) (439)
PARHAM, Leona 45, (465)
PARHAM, Lucy 31* (B) (500)
PARHAM, Martha? 60 (B) (445)
PARHAM, Phillis 75* (B) (422)
PARHAM, Tom 45 (B) (438)
PARHAM, Wm. 44, (464)
PARIS, James 20* (B) (369)
PARISH, Henry 51* (B) (383)
PARISH, James 21* (B) (426)
PARISH, Marker? 56 (m)* (B) (382)
PARISH, Oty 17 (m)* (B) (176)
PARISH, Robt. 22* (B) (164)
PARISH, Sallie 35* (B) (162)
PARISH, Tucker 24 (B) (395)
PARK, Ana? 22* (B) (206)
PARKER, Anna 50* (420)
PARKER, Dora 17* (285)
PARKER, Elizabeth 37* (206)
PARKER, Erastus 31, (198)
PARKER, Francis 33* (198)
PARKER, George 23* (B) (341)
PARKER, George 24* (B) (372)
PARKER, Gus 34* (B) (446)
PARKER, H__ 50 (m) (B) (462)
PARKER, Harris 40 (B) (439)
PARKER, Henry 7* (B) (480)

PARKER, Hiram 35* (B) (349)
PARKER, James 25 (B) (477)
PARKER, James 28* (280)
PARKER, James 52, (487)
PARKER, M. H. 45 (m), (281)
PARKER, Pres 36 (m)* (B) (341)
PARKER, Sallie 26, (438)
PARKER, Washington 62?* (198)
PARKER, Willie 20 (m)* (280)
PARKES, George 35, (445)
PARKES, Red 33* (B) (492)
PARKES, ____ 28 (m)* (B) (390)
PARKS, Ardell 12 (f)* (B) (479)
PARKS, Bob 31 (B) (471)
PARKS, Charly 39* (B) (470)
PARKS, Esqre. 28 (m)* (B) (223)
PARKS, Frank 35 (B) (387)
PARKS, Henry 37 (B) (467)
PARKS, James 75 (B) (468)
PARKS, Mose 57* (466)
PARKS, Samuel 70* (376)
PARKS, Willie 19 (m)* (237)
PARMER, Henry 24 (B) (434)
PARMER, Sam 22* (B) (287)
PAROTT, Henry 30* (B) (387)
PAROTT, Henry 87* (B) (387)
PARR, Felix 19* (B) (430)
PARR, Jennie 12* (B) (441)
PARR, Wm. 51* (430)
PARREL?, W. B. 22 (m)* (338)
PARRISH, Abraham 21* (B) (351)
PARRISH, Ben 26 (B) (456)
PARRISH, Cate 40 (f)* (488)
PARRISH, J. R. 27 (m), (474)
PARRISH, Lucy 22?* (492)
PARRISH, Scot 22* (B) (471)
PARROTT, M. C. 32 (m)* (481)
PARSONS, J. 29 (m)* (497)
PARSONS, MAnson 63* (183)
PARTIN, Lewis B. 32* (184)
PARTIN, Mary A. 55* (184)
PATE, B. R. F. 13 (m)* (335)
PATE, John 69, (359)
PATEN?, V. W. 25 (m)* (315)
PATERSON, C. C. 22 (m)* (306)
PATES?, Eliza 33, (408)
PATISON, ____ 41 (m), (393)
PATRICK, Alace 35* (B) (215)
PATRICK, Dolphin? 33 (m) (B) (451)
PATRICK, Green 45 (B) (373)
PATRICK, Henry 40 (B) (355)
PATRICK, Howard 23* (B) (215)
PATRICK, James 41 (B) (384)
PATRICK, Nolan 60, (444)
PATTERSON, Bill 25 (B) (433)
PATTERSON, Caroline 54* (189)
PATTERSON, Cary 27 (m) (B) (223)
PATTERSON, Daniel 35* (B) (180)
PATTERSON, Frank 26 (B) (214)
PATTERSON, Hiram 30 (B) (358)
PATTERSON, James 18* (208)
PATTERSON, Josiah 50* (B) (256)
PATTERSON, Lee 10 (f)* (B) (493)
PATTERSON, Mary 5* (189)

PATTERSON, Nelson 85 (B) (358)
PATTERSON, Price 40 (f) (B) (484)
PATTERSON, R. G. 62 (m)* (473)
PATTERSON, Simon 40 (B) (167)
PATTERSON, Tilda 30* (B) (433)
PATTERSON, Wassie? 20 (f)* (B) (201)
PATTILLO, John 52* (185)
PATTILLO, Julia 50, (185)
PATTON, Bob 25 (B) (220)
PATTON, Felix 37 (B) (353)
PATTON, Joseph 25, (455)
PATTON, Thomas 32, (443)
PATTON, Wm. 22* (B) (164)
PATTON, Wm. 24* (B) (167)
PAYNE, Bluford 28 (B) (345)
PAYNE, Hiram A. 53* (365)
PAYTON, John 4 (B) (448)
PAYTON, Mary 20* (B) (438)
PEALER, Smith 14* (B) (368)
PEARLE, James 38, (424)
PEARMAN, Henry 25* (B) (203)
PEARMAN, Susan 50* (B) (203)
PEARSON, Acy L. 66 (m), (370)
PEARSON, Jane 22* (B) (427)
PEARSON, P. M. 48 (m), (472)
PEARSON, Robert 32 (B) (372)
PEARSON, Sarah 28* (370)
PEATERSON, John 14* (386)
PEDRICK, Tom 20 (B) (258)
PEEBLES, Alfred 33 (B) (191)
PEEBLES, Allen 18* (B) (228)
PEEBLES, Atlas J. 63, (179)
PEEBLES, Crocket 24* (B) (185)
PEEBLES, E. 4 (f)* (B) (181)
PEEBLES, Eddie 21* (237)
PEEBLES, Elijah 59? (B) (164)
PEEBLES, Fereby 57* (B) (163)
PEEBLES, Henry __ (B) (165)
PEEBLES, Joseph W. 45* (171)
PEEBLES, Rufus 29?* (B) (172)
PEEBLES, Sarah L. 47* (162)
PEEKS, L. J. 24 (m)* (331)
PEELE, Dilphia? 30 (B) (261)
PEELER, F. 57 (f)* (B) (500)
PEELER, Peter 25 (B) (401)
PEEPLES, Harriett 47 (B) (451)
PEGEE, Lot 28 (B) (233)
PEGGEE, JAcob 45 (B) (230)
PEGRAM?, Willis 33 (B) (455)
PELLAM, MAjor 49* (B) (254)
PELLIT?, James 20* (433)
PELLMAN?, Ben 27 (B) (356)
PELLMAN?, Norah 25* (B) (354)
PENN, Alec 50* (B) (372)
PENNEY, David 40 (B) (273)
PEOPLES, Rufe 25* (B) (339)
PEPPER, R. G. 35 (m), (205)
PERCEY?, Ellen 23* (B) (376)
PERCY, Randal 59 (m) (B) (496)
PERKES?, Robert 1, (412)
PERKINS, Anna 25* (440)
PERKINS, Chas. 23, (279)
PERKINS, Elbert 25 (B) (458)
PERKINS, James 40* (B) (414)
PERKINS, Wm. H. 68, (177)
PERKINS, ____ 26 (f) (B) (457)

PERKS, Lucy 40* (B) (359)
PERN, Edward 74* (372)
PERRICK, T. J. 30 (m), (483)
PERRIN, Warren 26 (B) (388)
PERRSON, John K. 23* (375)
PERRY, Arthur 21* (B) (190)
PERRY, Asa 58, (200)
PERRY, Barbery 45 (f)* (B) (211)
PERRY, Ben 38 (B) (210)
PERRY, Ch. 48 (m), (436)
PERRY, Charles 15* (B) (210)
PERRY, Doney 16 (f) (B) (208)
PERRY, Eathran 30 (f), (278)
PERRY, Eliza 7* (B) (194)
PERRY, Fannie 30* (B) (415)
PERRY, Freelan 26 (B) (461)
PERRY, Gorge 47 (B) (210)
PERRY, Gus 35* (B) (242)
PERRY, H. H. 47 (m)* (208)
PERRY, J. 24 (B) (496)
PERRY, J. T. 37 (m), (210)
PERRY, Jeff 50 (B) (416)
PERRY, Joe 40 (B) (191)
PERRY, John J. 58* (267)
PERRY, Lee 13 (m)* (B) (192)
PERRY, Lewis C. 20* (201)
PERRY, M. W. J. 33 (m)* (392)
PERRY, Mary 57, (348)
PERRY, Peter 25 (B) (211)
PERRY, Preston 27* (B) (262)
PERRY, Robert __* (B) (416)
PERRY, Rose 5* (B) (206)
PERRY, Rosie 4* (317)
PERRY, Sam A. 63* (224)
PERRY, Solomon 30, (342)
PERRY, Solomon 49* (198)
PERRY, Solomon __, (317)
PERRY, Warner 25 (B) (236)
PERRY, Willis 50* (B) (205)
PERRY, Winnie 10* (B) (415)
PERRY, Wm. 24 (B) (351)
PERRY?, Camden 60 (B) (189)
PERSONS, Benjamin 10 (B) (176)
PERSONS, Emanuel 32 (B) (163)
PERSONS, Isaac 36 (B) (336)
PERSONS, Man 46 (m) (B) (336)
PERSONS, Mary 53* (421)
PERSONS, Mose 45 (B) (336)
PERSONS, Peter 56* (B) (178)
PERTLE, ____ 25 (f)* (B) (213)
PETERS, Delila 30 (B) (452)
PETERSON, Elbert 3* (B) (419)
PETERSON, Mary 17* (B) (419)
PETFOT?, John 39* (B) (380)
PETTIS, Sarah 50* (B) (475)
PETTIT, Caladonia 12 (B) (179)
PETTIT, Cireda 20 (f)* (B) (177)
PETT__, Charley 18* (B) (484)
PEW, James 17* (393)
PEW, MAry 7* (B) (208)
PEWETT, Calie 24* (B) (223)
PEWETT, Edmon 20* (B) (222)
PEWETT, Florance 2* (B) (224)
PEWETT, Isham 32* (B) (216)
PEYTON, Henry 45 (B) (289)
PEYTON, John 45 (B) (452)
PHASON, Betsy 25* (B) (414)
PHELTS, Henry 50, (486)
PHILIP, Maxwell 40 (B) (446)
PHILIPS, Marion 25* (200)

PHILLIP, J. W. 29 (m)* (304)
PHILLIP, Rufus 35* (322)
PHILLIPS, A. J. 44 (m), (293)
PHILLIPS, Ada 24* (B) (382)
PHILLIPS, Andrew 60* (295)
PHILLIPS, Anna 14* (B) (436)
PHILLIPS, B. 22 (f)* (B) (341)
PHILLIPS, Calie 6* (B) (228)
PHILLIPS, Celia 31* (B) (433)
PHILLIPS, D. __ (f)* (317)
PHILLIPS, Daisy 8* (342)
PHILLIPS, Dulan? 14 (m)* (278)
PHILLIPS, Easter 25 (B) (325)
PHILLIPS, Emmer 33?* (B) (469)
PHILLIPS, Erwin 25* (B) (291)
PHILLIPS, J. E. 34 (m)* (207)
PHILLIPS, J. P. 24 (m), (204)
PHILLIPS, J. W. 43 (m)* (483)
PHILLIPS, John 21* (B) (469)
PHILLIPS, Judge 39* (B) (421)
PHILLIPS, L.? 29 (m), (202)
PHILLIPS, Louis 24 (f)* (B)
   (395)
PHILLIPS, M. 53 (m) (B) (225)
PHILLIPS, Nancy 27* (B) (434)
PHILLIPS, Rachal 16* (B) (290)
PHILLIPS, S. P. 61 (m)* (469)
PHILLIPS, Sallie 35* (B) (341)
PHILLIPS, Sam 26 (B) (469)
PHILLIPS, Shannon 24 (m),
   (277)
PHILLIPS, Silus 67? (B) (460)
PHILLIPS, Tom 22 (B) (469)
PHILLIPS, Wash 24 (B) (469)
PHILLIPS, _. R. 20 (m), (204)
PHILLIS, Sallie 13* (B) (405)
PICKARD, W. H. M. 30 (m),
   (207)
PICKENS, Roxan 25 (f)* (B)
   (241)
PICKENS, Sallie 78* (413)
PICKINGS, John 27 (B) (368)
PICKINS, Flem 63 (m)* (B) (368)
PICKINS, Hepsibeth? 76 (f)*
   (176)
PICKINS, James K. 34, (373)
PICKINS, Willie 31 (m)* (485)
PIERCE, Andy 27 (B) (324)
PIERCE, J. C. 18 (m)* (316)
PIERCE, J. C. 18 (m)* (344)
PIERCE, James 31 (B) (324)
PIERCE, John 41* (425)
PIERCE, Sam 36 (B) (324)
PIERCE, Tennessee 35 (f), (425)
PIERCE, W. C. 17 (m)* (316)
PIERCE, W. C. 17 (m)* (344)
PIERCE, W. C. 45 (m)* (339)
PIERCE, Wm. 25* (B) (367)
PIERCE?, John C. 54* (324)
PIERSON, Leatty 60 (f)* (B)
   (222)
PINCH?, Joseph 60 (B) (444)
PINKNEY, James 39 (B) (383)
PINKNEY, Sam? 23* (305)
PINNEY, Esau 22 (m)* (B) (287)
PIPER, Samuel 50* (389)
PIPPIN, B. 55 (f)* (280)
PIPUS?, James 63 (B) (455)
PIRSER, Frank 22* (B) (320)
PIRTLE, A. Duglass 22 (B) (207)

PIRTLE, Ambrus 14* (B) (207)
PIRTLE, Ruben 52* (B) (205)
PIRTLE, Susen 13* (B) (205)
PITTMAN, H. 6_ (m) (B) (296)
PITTMAN, Henry 64 (B) (303)
PLAMPLIN?, Peter 37 (B) (436)
PLEASANT, Charley 30, (450)
PLEASANT, Mary? 45* (B) (313)
PLEASANT, S. F. 33 (f)* (329)
PLEASANT, Wm. 21* (B) (360)
PLEASANTS, Charles 53, (408)
PLEASANTS, Joseph A. 24*
   (366)
PLEDGE, John 20* (B) (402)
PLEDGE, Sam 30 (B) (457)
PLIETE?, Willie 1 (m)* (163)
PLUMMER, Yerger 12 (m)* (163)
POARTER?, Ax__ 60 (m)* (B)
   (369)
POARTER?, Sallie 45 (B) (369)
POINDEXTER, Albert 22, (289)
POINDEXTER, H. 50 (f) (B)
   (321)
POINDEXTER, J. 52 (m) (B)
   (282)
POINDEXTER, JAck 59 (B)
   (289)
POINDEXTER, Jack 27 (B) (289)
POINDEXTER, Lizzie 35 (B)
   (287)
POINDEXTER, W. J. 64 (m),
   (282)
POINTDEXTER, C. C. 37 (m),
   (271)
POINTDEXTER, Daniel? 50 (B)
   (271)
POINTDEXTER, Jon 1* (B)
   (269)
POINTDEXTER, M. 13 (f)* (B)
   (269)
POINTDEXTER, M. 70 (f)* (B)
   (270)
POINTDEXTER, R. 45 (m)*
   (270)
POINTDEXTER, Raleigh? 69*
   (271)
POINTDEXTER, Strom 23 (m)
   (B) (270)
POINTDEXTER, W. 16 (f)* (B)
   (270)
POINTDEXTER, _. M. 40 (f) (B)
   (271)
POINTDEXTER, _____ 40 (m)*
   (B) (267)
POINTER, Jessy 42 (m) (B) (439)
POLK, Britton 40 (B) (247)
POLK, Elisebeth 56* (477)
POLK, James K. 42* (351)
POLK, Silis 75 (B) (376)
POLK, Wm. 55 (B) (377)
POLK, Wm. 63* (314)
POLLARD, Green 43 (B) (369)
POND, James 65, (441)
POOL, G.? 25 (m)* (B) (389)
POOL, J. W. 32 (m)* (283)
POOL, Jeremiah 27 (B) (364)
POOL, Louisa 23* (B) (364)
POOL, Penelopy 40, (465)
POOL, Rachel 50* (B) (364)
POOLE, _____ 44 (f)* (422)

POOR, Esther 15* (B) (500)
POORE, George 58* (B) (473)
POO__, E. H. 36 (m)* (476)
POPE, J. 19 (f)* (300)
POPE, John 40 (B) (381)
POPE, John A. 56, (297)
POPE, Malinda 35 (B) (385)
POPE, Mary A. 60, (384)
POPE, Sarah _0* (B) (383)
POPE, T. M. 26 (m)* (315)
POPE, Thomas 75* (B) (386)
PORTER, AThey 16 (f)* (B)
   (273)
PORTER, Abbey 18* (427)
PORTER, Alace 14* (B) (234)
PORTER, C. T. 39 (m) (B) (343)
PORTER, Edward 25* (B) (428)
PORTER, Elizabeth 50, (407)
PORTER, Gardner 25 (B) (246)
PORTER, Gipp 30 (m) (B) (332)
PORTER, Henry 36 (B) (401)
PORTER, J. F. 43 (m), (282)
PORTER, Jessee 23 (B) (428)
PORTER, Lot 70 (B) (345)
PORTER, Louis 17* (B) (339)
PORTER, Robert 23 (B) (273)
PORTER, Sallie 50* (B) (422)
PORTER, Willis 54* (B) (174)
PORTER, Wm. 40 (B) (403)
PORTER, Wm. B. 40, (406)
PORTER, _____ 67 (m) (B) (301)
PORTER, _____ 7 (f)* (B) (246)
POTTS, Jim 19* (B) (355)
POTTS?, R. M. 30 (m), (334)
POWEL, Henry 24* (B) (223)
POWELL, Anica 80 (f)* (B)
   (251)
POWELL, James C. 35, (359)
POWELL, Link 24 (B) (225)
POWELL, Miles? 32* (B) (201)
POWELL, Willy 17 (m)* (327)
POWELL, Wm. 35 (B) (282)
POWELL, _____d 30 (m) (B)
   (449)
PRATER, Cl_____ 47 (m)* (B)
   (418)
PRATT, George 37, (434)
PREVETTE?, Mary 53* (280)
PREWETT, M. M. 34 (m)* (203)
PREWETT?, Charls 24* (B)
   (211)
PREWIT, M. 49 (m)* (B) (498)
PRICE, Dave 30* (B) (433)
PRICE, Diller 18 (f)* (B) (440)
PRICE, Frances 45, (470)
PRICE, James 41, (410)
PRICE, John 33, (428)
PRICE, Katy B. 21* (162)
PRICE, Peter 27* (B) (346)
PRICE, R. L. 76 (m), (470)
PRICE, Wm. 14 (B) (493)
PRICE, Wm. 5* (B) (192)
PRICE?, Sam 28* (B) (243)
PRIDDY, Walter? 11* (B) (301)
PRINDLER, Andrew 22* (B)
   (423)
PRIOR, Emiline 60* (B) (270)
PROCTOR, Jas. 27* (287)
PROYOR, Tom 48 (B) (346)
PRUETT?, Lou 20 (f)* (444)

PRUETTE?, Henry 48 (B) (446)
PRUIT, Sam 40* (B) (482)
PRU___, Baley N. 31 (m), (409)
PRYER, Davy? 40 (m) (B) (463)
PUDLE?, Tom 25* (B) (223)
PUGH, Ephram 29 (B) (455)
PUGH, Mahala 26 (B) (261)
PUGH, Wm. 21* (B) (360)
PULIA?, Nelson 45 (B) (458)
PULLIAM, A. B. 42 (m)* (160)
PULLIAM, Abe 17?* (B) (189)
PULLIAM, Abe 50 (B) (466)
PULLIAM, Alex 33 (B) (416)
PULLIAM, Bettie 42* (189)
PULLIAM, Compton 47 (B)
   (416)
PULLIAM, David 33, (409)
PULLIAM, Fayette 40, (410)
PULLIAM, Frances 50* (B) (189)
PULLIAM, Frank 36* (B) (415)
PULLIAM, Harvey 60* (B) (416)
PULLIAM, John 36 (B) (416)
PULLIAM, Junius? 54, (455)
PULLIAM, Lucreasa? 16 (f)* (B)
   (466)
PULLIAM, Mary 38* (B) (174)
PULLIAM, Parham 52 (B) (416)
PULLIAM, Richard 29, (409)
PULLIAM, Wash 35 (B) (466)
PULLIAM, Zeb 32* (B) (413)
PULLIAM?, Edward 24, (417)
PUTNEY, B. 55 (m) (B) (498)
P_ARTE, Tom 19* (B) (382)
QUALLS, Burton 21* (B) (248)
QUALLS, Dary 36 (m) (B) (248)
QUALLS, James 60 (B) (455)
QUALLS, Joseph 50 (B) (457)
QUENER, Sela 19* (B) (500)
QUENER?, Baker 20* (498)
QUENER?, Pleas 60 (B) (500)
QUENER?, R. 52 (m)* (B) (499)
QUENER?, R.? 25 (m) (B) (500)
QUINLEY, Richard 22, (274)
QUINLY, Edward 30, (278)
QUINN, James 25* (226)
QUINN, Jerry 45 (m), (278)
QUNHUR?, Jeff 27 (B) (415)
RADICK, Laura 12* (B) (397)
RAGGLAND, Charles 12?* (B)
   (213)
RAGGLAND, M. E. 40 (m), (216)
RAGLAND, Eliza 52* (B) (356)
RAGLAND, Felix 27* (B) (336)
RAGLAND, Frank 6/12* (B)
   (338)
RAGLAND, Hellen 14* (B) (173)
RAGLAND, Isaac 40 (B) (337)
RAGLAND, James 8* (B) (361)
RAGLAND, Jim 23* (B) (212)
RAGLAND, Minnie 7/12* (B)
   (336)
RAGLAND, T. A. 22 (f)* (B)
   (204)
RAGSDALE, Edward? 57, (267)
RAGSDALE, W. M. 32 (m)* (168)
RAINWATER, Mack 40* (B)
   (279)
RALPH, Leona 14* (278)
RANDEL, Alx. 35 (m) (B) (394)
RANDEL, Lizzie 24* (B) (263)

RANDELL, Alex. 25 (B) (400)
RANDOLPH, Anthony 58* (B) (366)
RANDOLPH, John 49 (B) (259)
RANDOLPH, Lewis 19* (B) (353)
RANKIN, Joseph 26 (B) (379)
RASKIN?, Anderson 28 (B) (231)
RATTIES?, Joe 50 (B) (417)
RAWLINGS, Mary 21* (B) (426)
RAY, Amy 45 (B) (279)
RAY, Eveline 50* (B) (276)
RAY, Fanny 22* (292)
RAY, NAncy 16* (B) (279)
RAY, Nancy 17* (B) (279)
RAY, Robert 53 (B) (472)
RAY, Willis 22 (B) (268)
RAY, Wm. 16* (B) (290)
RAYMON?, D. 66 (m) (B) (318)
RAYNER, John 25 (B) (404)
RAYNER, Wm. 55* (B) (353)
RAYNER?, E. J. 52 (f)* (B) (311)
RAYNOR, Alf 21 (B) (333)
RAYNOR, Blunt 27 (B) (333)
RAYNOR, Carline 4_ (B) (333)
RAYNOR, Hill 35 (B) (332)
RAYNOR, Ples 22 (f) (B) (333)
RAYNOR?, Guss 25 (B) (324)
RAYNS, Allace 2* (480)
READ, Davis 46 (B) (385)
READ, George 25 (B) (378)
READ, Jacob __ (B) (391)
REAMES, George 40, (319)
REAMES, J. B. 34 (m)* (187)
REAMES, M. J. 31 (m)* (334)
REAMES, W. A. 44 (m), (328)
REAMES?, _. 24 (m)* (254)
REAMS, Lewis 28* (B) (307)
REANICKS, Billie 31, (481)
REANICKS, S. 50 (f)* (B) (481)
REAR, Edward 50 (B) (427)
REAVES, Edward 20* (B) (429)
REAVES, Sallie 100* (B) (172)
REDD, Ada 18* (357)
REDD, Dabney 25 (B) (358)
REDD, Vina 7?* (B) (166)
REDDICK, Edward J. 70, (407)
REDDICK, Sam 35 (B) (293)
REED, Aron 20 (B) (423)
REED, Betsy 45 (B) (247)
REED, Clem 46 (m)* (B) (212)
REED, Eafrum 14 (m)* (B) (215)
REED, Etta 8* (B) (428)
REED, Fannie 13* (B) (328)
REED, George 51 (B) (328)
REED, Horace 30 (B) (400)
REED, James 44 (B) (225)
REED, James 7* (B) (355)
REED, John 13* (B) (346)
REED, John 22* (B) (220)
REED, John B. 48, (407)
REED, Josheph 48 (B) (423)
REED, Lucy 24* (B) (209)
REED, Peter 20* (B) (349)
REED, Richard 36* (B) (359)
REED, Richard 57 (B) (187)
REED, Tom 70 (B) (219)
REED, Ton? 58 (m) (B) (219)
REED, Wm. 30* (B) (270)
REED?, Hattie? 24* (B) (169)
REEDLES?, Robt. 26 (B) (167)

REEVES, Anna 6* (B) (336)
REEVES, Hattie 10* (B) (165)
REEVES, Isabella 68 (B) (182)
REEVES, John 41 (B) (164)
REEVES, John C. 68, (242)
REEVES, Josephene _* (B) (164)
REEVES, N. W. 60 (f), (472)
REEVES, Robert 23 (B) (242)
REEVES, Tom 31* (327)
REEVES, W. C. 64 (m)* (494)
REEVES, Wm. 24* (183)
REEVES, _____ 70 (m) (B) (172)
REEVES?, Hanah 35 (B) (303)
REGAN, Kate 23 (B) (362)
REGAN, Rudd 40* (B) (417)
REICHARDT, Gus 32* (237)
REIC__, ___st 68 (m)* (185)
REMAS, HAttie 2* (253)
RENELS, Bee 2_ (m), (384)
RENFROE, A. J. 39 (f)* (482)
RENFROE, Jno. S. 37, (190)
RENNOLDS, Willis 20* (B) (436)
REVES, Jef 22* (B) (250)
REVES, Richard 20 (B) (250)
RE_____N, Geo. 30* (B) (256)
RHEA, Celia 22?* (B) (160)
RHEA, Elick 28* (B) (253)
RHEA, James S. 31* (264)
RHEA, John R. 24* (187)
RHEA, Mary 75?* (188)
RHEA, Mathew 33* (226)
RHEA, Milley 53* (B) (175)
RHEA, Minerva 60 (B) (164)
RHEA, Walter P. 38* (181)
RHEA, Wm. A. 36* (186)
RHINER?, Wm. 27, (276)
RHODA, Thomas 20* (B) (200)
RHODES, Amanda 50 (B) (194)
RHODES, Anna 26* (B) (291)
RHODES, Austin 39* (B) (196)
RHODES, Jesse 18 (m) (B) (201)
RHODES, John 30* (B) (400)
RHODES, John 30 (B) (276)
RHODES, Jordon 80 (B) (419)
RHODES, Lee 51 (m)* (B) (201)
RHODES, Lue 7 (f)* (B) (215)
RHODES, Luella 10* (B) (356)
RHODES, Luraner 43 (f)* (B) (212)
RHODES, Martin 45 (B) (494)
RHODES, Mat 29 (m)* (B) (495)
RHODES, Robert 31* (B) (192)
RHODES, Robert J. 35* (195)
RHODES, S. __ (m)* (195)
RHODES, Silas 26 (B) (212)
RHODES, Simon 38 (B) (205)
RHODES, Turner 35 (B) (205)
RHODES, Wm. 8* (B) (206)
RHODES?, Albert 29* (B) (184)
RICE, Cain 28* (B) (232)
RICE, Edmond 43* (424)
RICE, Emily 49* (B) (400)
RICE, HArry 54* (B) (232)
RICE, Isaac 23* (B) (285)
RICE, Jim 45* (B) (290)
RICE, Wm. F. 24, (369)
RICH, James 49* (235)
RICHARDS, _____ 21 (m)* (B) (500)

RICHARDSON, A. 21 (m)* (B) (370)
RICHARDSON, Billy 48* (B) (233)
RICHARDSON, Dennis 34 (B) (399)
RICHARDSON, Fannie 60 (B) (389)
RICHARDSON, Henry 30 (B) (413)
RICHARDSON, Sam 30* (202)
RICHE, Charles 55* (422)
RICHERSON, Mary 5* (B) (477)
RICHERSON, Newton 55* (483)
RICHERSON, _. 85 (m) (B) (466)
RICHEY, A. G. 33 (m)* (469)
RICHEY, Christopher 26, (200)
RICHEY, J. B. 57 (m), (466)
RICHEY, Jesse 38 (m), (194)
RICHEY, Wash 47* (466)
RICHMON, Y. 35 (m) (B) (474)
RICKET, Alax 30* (B) (236)
RICKET, Ann 47* (B) (253)
RICKET, Ida 19* (B) (337)
RICKET, Liz Z. 12 (f)* (B) (254)
RICKET, Martha _0* (B) (257)
RICKET, Sandy 19 (m)* (B) (256)
RICKET, Thomas 50* (B) (258)
RICKET, Vinie 70 (f)* (B) (257)
RICKETS?, L. 16 (m)* (255?)
RIDDICK, Andrew? 35 (B) (476)
RIDDICK, Fillis 65* (B) (477)
RIDDICK, Mary 35* (B) (333)
RIDDICK, T. K. 29 (m)* (165)
RIDDICK, W. M. 27 (m)* (316)
RIDDICK, W. M. 27 (m)* (344)
RIDLY, Elisa 60* (187)
RIEVES, Mattie 35 (f)* (170)
RIGAN, George 25* (362)
RIGGS, David 90?* (488)
RIGGS, Jas. 56* (488)
RIGGS, Joe 21, (478)
RIGGS, Tom 55, (474)
RIGHT, Ellen 24 (B) (464)
RIGHT, Frank 27 (B) (459)
RIGHTDALE, Callie 22 (B) (484)
RIGHTEL, Anna 13* (B) (471)
RIGHTEL, D. 65 (f)* (B) (483)
RIGHTEL, John 17* (B) (474)
RIGSBY, Aron 50, (282)
RIGSBY, Lizzie 24* (329)
RIGSBY, Mattie 22 (f)* (331)
RIKE, B. L. 46 (m), (293)
RILEY, Mary 40* (B) (345)
RINER, Wm. 68, (351)
RISER, Wm. 59* (B) (419)
RIVERS, Alford 31 (B) (220)
RIVERS, Amos __, (492)
RIVERS, Auston 54* (B) (215)
RIVERS, Cick 35 (m) (B) (169)
RIVERS, Dathula 15* (B) (174)
RIVERS, Faney 25 (B) (215)
RIVERS, G. 18 (m)* (B) (488)
RIVERS, Green 60 (B) (171)
RIVERS, H. 23 (m)* (B) (502)
RIVERS, Humphrey 32, (502)
RIVERS, Isreal 50 (B) (400)
RIVERS, J. M. 20 (m)* (B) (340)
RIVERS, James 35 (B) (180)
RIVERS, James? 30 (B) (502)

RIVERS, Lucy M. _* (B) (166)
RIVERS, Margarett 60* (B) (489)
RIVERS, Maria? 40* (B) (502)
RIVERS, Mark 54? (B) (169)
RIVERS, Mason 55* (B) (172)
RIVERS, P. 14 (m)* (B) (214)
RIVERS, Pleas 55* (B) (488)
RIVERS, R. H. 19 (m)* (489)
RIVERS, Richard 29 (B) (182)
RIVERS, Thomas 26 (B) (183)
RIVERS, Thomas 45* (B) (169)
RIVERS, Tomas J. 10* (B) (170)
RIVERS, Wm. 45 (B) (492)
RIVERS, _____ 28 (m) (B) (212)
RIVERS, _____ 36 (m) (B) (214)
RIVERS, _____ 46 (f) (B) (214)
RIVES, Alexander 17* (B) (172)
RIVES, Jane 32* (B) (460)
RIVES, Lycurges 49* (267)
RIVES, M. A. 49 (m), (271)
RIVES, Mary P. 70* (263)
RIVES, Rich H. 25, (271)
RIVES, Robert 14* (B) (440)
RIVES, Susen 28* (B) (243)
RIVES, Th. 27 (m) (B) (464)
RIVES, Thos. 65, (439)
RIVES, Wm. C. 31, (224)
RIVES?, Andrew 5_ (B) (447)
ROACH, Columbus 19* (B) (243)
ROACH, Eaton 59* (370)
ROACH, George M. 29* (368)
ROACH, JAmes 22* (335)
ROACH, James 27, (372)
ROACH, Louisa 30* (B) (431)
ROACH, Walker 20* (B) (391)
ROADE, Guss 22 (B) (466)
ROARK?, Sam 21, (413)
ROBBINS, W. D. 31 (m), (289)
ROBERSON, Abie 18* (258)
ROBERSON, Ann 25?* (B) (160)
ROBERSON, Ben 40 (B) (225)
ROBERSON, Billy 50 (B) (225)
ROBERSON, Burrell 40 (B) (432)
ROBERSON, Dave 27* (326)
ROBERSON, Ed 13* (B) (212)
ROBERSON, Edmon 24, (226)
ROBERSON, Ella 11* (B) (165)
ROBERSON, Gabe 30* (B) (164)
ROBERSON, Hattie L. 4* (B) (483)
ROBERSON, Ira S. 31, (235)
ROBERSON, J. 27 (m), (480)
ROBERSON, James 33, (409)
ROBERSON, James 49, (410)
ROBERSON, James 60, (235)
ROBERSON, Jim 53 (B) (226)
ROBERSON, Joe 81* (467)
ROBERSON, Jordan 21* (B) (330)
ROBERSON, Lillie 2* (430)
ROBERSON, Mary 39* (B) (160)
ROBERSON, Nannie 25 (B) (251)
ROBERSON, Richard 22* (427)
ROBERSON, Sallie 25* (B) (167)
ROBERSON, Sallie 75, (412)
ROBERSON, Sam 35* (B) (169)
ROBERSON, Sam 50* (B) (468)
ROBERSON, Sam 64* (B) (216)
ROBERSON, Sarah 11* (B) (165)
ROBERSON, Sarah 40* (B) (225)
ROBERSON, Sarah 71* (B) (172)

ROBERSON, Tom 25 (B) (479)
ROBERSON, Wm. 26* (431)
ROBERSON, Wm. 46 (B) (404)
ROBERSON?, Willis 31* (237)
ROBERTS, Ambus 23 (m) (B) (435)
ROBERTS, Charles 27* (B) (432)
ROBERTS, Henry 23* (B) (349)
ROBERTS, Isaac 59 (B) (173)
ROBERTS, John 28, (450)
ROBERTS, John 45 (B) (435)
ROBERTS, Mildred A. 57, (361)
ROBERTS, N. 37 (m), (450)
ROBERTS, R. M. 60 (m), (474)
ROBERTS, Sara 41* (430)
ROBERTS, Sarah 16, _____ 2 (435)
ROBERTS, Wm. 31 (B) (357)
ROBERTS, Wm. 33* (B) (436)
ROBERTSON, Belton 22 (B) (494)
ROBERTSON, Bill 35 (B) (295)
ROBERTSON, Green 27* (B) (196)
ROBERTSON, Henry 28* (B) (284)
ROBERTSON, Hiram 30 (B) (294)
ROBERTSON, Isaac 24* (B) (206)
ROBERTSON, Isaac 40 (B) (287)
ROBERTSON, J. 9 (m)* (494)
ROBERTSON, Joh? 10 (m)* (B) (208)
ROBERTSON, Tom 22 (B) (206)
ROBERTSON, Tom 48, (326)
ROBERTSON, Wash 47 (B) (207)
ROBERTSON?, Christohper 31* (166)
ROBIN, Wm. M. 47, (410)
ROBINSON, Aaron 22 (B) (354)
ROBINSON, Drusilla 79* (357)
ROBINSON, Edmond 30 (B) (379)
ROBINSON, Jesse 26 (m) (B) (348)
ROBINSON, John 23, (375)
ROBINSON, John 53 (B) (378)
ROBINSON, Paul 27* (B) (358)
ROBINSON, Willis 29* (B) (389)
ROBINSON, Wm. 54* (B) (199)
ROBINSON?, George A. 36 (f)* (B) (391)
ROBISON, Candas 35* (B) (340)
ROBISON, David 24 (B) (424)
ROBISON, H. F. 41 (m), (336)
ROBY, Wm. 46* (B) (306)
ROCKER, Dallas 30* (278)
ROCKET, Fibbie 27 (f)* (B) (254)
ROCKET?, Ed 22?* (B) (254)
RODGERS, Ellen 35 (B) (340)
RODGERS, Haris 30* (B) (370)
RODGERS, James 15* (B) (390)
RODGERS, James 40, (425)
RODGERS, Jane 65, (431)
RODGERS, Kildy 25 (f) (B) (373)
RODGERS, Martha T. 72* (270)
RODGERS, Moses 26 (B) (397)
RODGERS, Robt. 39, (271)
RODGERS, Will 22 (B) (373)
RODGERS, Wm. 40, (431)
RODGERS, _____ __ (m)* (B) (457)

RODICK, Tenny 60 (f)* (B) (297)
ROGERS, Galen P. 39, (198)
ROGERS, H. M. 34 (m), (217)
ROGERS, L. M. 37 (m), (220)
ROGERS, Martin 35 (B) (353)
ROGERS, Simon 26 (B) (347)
ROGGERS, Charley 30 (B) (481)
ROLF, Harry 30* (B) (269)
ROLLINS, Charles 35 (B) (398)
ROMAN?, JAcob 29* (B) (268)
RONEY, Queen 12* (B) (349)
ROOK, Squire 35 (B) (435)
ROOK, Thomas 23* (B) (431)
ROOKEN, Fred 30* (B) (333)
ROOKEN, James 27 (B) (333)
ROOKS, Mariah J. 23* (B) (186)
ROOKS, STack 50 (m)* (B) (181)
ROOT, Malinda 69* (170)
ROSE, Alexander 49* (444)
ROSE, Alfred 35* (447)
ROSE, Alph___ 35 (m), (464)
ROSE, Bob _____ 45 (m)* (B) (444)
ROSE, Brooks 38 (B) (436)
ROSE, Dulcinea 13* (201)
ROSE, G. 54 (m), (495)
ROSE, Jefferson 18* (202)
ROSE, Loucas 23 (B) (444)
ROSE, Samuel 27* (B) (451)
ROSON, C. T. 33 (m)* (263)
ROSS, Charlie 35 (B) (228)
ROSS, Cornelia 24, (165)
ROSS, Francis M. 43, (235)
ROSS, J. G. 40 (m), (204)
ROSS, JAck 18* (B) (284)
ROSS, Lee 47 (m) (B) (181)
ROSS, Maggie 10* (285)
ROSS, Rebecca 68* (B) (171)
ROSS, Thomas 13* (197)
ROSS, Thomas 52* (B) (351)
ROSS, Tom 30* (B) (208)
ROSS, Warren R. 26 (B) (366)
ROSSER, James 33 (B) (435)
ROSSER, Jiles 25* (B) (418)
ROSSER, Lawrence 36 (B) (285)
ROSSER, Thomas 21 (B) (435)
ROSUR, Alex 39* (420)
ROTA, Lou E. 5 (f)* (485)
ROTA, Mary A. 45* (485)
ROY, Wyly 50 (B) (306)
ROYAL, Thomas? 51, (449)
RO__INE 35, Annie 35, (442)
RUBIN, Andrew 35 (B) (374)
RUDD, Sallie 27* (430)
RUFFIN, Mose 25 (m)* (B) (222)
RUGG__, Moses 50 (B) (266)
RUSSEL, Edd 40 (B) (474)
RUSSEL, Sam 29* (B) (234)
RUSSELL, Charles 30 (B) (404)
RUSSELL, Cornelius 25 (B) (396)
RUSSELL, Louis 52 (B) (459)
RUSSELL, Lyle 27 (f)* (B) (183)
RUSSELL, Q. C. 50 (m), (212)
RUSSELL, R. P. 45 (m), (210)
RUSSELL, S. C. 40 (m), (211)
RUSSELL, _____ 23 (m)* (B) (214)
RUSSELL, _____ 52 (m), (210)
RUSSLE, Wm. 45* (B) (389)
RUTH, Edwin 40?* (432)

RUTLAGE?, Monroe 25 (B) (388)
RUTLAND, C. __ (m)* (B) (290)
RUTLEDGE, Betsy 20* (B) (226)
RUTLEDGE, Jack 65 (B) (232)
RUTLEDGE, Mat 35 (m) (B) (223)
RUTLEGE, James B. 35, (348)
RYALE?, J. B. 38 (m), (474)
R____, Charlotta 34* (B) (219)
SACKETT, Joseph 24 (B) (456)
SADLER, Jerry 48* (428)
SADLER, Louis 24* (B) (423)
SADLER, Marion 27 (m) (B) (455)
SAINS, John 31* (B) (488)
SALE, Alphonso 18* (B) (435)
SALE, John 61* (435)
SALE, Moses 45* (B) (435)
SALLARD, Edy 80 (f)* (B) (352)
SALMON, JAke 23* (B) (235)
SAMMERS?, James 38, (373)
SAMPSON, J. 65 (m) (B) (346)
SAMPSON?, Sam 30* (B) (464)
SANDELAN, Med__ 60 (m) (B) (214)
SANDERS, A. T. 31 (m), (268)
SANDERS, Agnes 30* (B) (346)
SANDERS, Charles 12* (B) (202)
SANDERS, David 47, (414)
SANDERS, Ed 26 (B) (173)
SANDERS, Enoch 30 (B) (456)
SANDERS, Felir? 40 (m)* (B) (248)
SANDERS, H. 25 (m) (B) (498)
SANDERS, Henry 25* (B) (437)
SANDERS, James 40 (B) (454)
SANDERS, Jas. 41?, (197)
SANDERS, John W. 39* (196)
SANDERS, Mary 103* (B) (471)
SANDERS, Nathan 25, (413)
SANDERS, S. H. 36 (m), (212)
SANDERS, Sarah 7_* (B) (197)
SANDERS, Willie 9 (m)* (B) (170)
SANDERS, Willis 27* (B) (303)
SANDRIDGE, Samuel 29* (B) (393)
SANE, Charles 14* (B) (360)
SANE, Edmond 55 (B) (363)
SANSING, S. A. 50 (f)* (285)
SANSONG, S. H. 28 (m)* (283)
SAUNDERS, Joe 46* (B) (427)
SAWYER, John 54 (B) (293)
SAWYER, John? 36* (254)
SAWYERS, Anna 13* (293)
SAWYERS, James 23* (253)
SAWYERS, Ruben 24 (B) (289)
SAXTON?, Alison? 50 (m) (B) (446)
SCALE, John? 30* (B) (271)
SCALES, Lafayett 26 (B) (271)
SCALES, Weston 55 (B) (271)
SCERATT, J. H. 40 (m), (309)
SCHIELE?, Hugh 36* (419)
SCHINDER, L. 42 (m), (274)
SCOT, Paton 21* (B) (337)
SCOT, Shed 38 (B) (329)
SCOTT, Ab 35? (B) (389)
SCOTT, Abram 26 (B) (219)
SCOTT, Alex 22* (B) (419)

SCOTT, Alex 62* (B) (267)
SCOTT, Allice 30* (B) (187)
SCOTT, Berry 30* (B) (501)
SCOTT, Charles 39* (249)
SCOTT, Cotton 69 (B) (395)
SCOTT, Dock 35 (B) (394)
SCOTT, Edmon 64 (B) (251)
SCOTT, Edward 29 (B) (300)
SCOTT, Eveline 50* (B) (219)
SCOTT, Flora 53* (187)
SCOTT, H. F.? 43 (m)* (460)
SCOTT, Harriet 44* (B) (437)
SCOTT, Haymon 36 (B) (493)
SCOTT, Henry 18* (B) (257)
SCOTT, JOhn 37 (B) (275)
SCOTT, James? 69, (388)
SCOTT, Jane 34, (389)
SCOTT, Joe 36 (B) (485)
SCOTT, Katie 37 (B) (258)
SCOTT, Lena 12* (B) (437)
SCOTT, Lou 14 (f)* (B) (437)
SCOTT, M. 30 (m)* (392)
SCOTT, Morning 40 (f) (B) (221)
SCOTT, Nathan 52 (B) (199)
SCOTT, Patsy 75* (B) (251)
SCOTT, Prince 26* (B) (188)
SCOTT, Thomas 42, (388)
SCOTT, W. H. 46 (m), (216)
SCOTT, Wm. 55 (B) (455)
SCOTT?, Jack __ (B) (245)
SCOTTE, Zenith 35 (m) (B) (445)
SCRIBNER, Price 58 (B) (423)
SCRIBNER, Robert 19 (B) (423)
SCRUGGS, Carter 40 (B) (286)
SCRUGS, E. R. 41 (m)* (161)
SC____D, Easter 50?* (B) (341)
SEA, Wm. 30 (B) (249)
SEAMSTER, Eliza 22* (B) (166)
SEARGEANT?, D. 48* (B) (428)
SELARS, Arch 27 (B) (203)
SELBA, JEff 27 (B) (492)
SELBY, Warren C. 38* (345)
SELLARS, Jim 7* (B) (211)
SELLERS, James 30, (415)
SELLERS, John 52, (415)
SERLAND?, Andy 51* (B) (419)
SESSIONS, Charles? __* (B) (253)
SETTLE, Abe 45* (B) (370)
SETTLE, Benjamin 30, (370)
SETTLE, Green 23 (B) (370)
SETTLE, Harry 24 (B) (374)
SETTLE, Sarah P. 61* (370)
SEWARD, E. 30 (m), (302)
SEWARD, G. L. 17 (f)* (351)
SEWARD?, Frank 40 (B) (299)
SEXTON, Arnold 29 (B) (414)
SEYMORE, Caladonia 10* (B) (238)
SEYMORE, Callie 23* (B) (330)
SEYMORE, Curtis 28 (B) (243)
SEYMORE, Harriett 43 (B) (243)
SEYMORE, Joseph 60 (B) (243)
SEYMORE, Liza 55* (B) (338)
SEYMORE, Lucy __* (B) (242)
SEYMORE, Simon 24* (B) (243)
SEYMORE, Thomas 36 (B) (242)
SEYMORE, _____ _ (m)* (242)
SEYMORE?, _____ __ (B) (166)
SEYMOUR, Allen 50* (B) (163)

SHACKLEFORD, Zack 59, (409)
SHADIN___, Nathan 55, (242)
SHAFFER, Fannie 70* (B) (430)
SHAFFER, Frank 20* (B) (230)
SHAMBLET, Byron? 19* (B) (429)
SHARP, J. F. 34 (m), (298)
SHARP, Richard 26* (273)
SHARP, Sam 56 (B) (296)
SHARP, W. F. 39 (m), (285)
SHAW, Anderson 18* (B) (201)
SHAW, C. A. S. 37 (m)* (168)
SHAW, Cary 25 (f)* (B) (405)
SHAW, Cornelia 22* (B) (242)
SHAW, Daniel? 20* (B) (215)
SHAW, Eliza 21* (B) (188)
SHAW, Fannie 29* (B) (244)
SHAW, Frank 30* (B) (194)
SHAW, Frank 40* (B) (294)
SHAW, Gorge 24 (B) (216)
SHAW, H. S. 21 (m), (483)
SHAW, Henerson 30 (B) (479)
SHAW, Henry 30 (B) (221)
SHAW, Isham 25* (223)
SHAW, Isom 64 (B) (325)
SHAW, J. Q. 70 (m), (188)
SHAW, John 27* (B) (218)
SHAW, John W. 23?* (164)
SHAW, Julia 21* (B) (290)
SHAW, Lucy 62* (B) (218)
SHAW, Mary 40 (B) (401)
SHAW, Narcissus 9 (f)* (B) (196)
SHAW, Ophy? 50 (m)* (B) (176)
SHAW, Peggy 25? (B) (245)
SHAW, Penny 14* (B) (494)
SHAW, Peter 46 (B) (479)
SHAW, Pomp 14 (m)* (B) (480)
SHAW, Prince 53, (223)
SHAW, Robe 23 (m) (B) (479)
SHAW, Sallie 40 (B) (236)
SHAW, Solomon 53 (B) (431)
SHAW, Taylor 60 (B) (326)
SHAW, Thos. J. W. 40* (168)
SHAW, Tom 15* (B) (241)
SHAW, Tom 28 (B) (248)
SHAW, V. 23 (m) (B) (325)
SHAW, Vigg? 31 (m) (B) (399)
SHAW?, Cain 33* (B) (181)
SHEALS, Dixie 6 (f)* (B) (377)
SHEALS, Lee 24 (m) (B) (374)
SHEALS, Matt 40 (m) (B) (378)
SHEALS?, Van 25 (B) (376)
SHEDRICH, Mary 32* (B) (218)
SHEDRICK, Nelson 62 (B) (289)
SHEE?, Dan 55* (498)
SHEFFIELD, W. R. 29 (m), (332)
SHEGRO, Thomas 24* (B) (424)
SHELL, Raleigh 53 (B) (176)
SHELTON, Andrew 21 (B) (312)
SHELTON, Charley 24* (B) (461)
SHELTON, Daniel? 48 (B) (304)
SHELTON, Dennis 14* (B) (229)
SHELTON, Frank 9* (161)
SHELTON, Freeman 25 (B) (353)
SHELTON, Gilbert 55 (B) (247)
SHELTON, Henry 27 (B) (365)
SHELTON, Isaac? 40, (462)
SHELTON, Isham 22 (B) (247)
SHELTON, J. W. 38 (m)* (310)
SHELTON, Jack 51 (B) (245)

SHELTON, John 50 (B) (461)
SHELTON, Jonas 35 (B) (313)
SHELTON, L. V. 45 (m), (313)
SHELTON, Mag 1 (f)* (B) (247)
SHELTON, Olley 56 (f)* (B) (312)
SHELTON, Pomp 35 (m) (B) (464)
SHELTON, T. J. jr. 41, (443)
SHELTON, Thomas 75* (461)
SHELTON, Thomas? 39* (B) (312)
SHELTON, Tom 26* (B) (304)
SHELTON, Wilson 17* (B) (351)
SHELTON, Wm. 17* (B) (351)
SHELTON, Wm. 25, (272)
SHELTON, Wright 62 (B) (359)
SHEPARD, History 40 (f)* (B) (485)
SHEPARD, Pres 18 (m)* (B) (222)
SHEPERD, S. 29 (m) (B) (499)
SHEPHERD, James 26* (191)
SHEPHERD, Robert 49?, (451)
SHEPPARD, Ike 33 (B) (420)
SHEPPARD, Sarah 75* (B) (386)
SHEPPERD, Birdie 16 (f)* (460)
SHERADEN, Thos. A. 32, (406)
SHEROD, Florady 24 (f)* (B) (164)
SHERRARD?, George 32* (305)
SHERRILL, John 28, (456)
SHERROD, Alfred 30 (B) (293)
SHERROD, Ellison 56* (B) (303)
SHERROD, H. R. 52 (m)* (293)
SHERROD, Robert 51* (B) (280)
SHERROD, Willie 16 (m)* (B) (348)
SHERRON, Felix K. 21, (375)
SHERRON, Mary 33, (484)
SHIELDS, Mary 48* (310)
SHIELDS, Mollie 70* (B) (460)
SHINAULT?, John 34* (198)
SHINE, Dick 30* (B) (351)
SHINE?, Eliza 20* (B) (355)
SHIVERS, Oliver 34 (B) (211)
SHOALS, Napoleon 13* (B) (389)
SHOEMAKER, Wm. 60, (375)
SHOETER?, Z.? 19 (m)* (B) (500)
SHOFFNER, James 43, (433)
SHORT, JOe 25* (B) (222)
SHORTER, John 60* (B) (443)
SHORTER, Osker 21 (B) (459)
SIDER?, Hiram 22, (423)
SIDY?, Absent 26 (f)* (B) (203)
SILMAN, Nathan 26 (B) (455)
SIMERSON, Nannie? 45* (344)
SIMERSON?, S. 55 (f), (314)
SIMINGTON?, Jennie 18* (B) (419)
SIMISON?, Nannie 45* (316)
SIMMONS, Alford 42 (B) (395)
SIMMONS, Anna 69* (428)
SIMMONS, Bartlet 47* (433)
SIMMONS, Bascomb 29, (428)
SIMMONS, Henry 30* (B) (481)
SIMMONS, James 51, (426)
SIMMONS, Jessee 35 (m)* (B) (301)

SIMMONS, Jno. 45, (194)
SIMMONS, John 35* (428)
SIMMONS, M. 35 (f) (B) (490)
SIMMONS, Sam 32 (B) (232)
SIMMONS, Tom 24* (421)
SIMMONS, W. J. 37 (m)* (168)
SIMMONS, Zelph 75 (f)* (B) (479)
SIMMONS?, Dock 23* (B) (260)
SIMMONS?, Westley 32 (B) (428)
SIMMS, James 24, (443)
SIMMS, Jas. A. 27, (440)
SIMONS, Emelie 60* (B) (210)
SIMPSON, Mabe 27 (m)* (B) (172)
SIMPSON, Thomas 25* (436)
SIMPSON, Thomas 27 (B) (365)
SIMPSON, Tobe 28 (B) (386)
SIMS, Abb 25 (m)* (B) (251)
SIMS, Brooks 19* (B) (233)
SIMS, Ginny 30 (m)* (B) (233)
SIMS, Hubbard 35 (B) (447)
SIMS, Laurer? 23 (f)* (B) (441)
SIMS, Walter 40* (B) (348)
SIM___, John 44* (B) (284)
SINES?, Peter 79? (B) (446)
SINGLETON, Mollie 26* (B) (357)
SINGLETON, Ned 52 (B) (434)
SINGLETON, Perry 26, (490)
SISCO, James C. 33, (410)
SISCO, John W. 23, (410)
SISCO, Wm. 59, (410)
SISTER?, W. P. 34 (m)* (312)
SKALLER, Jake 35* (168)
SKALLER, Mark 37* (168)
SKIDMORE, J. S. 35 (m), (483)
SKIDMORE, J. S. 38 (m)* (168)
SKILLER, J. F. H. 55 (m), (408)
SKINNER, John 27* (487)
SKINNER, M. 55 (m), (486)
SKIPPER, Jacob 22 (B) (260)
SLADE, Fannie 56* (443)
SLATES, Daniel 40 (B) (431)
SLAUGHTER, A. C. 25 (m)* (494)
SLAUGHTER, A.? J. 25 (m), (370)
SLAUGHTER, Dora 23, (469)
SLAUGHTER, G. 36 (m), (495)
SLAUGHTER, J. 29 (m), (502)
SLAUGHTER, Joseph 45* (B) (386)
SLAUGHTER, P. E. 51 (f)* (370)
SLAYTER?, S. H. 51 (m)* (318)
SLOAN, R. 61 (m), (300)
SLOAN, R. 64 (f)* (301)
SLOAN, Rachal 37 (B) (290)
SLOOP, J. C. 29 (m), (278)
SLOSIP?, S. J. 30 (f)* (324)
SMALL, Wm. 47* (165)
SMITH, A. C. 46 (m)* (272)
SMITH, A. E. 61 (f)* (440)
SMITH, Abe 19? (B) (467)
SMITH, Add__ 23 (m)* (B) (332)
SMITH, Adeline 45* (B) (268)
SMITH, Allen 27 (B) (375)
SMITH, Bance? 6 (f)* (B) (419)
SMITH, Briant 25* (B) (482)
SMITH, Carrie 12* (B) (366)

SMITH, Chaney 38 (f) (B) (357)
SMITH, Charles 20 (B) (398)
SMITH, Charles 23* (427)
SMITH, Charles 35 (B) (468)
SMITH, Cora 20* (B) (306)
SMITH, Cora 21 (B) (255)
SMITH, Crawford 30 (B) (381)
SMITH, Davey 67 (m)* (B) (214)
SMITH, Delia 22* (B) (433)
SMITH, Ed H. 46, (165)
SMITH, Edward 24 (B) (435)
SMITH, Edward 31* (B) (418)
SMITH, Egbert 20* (168)
SMITH, Eliza 60* (B) (177)
SMITH, Emily 40 (B) (305)
SMITH, Enoch H. 43, (360)
SMITH, F. 20? (m) (B) (312)
SMITH, Francis J. 30* (198)
SMITH, G. F. 47 (m)* (483)
SMITH, G. W. 51 (m)* (324)
SMITH, George 30* (B) (381)
SMITH, George 33* (B) (195)
SMITH, George 48 (B) (419)
SMITH, Gracy 4* (B) (174)
SMITH, HArriett 35 (B) (306)
SMITH, Hannah 60* (B) (416)
SMITH, Hansel 28, (203)
SMITH, Harry 25* (201)
SMITH, Henry 22* (B) (250)
SMITH, Henry 30* (B) (303)
SMITH, Henry 40 (B) (310)
SMITH, Henry 47, (332)
SMITH, Henry 52 (B) (398)
SMITH, Henry 56* (226)
SMITH, Huldie 75 (f)* (B) (330)
SMITH, Ike 33* (B) (325)
SMITH, J. A. 49 (m)* (300)
SMITH, J. G. 28 (m)* (316)
SMITH, J. G. 28 (m)* (344)
SMITH, J. L. 22 (m), (204)
SMITH, J. N. 44 (m), (220)
SMITH, J. P. 42 (m)* (332)
SMITH, James 9* (183)
SMITH, Jane 15 (B) (303)
SMITH, Jane? 19* (198)
SMITH, Jasper 41* (197)
SMITH, Jessee 40 (m) (B) (184)
SMITH, Jessie 42 (m) (B) (473)
SMITH, John F. 25* (374)
SMITH, Joseph 25* (B) (269)
SMITH, Julia 9* (B) (315)
SMITH, Katie 29* (447)
SMITH, Lewis 56 (B) (384)
SMITH, Lieu 25 (f) (B) (340)
SMITH, Lizie 35* (B) (483)
SMITH, M. 19 (f)* (B) (254)
SMITH, M. J. 38 (f)* (285)
SMITH, Mary 60* (376)
SMITH, Matt 24 (f)* (B) (405)
SMITH, Mealie 23 (f)* (B) (481)
SMITH, Melissa 54* (425)
SMITH, Morgan 28 (B) (372)
SMITH, NEwman 60* (B) (254)
SMITH, Newman 50 (B) (276)
SMITH, P. 46 (m)* (261)
SMITH, Phill 44 (B) (467)
SMITH, Polly 60* (B) (339)
SMITH, Prestley 22 (m)* (B) (276)
SMITH, R. 30 (m)* (502)

SMITH, Robert 22* (B) (284)
SMITH, Robert 75* (B) (178)
SMITH, S. 19 (m)* (335)
SMITH, S. J. 46 (m), (203)
SMITH, Samuel 27 (B) (426)
SMITH, Silus 28* (B) (162)
SMITH, Silus 29* (B) (166)
SMITH, Stephen 25 (B) (435)
SMITH, Sylvester 29 (f) (B) (250)
SMITH, Thomas 19* (B) (418)
SMITH, Thos. J. 50* (194)
SMITH, Tobia 28 (m)* (B) (484)
SMITH, Violet 42 (B) (324)
SMITH, W. H. 31 (m) (B) (312)
SMITH, Willy 6 (m)* (B) (338)
SMITH, Wm. 18* (335)
SMITH, Wm. 32* (377)
SMITH, Wm. 54* (213)
SMITH, Wm. H. H. 40, (406)
SMITH, Zilpha 80* (B) (268)
SMITH, _. M. 52 (m), (204)
SMITH, _aker 33 (m)* (B) (168)
SMITH?, Tom 50? (B) (329)
SMITHSON, J.? M. 51 (m), (286)
SMITHWICK, Joe 18* (427)
SNEED, John 4* (B) (415)
SNEED, John 54, (293)
SNEED, Jonathan 32, (293)
SNEED, Lucey 38 (475)
SNEED, Nat 25, (293)
SNEED, Willie 8 (m)* (B) (401)
SNELL, ____ 70* (197)
SNELLING, ____ 35 (f)* (473)
SNOW, George 20* (B) (435)
SNOW, Lucretia 52* (201)
SOINS, Solomon 33 (B) (471)
SOLAMON, Crook 45, (409)
SOLOMON, Ann 19* (B) (232)
SOLOMON, Jas. E. 16* (406)
SOLOMON, Sydner 50 (m)* (235)
SOLONE?, MArgaret 15* (B) (350)
SOMERS?, Perry 26, (420)
SOMERVILLE, Ben 48 (B) (288)
SOMERVILLE, Sesar 83 (m)* (B) (225)
SOMERVILLE, Sylva 23* (B) (227)
SOWARD, Charles 50* (B) (340)
SOWER?, Cora __* (305)
SPAIN, Robert 23 (B) (361)
SPAIN, Wm. 47* (250)
SPARKS, James 54, (282)
SPARRIS?, George 43 (B) (460)
SPENCE, Harriet _* (B) (417)
SPENCE, ____ 18 (f) (B) (418)
SPENCER, Annie 7* (201)
SPENCER, Emily 51 (B) (457)
SPENCER, H. 23 (m)* (B) (494)
SPENCER, Isham 33 (B) (362)
SPENCER, John 21* (200)
SPENCER, John 24 (B) (243)
SPENCER, Melzer 52 (m), (198)
SPENCER, Susan 50* (198)
SPENCER?, Louisa 27 (B) (432)
SPIKE, Sam 9* (B) (164)
SPILLER, Alexander 26 (B) (179)
SPILLER, C. E. 14 (m)* (334)
SPILLER, G. F. A. 53 (m), (320)
SPILMAN, Lou 9 (m)* (289)

SPINKS, Jo. 61 (m) (B) (497)
SPITE, Marietta 11* (B) (461)
SPRINGER, Tom 30, (336)
SPRINGFIELD, B. 48 (m) (B) (224)
SPRINGFIELD, Ike 25 (B) (246)
SPRINGFIELD, Liza 45* (B) (229)
SPRINGFIELD, Louis 23 (B) (238)
SPRINGFIELD, Sarah 23 (B) (246)
SPRINGFIELD, Stephen 55 (B) (251)
SPRINGFIELD, __tna 65 (m)* (B) (252)
STAFFORD, B. R. 74 (m), (336)
STAFFORD, G. M. 42 (m), (328)
STAFFORD, G. R. 24 (m), (321)
STAFFORD, G.? 71 (f)* (501)
STAFFORD, H. M. 51 (f)* (461)
STAFFORD, Heck 61 (m), (331)
STAFFORD, J. O. 29 (m)* (330)
STAFFORD, JOhn 44, (330)
STAFFORD, N. 40 (m), (490)
STAFFORD, Pinckney 44?* (258)
STAFFORD, T. L. 58 (m)* (321)
STAFFORD, Tom 29* (331)
STAFFORD, Will 40 (B) (319)
STAFFORD, ____ 14 (f)* (331)
STAFFORD, ____ jr. 48 (m), (336)
STAFFORD?, Preston 10* (185)
STAINBACK, Catherin 60* (228)
STAINBACK, Giles 33 (B) (251)
STAINBACK, Hender? 31 (m)* (B) (224)
STAINBACK, Will 40* (259)
STALLINGS, W. S. 42 (m)* (334)
STALLION, Allen 25 (B) (272)
STALLIONS, Ben 53* (B) (276)
STALLIONS, Fred 22 (B) (292)
STAMPER, Fillmore 23, (198)
STAMPER, Henry 47* (196)
STANCEL?, Lizia 12* (183)
STANLEY, J. W. 17 (m)* (280)
STANLEY, M. F. 35 (f)* (469)
STANLEY, Samuel 46 (B) (362)
STANLY, Robert 8* (429)
STAPLES, David G. 30 (B) (361)
STARK, Isaac 17* (B) (419)
STARKS, Angline 26* (B) (392)
STARNBACK, _. 28 (m)* (160)
STARTS, Olavar 30 (B) (378)
STEDMAN, Mary 22* (435)
STEEL, Lucy 15* (B) (243)
STEELE, Jane 55, (201)
STEELE, P. 50? (f)* (198)
STEE_, Allice 15* (185)
STEGER, Armsted 68 (B) (374)
STEGER, Charles J. 29* (392)
STEGER, Edward 70* (426)
STEGER, John 38* (433)
STEGER, Robert 23* (433)
STEGER, Verge 18 (m), (433)
STEGER, Wm. 25* (B) (374)
STEGER, Wm. 30, (434)
STEGER, ____ 29* (434)
STEPHENSON, Mary 34, (190)
STEPHERN, Mary 50* (441)

STEPHS?, Conway 25 (B) (456)
STEVENS, Alex 18* (B) (317)
STEVENS, W. H. 53 (m), (323)
STEVENS?, ____ 18 (m)* (B) (342)
STEWARD, Celia 40 (B) (340)
STEWART, Aggy 78 (f)* (B) (186)
STEWART, Albert 21* (B) (376)
STEWART, Charles 44* (B) (193)
STEWART, Emeline 50?* (B) (255)
STEWART, Fanny 26* (B) (186)
STEWART, Henry 22 (B) (376)
STEWART, James 28, (455)
STEWART, James 43* (237)
STEWART, Mary 43* (238)
STEWART, Mat 78* (B) (289)
STEWART, Paul 30 (B) (376)
STEWART, Robert 25 (B) (450)
STEWART, Rose 17* (B) (282)
STEWART, Thomas 28 (B) (383)
STEWART, Tom 35* (B) (236)
STEWART, Tomy 39 (B) (378)
STEWART, Wm. 8* (427)
STEWART, Wm. J.? 53, (265)
STIEVENS, Jule 24 (m)* (320)
STIGALL, Robert 23 (B) (388)
STIGALL, Wash 21 (m)* (B) (388)
STIGOR, Gus F. 24* (392)
STINSON, Eli P. 38, (194)
STINSON?, Louis 50* (B) (379)
STITONS?, Cl___ 25 (m)* (B) (482)
STITT, Isaac 30* (B) (161)
STITT, JAcob 24 (B) (171)
STITT, Thomas 63* (B) (174)
STITT, Tobias 28* (B) (172)
STITTUM, John 16* (B) (374)
STITT___, Chessy? 21 (f)* (B) (474)
STOACKARD, Bill 25 (B) (210)
STOKELY, Bell 20 (B) (396)
STOKES, John 27 (B) (396)
STOKES, Louis 27 (B) (396)
STONE, Clark 39* (392)
STONE, Thomas 30 (B) (358)
STORER?, Robert 40, (433)
STOTT, Henry 39 (B) (175)
STOTT?, MArtha 7* (B) (169)
STOVALL, Jack 22* (339)
STRADHAM?, Ned 22 (B) (403)
STRAWN, T. J. 30 (m), (208)
STREADHAM, John 45* (B) (403)
STREET, Dorcas 62* (B) (366)
STREET, George M. 23* (162)
STREIGHOR, J. T. 32 (m), (274)
STRICKLAND, J. H. 26 (m) (B) (163)
STRONG, Heet? 45 (f)* (B) (198)
STUART, R. 23 (m)* (B) (493)
STUART, W. 24 (m) (B) (498)
STUART, Yancy? 38 (m) (B) (493)
STUBBLEFIELD, Lee 25 (m)* (B) (482)
STULL, George 23 (B) (240)
STULL, Nicy 45 (B) (180)

STURM, Jacob 27* (434)
SUCADA?, Wat 65 (m) (B) (205)
SUERLINGS, B. V. 35 (m)* (331)
SULAVAN, Nancy 56* (368)
SULAVAN, Wesley 18* (368)
SULCER?, George 58* (304)
SULLIVAN, E. 68 (f)* (489)
SULLIVAN, Edward 16* (430)
SULLIVAN, H. 26 (m)* (B) (487)
SULLIVAN, Rolina? 50 (f) (B) (465)
SULLIVANT, Jona 18* (201)
SUMMER, Alice 28 (B) (325)
SUMMERS, J. 35? (m)* (480)
SUMMERS, J. A. 41 (m), (476)
SUMMERS, Penny 28 (m), (410)
SUTHERLAN, James 53, (459)
SUTTERS, Sam? 53 (m)* (B) (315)
SUTTON, Bartlett 40, (427)
SUTTON, Calvin 27 (B) (353)
SUTTON, Elijah 92 (B) (349)
SUTTON, Martha 26* (B) (366)
SUTTON, Viney 29 (f)* (B) (349)
SWAN, Jno. Thos. 28, (194)
SWAN?, Steve 26 (B) (500)
SWEENY, Henry 18* (292)
SWEET, Frank 40 (B) (458)
SWIFT, Abraham 25 (B) (399)
SWIFT, Armstead 62 (B) (458)
SWIFT, Eliza A. 79* (361)
SWIFT, Frank 23, (440)
SWIFT, Harvey 21* (B) (345)
SWIFT, Henry 30, (440)
SWIFT, Jacob 30 (B) (334)
SWIFT, James 30* (B) (444)
SWIFT, Jane 25* (B) (333)
SWIFT, John 22 (B) (394)
SWIFT, John jr. 36 (B) (395)
SWIFT, Julian 29, (442)
SWIFT, Lucy 90* (B) (313)
SWIFT, Mat 17 (f)* (B) (394)
SWIFT, Matilda 25* (B) (395)
SWIFT, Samuel 25 (B) (363)
SWIFT, Wm. 5* (B) (360)
SYKES, Edward 38 (B) (418)
TABOR, Wm. 17* (B) (419)
TALL, Nelson 25* (B) (395)
TALTON, Ely 33, (375)
TANANDERS?, Robert 13* (B) (369)
TAPP, Nimrod 72, (240)
TAPP?, Louis 34?, (240)
TAPPAN, S. W. 38 (m), (281)
TARPLEY, Charlie 26* (B) (346)
TARPLEY, Henry 39 (B) (397)
TARPLEY, M. 29 (m) (B) (497)
TARPLEY, Wm. H. 82* (407)
TARPLY, Eveline 16* (B) (405)
TATE, Andew 40* (B) (402)
TATE, Claborn 30 (B) (403)
TATE, David 50 (B) (163)
TATE, Easter 20 (f)* (B) (222)
TATE, Edward 24 (B) (255)
TATE, Edward 24 (B) (274)
TATE, Edward 28 (B) (227)
TATE, Harry 55 (B) (403)
TATE, Henry 25 (B) (260)
TATE, John 14* (B) (175)
TATE, Mumford 21 (B) (402)

TATE, Nancy 16* (B) (403)
TATE, Peter 55 (B) (402)
TATE, Pollie 65* (B) (394)
TATE, Sandy 20 (B) (215)
TATE, Sarah 17* (B) (166)
TATE, Swail 2 (f)* (B) (222)
TATE, T. C. 33 (m), (207)
TATE, Wm. 26 (B) (403)
TATE, Wm. 26 (B) (403)
TATEM, Bill 24 (B) (395)
TATEM, Hannibal 26 (B) (349)
TATIM, Abe 25 (B) (394)
TATTUM, Gorge 55* (B) (204)
TATUM, Betty 26 (B) (200)
TATUM, E. W. 69 (m), (170)
TATUM, Ellen 37* (B) (197)
TATUM, G. W. 53 (m), (286)
TATUM, Henry? _* (B) (200)
TATUM, Major 35* (B) (161)
TATUM, Mattie L. 35 (f), (165)
TATUM, Ples? J. 19 (m)* (254)
TATUM, R. G. 52 (m)* (173)
TATUM, Rachel 48* (B) (173)
TATUM, Richd. 33* (B) (166)
TATUM, Sallie 21 (B) (167)
TATUM, Wm. 45 (B) (211)
TATUM?, Frank 36 (B) (197)
TATUM?, Mary 33, (193)
TAYLER, Nancie 13* (469)
TAYLOR, A. 22 (m)* (B) (501)
TAYLOR, A. E. 54 (m)* (281)
TAYLOR, Abram 42 (B) (219)
TAYLOR, Alax? 27 (B) (245)
TAYLOR, Alex 25* (B) (430)
TAYLOR, Alfred 53 (B) (431)
TAYLOR, Allen? 26 (B) (495)
TAYLOR, Andrew 25* (B) (383)
TAYLOR, Ann 68* (B) (222)
TAYLOR, Arthey 46 (m)* (B) (219)
TAYLOR, Arvit? 19 (m) (B) (490)
TAYLOR, Bell 46 (B) (495)
TAYLOR, Bevley 52 (m)* (B) (218)
TAYLOR, C. 40 (m)* (B) (292)
TAYLOR, Charles 26* (B) (217)
TAYLOR, Charles 63 (B) (495)
TAYLOR, Charley 9* (B) (215)
TAYLOR, Cinse? 31 (m)* (B) (433)
TAYLOR, Cumba 35 (m) (B) (394)
TAYLOR, Dan 18* (B) (495)
TAYLOR, David 19* (B) (397)
TAYLOR, David 46 (B) (219)
TAYLOR, Dick 70* (B) (221)
TAYLOR, Dunkin 46 (B) (248)
TAYLOR, Ed 13* (B) (501)
TAYLOR, Ed__ 33 (m), (247)
TAYLOR, Emeline 30?* (B) (222)
TAYLOR, Fan? 18 (f)* (B) (495)
TAYLOR, Fannie 25 (B) (383)
TAYLOR, Frank 51 (B) (267)
TAYLOR, George 35 (B) (215)
TAYLOR, George 70 (B) (271)
TAYLOR, H. _ (f)* (486)
TAYLOR, Henderson 19 (B) (258)
TAYLOR, Henry 21* (268)
TAYLOR, Henry 21 (B) (324)
TAYLOR, Henry 39 (B) (219)

TAYLOR, Henry 41 (B) (467)
TAYLOR, Henry 45 (B) (259)
TAYLOR, Hettie 25 (f)* (B) (267)
TAYLOR, Hubbard 50* (B) (200)
TAYLOR, J. 14 (m)* (498)
TAYLOR, J. 25 (m)* (B) (501)
TAYLOR, J. J. 19 (m)* (168)
TAYLOR, James 82* (B) (488)
TAYLOR, James M. 61?* (B) (219)
TAYLOR, Jenny 28* (169)
TAYLOR, Jessee R. 43 (m), (411)
TAYLOR, Jim 56 (B) (218)
TAYLOR, Jim R. 30* (B) (217)
TAYLOR, Jno. S. 13* (195)
TAYLOR, John 16* (B) (218)
TAYLOR, John 33* (B) (263)
TAYLOR, John 41* (B) (329)
TAYLOR, John 44* (B) (488)
TAYLOR, John 50 (B) (363)
TAYLOR, Jos. 47 (B) (495)
TAYLOR, Kelley 67* (B) (381)
TAYLOR, L. 19 (f)* (B) (267)
TAYLOR, Lawson 27 (B) (262)
TAYLOR, Lewis 57 (B) (267)
TAYLOR, Liza Jane 4* (B) (270)
TAYLOR, Logan 40 (B) (218)
TAYLOR, Louis 33?* (B) (492)
TAYLOR, Louis 53* (B) (277)
TAYLOR, Lucy 15* (B) (195)
TAYLOR, M. 32 (m) (B) (260)
TAYLOR, M. 57 (m), (486)
TAYLOR, M. A. 45 (f), (285)
TAYLOR, MAt 43 (m)* (B) (217)
TAYLOR, Malida 65 (B) (370)
TAYLOR, Manda 50 (B) (448)
TAYLOR, Martha 4* (B) (217)
TAYLOR, Martha 46* (469)
TAYLOR, Mary 16* (B) (494)
TAYLOR, Mary 29 (B) (487)
TAYLOR, Mary? 5_* (263)
TAYLOR, Miles 19 (B) (258)
TAYLOR, Miles 23 (B) (221)
TAYLOR, Millie 20* (B) (376)
TAYLOR, Mont 22 (m)* (B) (488)
TAYLOR, Nathan 26 (B) (218)
TAYLOR, Nelson 24* (B) (239)
TAYLOR, O. 21 (m) (B) (488)
TAYLOR, Parlina 32, (183)
TAYLOR, Pempy 18 (m)* (B) (235)
TAYLOR, Permelia 47* (B) (218)
TAYLOR, Phillip 50* (B) (421)
TAYLOR, R. 22 (m) (B) (301)
TAYLOR, R. 38 (m) (B) (312)
TAYLOR, R. V. 59 (m)* (218)
TAYLOR, Rameus? 65 (B) (260)
TAYLOR, Robert 44 (B) (461)
TAYLOR, S. A. 55 (m), (219)
TAYLOR, Sallie B. 26* (310)
TAYLOR, Sarah 30* (B) (227)
TAYLOR, Sarah 49* (B) (487)
TAYLOR, Sol 54* (B) (494)
TAYLOR, Stephen 54 (B) (239)
TAYLOR, Steven 30 (B) (324)
TAYLOR, Susan 15* (467)
TAYLOR, Tampa 80* (B) (433)
TAYLOR, Thomas 14* (B) (190)
TAYLOR, Willis 25* (B) (378)

TAYLOR, Willis 50 (B) (258)
TAYLOR, Winnie 45* (B) (377)
TAYLOR, Wit 10* (B) (490)
TAYLOR, Wm. 18* (B) (418)
TAYLOR, Wm. 19* (B) (268)
TAYLOR, Wm. 20* (196)
TAYLOR, Wm. 25 (B) (366)
TAYLOR, Wm. 26* (B) (215)
TAYLOR, Wm. 26 (B) (190)
TAYLOR, Wm. 40 (B) (221)
TAYLOR, Wm. 52* (B) (227)
TAYLOR, _. 22 (m)* (B) (491)
TAYLOR, _ E. 51 (f)* (467)
TAYLOR, ___ 13 (m)* (485)
TAYLOR, ___ 23 (m)* (B) (388)
TA___, John 24* (307)
TEAGUE, Benjamin 47, (369)
TEAGUE, Burrel 31, (369)
TEAGUE, Caroll M. 48 (m), (369)
TEAGUE, Eady 45 (f)* (B) (379)
TEAGUE, Elizabeth 80* (369)
TEAGUE, Foster 33, (369)
TEAGUE, James 48, (369)
TEAGUE, John Z.? 56, (369)
TEAGUE, Mary T. 82, (369)
TEAGUE, Wilborn 58, (372)
TEAGUE, Wm. 60, (369)
TEAY?, Robert 35 (B) (236)
TEMPLES, Frank 24 (B) (326)
TEMPLES, Hope 50* (B) (335)
TEMPLES, James 26 (B) (335)
TEMPTON, Anga 10* (B) (231)
TENNER, Manuel 28 (B) (469)
TERRY, Bob 27 (B) (292)
TERRY, Clara A. 30* (164)
THARP, Amanda 45* (B) (340)
THARP, Ella 50* (B) (480)
THARP, Ellen 26 (B) (401)
THARP, Jacob 25 (B) (404)
THARP, Jessee L. 52* (407)
THARP, Laura 17* (B) (305)
THARP, Robert 55 (B) (310)
THARP, Sarah 58 (B) (325)
THARP, Steven 65* (B) (343)
THARP, Vira 70* (B) (285)
THARP, Zilphie 63? (f)* (B) (333)
THARP, ___ 35 (m)* (324)
THEGGO?, M. 40 (m), (486)
THIGPEN, John 34* (253)
THOMAS, A. 22 (m)* (B) (382)
THOMAS, Abraham 70* (B) (169)
THOMAS, Alas 12 (f)* (B) (217)
THOMAS, Allen 24 (B) (404)
THOMAS, Amanda 14* (168)
THOMAS, Amanda? 50, (198)
THOMAS, Ann 32* (B) (318)
THOMAS, C. C. 24 (m), (279)
THOMAS, Calvin 21* (B) (234)
THOMAS, Cass 23 (m)* (B) (329)
THOMAS, Curtis W. 33, (363)
THOMAS, D. 39 (m) (B) (439)
THOMAS, Daniel 60* (B) (255)
THOMAS, Daniel? 65 (B) (217)
THOMAS, David 62 (B) (281)
THOMAS, Doc 45 (B) (384)
THOMAS, Doc 55 (B) (386)
THOMAS, E. F. 62 (m), (274)

THOMAS, George 32* (B) (487)
THOMAS, Henry 25* (B) (298)
THOMAS, Henry 36* (B) (197)
THOMAS, Herey 22 (m)* (B) (203)
THOMAS, Ida 25* (386)
THOMAS, Ike 19* (B) (392)
THOMAS, James 29, (409)
THOMAS, Jane 49* (B) (378)
THOMAS, Jef D. 17* (234)
THOMAS, Jim 38 (B) (217)
THOMAS, John 19* (B) (246)
THOMAS, John 30 (B) (380)
THOMAS, John W. 17* (385)
THOMAS, Judia 20 (f)* (B) (256)
THOMAS, Laura 27* (B) (290)
THOMAS, Laura 35 (B) (496)
THOMAS, Mary 35 (B) (365)
THOMAS, Mat 50 (m)* (B) (447)
THOMAS, Mollie 46, (299)
THOMAS, Moses 7* (B) (256)
THOMAS, Neel 30 (B) (327)
THOMAS, Osey 21 (m)* (B) (226)
THOMAS, Plumber 19* (B) (226)
THOMAS, Rosa 20* (B) (382)
THOMAS, Simon 55* (B) (217)
THOMAS, T. J. 41 (m), (217)
THOMAS, Tom 22* (B) (222)
THOMAS, Wash 50 (B) (285)
THOMAS, Wm. 46 (B) (277)
THOMAS?, __ 44 (m), (166)
THOMASSON, J. H. 47 (m), (473)
THOMPSON, Andy 30 (B) (212)
THOMPSON, C. V. 40 (m)* (314)
THOMPSON, Dan 39? (B) (445)
THOMPSON, Dave? 45* (B) (318)
THOMPSON, Geo. M. 50, (407)
THOMPSON, Ida 14* (B) (434)
THOMPSON, Isac 22 (B) (393)
THOMPSON, J. O. 33 (m)* (392)
THOMPSON, Jake 44* (B) (499)
THOMPSON, Jas. 70, (318)
THOMPSON, John 60 (B) (279)
THOMPSON, Katie 60* (433)
THOMPSON, Kite? 55 (m) (B) (454)
THOMPSON, L. L. 45 (m), (275)
THOMPSON, M. 13 (m)* (B) (488)
THOMPSON, M. 34 (m) (B) (230)
THOMPSON, M. L. 44 (f), (166)
THOMPSON, Mary 55* (B) (301)
THOMPSON, Mose 54 (B) (290)
THOMPSON, Nancy 55? (B) (326)
THOMPSON, Peter 68 (B) (448)
THOMPSON, Polly 62* (B) (181)
THOMPSON, Rosana 65* (B) (296)
THOMPSON, W. 45 (m)* (494)
THOMPSON, Whit 18* (B) (188)
THOMPSON, Will 31, (322)
THOMPSON, Wm. 32, (353)
THOMPSON, _. 30 (m)* (495)
THOMSON, M. A.? 49 (f), (484)
THOMSON, Wesly 32 (B) (258)

THOMSON?, Harriet 6* (B) (259)
THORN, Sisse 18 (f)* (B) (422)
THORNTON, James B. 42, (393)
THORNTON, Mary 12* (422)
THORNTON, Ruben 16* (B) (413)
THORNTON, Ruben 34 (B) (415)
THORNTON, Simon 54 (B) (386)
THORNTON, Sue 9* (427)
THORNTON, Wm. 43, (426)
THORTON, James 7* (477)
THURMAN, Wash 26 (B) (480)
THURMON, Phillip R. 29* (177)
THURMON, W. D.? 64 (m), (176)
TIBBS, Daniel 23* (B) (189)
TILLER, Thomas 46* (422)
TILLUR, Mary 56, (431)
TILMON, Israel 64 (B) (174)
TIMBERLAKE, Bob 35 (B) (274)
TIMBERLAKE, Lena 10* (279)
TINES, Henry 30 (B) (452)
TINKLER, Joseph J. 53, (351)
TIPLETT, W. G. 26 (m), (210)
TIPPIN?, Tom 61* (B) (239)
TISSIAK?, Fred 30* (194)
TOD?, Jerey 20 (m)* (B) (209)
TODD, Ed 16* (501)
TODD, Tessia 22* (432)
TODD, Wm. 37* (494)
TOFTON, Ider 13 (f)* (B) (208)
TOLDS?, Jane 40 (B) (480)
TOLIN, S. A. 38 (f), (485)
TOLIVER, May 28 (B) (452)
TOLLEY, Bartlett 54 (m) (B) (303)
TOLTON, Mary 60* (375)
TOMAS, Henry 50 (B) (473)
TOMLIN, E. B. 24 (m), (480)
TOMLIN, J. 28 (m), (334)
TOMLIN, S. J. 32 (m), (342)
TOMLIN?, W. P. 61 (m)* (480)
TOMLINSON, J. 38 (m), (483)
TOMPSON, Annie 8* (B) (239)
TOMPSON, Ben 60 (B) (226)
TOMPSON, E. J. 60 (f), (211)
TOMPSON, Hecaba 20 (m) (B) (226)
TOMPSON, Jerry 23 (m) (B) (226)
TOMSON, El____ 56 (m) (B) (269)
TOMSON?, Eull 35 (m)* (B) (258)
TONY, John 44* (B) (259)
TOOMBS, A. G. 40 (m)* (460)
TOPIN, Polly 55* (B) (337)
TOPPIN, Beckie 16* (B) (337)
TOPPIN, Tom 32 (B) (338)
TOPPIN, ____ 25 (m)* (B) (338)
TORENCE, John 55 (B) (395)
TOTAN?, John 61* (310)
TOWLES, Innis 12 (m)* (B) (400)
TOWLES, J. T. 33 (m), (481)
TOWNS, Bob 35* (B) (246)
TOWNS, Conrad P. 30, (351)
TOWNS, Wm. 35* (B) (449)
TOWNSEND, hester 38* (B) (268)

TOWNSON, Alertt 65 (m)* (B) (384)
TOWNSON, Alford 50* (B) (382)
TRADOR, Daniel 30* (B) (355)
TRAILOR, Reese 22* (B) (356)
TRAINER, Barnet 69, (196)
TRAVIS, W.? 36 (m), (204)
TREDWAY, John 30, (171)
TREMAGE, Monroe 23 (B) (296)
TRENT, Cumberland 47 (m)* (B) (170)
TRENT, Fred 21* (B) (184)
TRENT, George 45 (B) (468)
TRENT, LEwis 35 (B) (180)
TRIGG, Adaline 51* (B) (161)
TRIMBLE, Frank 39* (164)
TRIPP, C. F. 34 (m)* (218)
TRIPP, W. R. 21? (m)* (208)
TROTTER, J. 25 (m)* (238)
TROTTER, James 33* (255?)
TROTTER, Mose 46 (B) (480)
TROTTER, Rachal 47* (B) (249)
TROTTER, Sam 47 (B) (225)
TROTTER, Willie 27* (236)
TROTTER?, W. B. 27 (m)* (290)
TROUT, Wm. H. 45* (255)
TROUT?, B. 20 (m)* (B) (405)
TROUT?, L. 25 (m), (486)
TROWELL, T. J. 41 (m)* (274)
TRUEHART, Eliza 55* (B) (356)
TRUSDALE, Alex 55 (B) (295)
TRUSDALE, Andrew 23* (B) (283)
TRUSDALE, JAck 35 (B) (273)
TRUSDALE, Wm. 35* (B) (273)
TR____, J. T. 30 (m), (271)
TUCKER, A. 25 (f) (B) (266)
TUCKER, Alfred? 32* (B) (160)
TUCKER, Anna 18* (B) (269)
TUCKER, B. 20 (m)* (B) (269)
TUCKER, Becca 55 (B) (265)
TUCKER, Chapel 47 (m)* (B) (231)
TUCKER, Charity 85* (B) (354)
TUCKER, Daniel 54* (B) (292)
TUCKER, Dud 22 (m) (B) (232)
TUCKER, E. J. 65 (m)* (164)
TUCKER, Edmond? 21* (B) (253)
TUCKER, Eliza 13* (B) (500)
TUCKER, Ellen 20* (B) (498)
TUCKER, Emma 12* (B) (429)
TUCKER, Emma 7* (B) (241)
TUCKER, James 18* (B) (467)
TUCKER, James 52?, (265)
TUCKER, Joseph C. 60* (232)
TUCKER, Lucy 35 (B) (241)
TUCKER, Lucy 4* (B) (261)
TUCKER, Lucy 59* (226)
TUCKER, Mary 35* (B) (470)
TUCKER, Mary E. 45, (442)
TUCKER, Mollie 12* (B) (372)
TUCKER, Pillip 51* (B) (262)
TUCKER, Sallie 50 (B) (438)
TUCKER, Wm. 21* (198)
TUCKER, Wm. 23 (B) (425)
TUCKER, Wm. 25* (440)
TURBIVILLE, Fountain M. 52, (345)
TURK, Ike 27* (B) (235)
TURNAGE, Daniel? 55 (B) (298)

TURNAGE, JEssee 40 (m) (B) (300)
TURNAGE, M. B. 49 (f), (301)
TURNAGE, ____ 22 (m) (B) (298)
TURNBUL, Nannie 39* (433)
TURNER, Ambros 21* (B) (226)
TURNER, Anna 28* (B) (352)
TURNER, Bettie 16* (B) (444)
TURNER, Beverly __ (m)* (B) (413)
TURNER, Bob? 25* (B) (259)
TURNER, Bruce? 30* (B) (341)
TURNER, Faun? 43 (m) (B) (497)
TURNER, George 30* (B) (174)
TURNER, Harry 60* (B) (453)
TURNER, John 35* (B) (475)
TURNER, John B. 52, (161)
TURNER, Julia 49, (406)
TURNER, Liza 15* (B) (231)
TURNER, MAry Jane 9* (B) (172)
TURNER, Martha 60* (B) (226)
TURNER, Martha 90* (B) (413)
TURNER, Mary 28 (B) (452)
TURNER, Mattie 9* (470)
TURNER, Mose 30* (B) (416)
TURNER, Richmond? 26* (B) (264)
TURNER, Willie 11 (m)* (B) (215)
TURNER, Willy? 50 (m) (B) (453)
TURNER, Wm. 41, (367)
TURNER, Wm. 50 (B) (453)
TURNER, ___ 25 (m)* (440)
TURNER?, ____ 24 (m)* (443)
TURNLEY, Asy 24 (m)* (B) (222)
TURNLEY, Chesley 50 (m) (B) (215)
TURNLEY, Edmond? 20* (B) (215)
TURNLEY, S. B. 26 (m) (B) (218)
TWEEDY?, Bradley 40 (B) (303)
TWINS?, W. C. 55 (m)* (161)
TYLER, G. W. 31 (m) (B) (320)
TYNE, Jim 70* (B) (288)
TYUS, Fred W. 42, (201)
ULMAN, Henry 38* (282)
UPCHURCH, A. 48 (m)* (B) (273)
VALENTINE?, J. 20 (m)* (B) (498)
VANALSTON, Sam 60* (B) (416)
VANBUREN, Martin 38 (B) (191)
VANCE, Caroline 20* (B) (269)
VANPELT, Alice 26* (B) (372)
VANPELT, David 18* (B) (430)
VANPELT, Jerry 51 (B) (430)
VANPELT, Katie 65* (430)
VANPELT, Mattie 20* (428)
VANPELT, Moses 28 (B) (435)
VANPELT, Samuel 33 (B) (435)
VANPELT, Samuel 40 (B) (431)
VANPELT, Squire 30* (B) (414)
VARPEL, Wm. 28 (B) (429)
VAUGHN, A. G. 50 (m), (465)
VAUGHN, Carrie 10* (434)
VEAL, Thomas 43, (190)

VEST, Wm. 33* (415)
VESTER, A. 35 (m)* (B) (310)
VIC, Cove 45 (m), (384)
VICK, Wm. 26, (171)
VINCENT, Anderson 58 (B) (355)
VINSON, Daniel 27? (B) (172)
VOGEL, Abram 26, (167)
VOLENTIN, B. 56 (m) (B) (501)
VOLUNTIN, Pink 53 (m) (B) (501)
VOSS, Washington 52* (B) (213)
WADDELL, Nancy 65 (B) (442)
WADDLE, Judy 56* (B) (424)
WADE, Anderson 50* (B) (178)
WADE, Antny 30 (m) (B) (403)
WADE, Claborn 25 (B) (398)
WADE, Clem 26* (B) (417)
WADE, Cynthia 18* (B) (399)
WADE, Frank 23* (B) (424)
WADE, Henry 2* (B) (419)
WADE, J. 36 (m) (B) (302)
WADE, John F. 29, (362)
WADE, Margret 50 (B) (460)
WADE, Milton 51 (B) (399)
WADE, Mollie 24* (B) (310)
WADE, Moses 47 (B) (358)
WADE, Paul 26* (B) (394)
WADE, Philip 30 (B) (403)
WADE, Pollie 65* (B) (394)
WADE, Richard 25 (B) (402)
WADE, Richard 48, (411)
WADE, Solomon 27 (B) (468)
WADEL, Ed 32* (B) (493)
WADEL, Wash 57?* (B) (493)
WADEL, _. 31 (m)* (B) (500)
WADKIN, Ely 48* (B) (390)
WADKINS, JAck 25 (B) (209)
WADKINS, Nancy 48 (B) (216)
WADKINS, Nelson 35 (B) (218)
WADKINS, Teff 50 (m)* (B) (208)
WADKINS, Tom 2?* (B) (206)
WADLEY, Samuel 37 (B) (442)
WADSEL, Samuel 25 (B) (422)
WAFFORD, Elisha 55 (B) (500)
WAGENER, J. L. 40 (m), (316)
WAGONER, J. L. 40 (m), (344)
WAINRIGHT, Nancy 7* (B) (217)
WAINRIGHT, Willie 12 (m)* (B) (219)
WAINWRIGHT, Ellen 15* (B) (241)
WAINWRIGHT, Good 47 (m) (B) (241)
WAINWRIGHT, John 26 (B) (251)
WAINWRIGHT, Lewis 18* (B) (173)
WAINWRIGHT, MAranda 39 (B) (241)
WAINWRIGHT, Payton 70 (B) (241)
WAINWRIGHT, Scott 48 (B) (251)
WAINWRIGHT, Tom 70 (B) (241)
WAINWRIGHT?, Jeanna 5* (B) (247)
WAIR, Nathan 25* (B) (378)
WALDEN, W. M. 75 (m), (472)

WALDREN, Louisa 48* (223)
WALKEN, Ruben 21 (B) (401)
WALKER, Andrew 20* (B) (387)
WALKER, Andrew 35* (467)
WALKER, Andy 50 (B) (420)
WALKER, Bedford 60* (B) (474)
WALKER, Carles 47 (m) (B) (378)
WALKER, Ed 19* (B) (234)
WALKER, Edward 24 (430)
WALKER, Fillis 6* (B) (483)
WALKER, Flora 22* (B) (263)
WALKER, Frank 22 (B) (210)
WALKER, George 28* (B) (381)
WALKER, George 55 (B) (348)
WALKER, Henry 25 (B) (239)
WALKER, Henry 35 (B) (280)
WALKER, J. T. 16 (m)* (203)
WALKER, J.? 55 (m) (B) (171)
WALKER, JAck 35* (B) (394)
WALKER, Jacob 44* (B) (346)
WALKER, James 24* (B) (333)
WALKER, James 42 (B) (360)
WALKER, Jane? 10* (B) (271)
WALKER, John 46* (280)
WALKER, John jr. 20* (443)
WALKER, Johnson 35* (B) (427)
WALKER, Louisa 50* (B) (349)
WALKER, Lula 14* (B) (235)
WALKER, M. J. _ (f)* (317)
WALKER, Mary J. 12* (B) (349)
WALKER, Matt 28 (B) (388)
WALKER, Mattie 23 (f)* (B) (473)
WALKER, Nelson 50 (B) (474)
WALKER, Phillip 30 (B) (390)
WALKER, Rachael 47 (B) (334)
WALKER, Rachel 23* (B) (213)
WALKER, Robert 30 (B) (387)
WALKER, Simon 33 (B) (343)
WALKER, Thomas 35 (B) (452)
WALKER, Truelove 60 (f) (B) (401)
WALKER, Will 25 (B) (470)
WALKER, _. J. 56 (m)* (483)
WALKER, ____ 25 (m) (B) (492)
WALKER?, Epps 55 (B) (446)
WALKINS, Dunk? 24 (m) (B) (485)
WALKINS?, Albert 7* (B) (473)
WALL, F. F. 47 (m), (279)
WALL, James 36, (247)
WALL, John 35* (198)
WALL, Nelson 54, (288)
WALL, Oney C. 38 (m), (229)
WALL, Sarah 22* (B) (490)
WALL, Tempsey? 66 (m) (B) (203)
WALL, Thomas 26* (424)
WALL, W. R. 53 (m), (283)
WALL, W. T. 46 (m)* (292)
WALLACE, Andy 21* (B) (432)
WALLACE, James 21* (478)
WALLACE, Jim 20* (B) (262)
WALLACE, T. C. 23 (m), (478)
WALLACE, Wm. 42, (163)
WALLACE, _ick 27 (f)* (B) (321)
WALLDEN, M. N. 18 (f)* (215)
WALLER, Ike 55 (B) (401)

WALLER, James T. 53, (408)
WALLER, John 52* (B) (364)
WALLER, Joseph 25 (B) (364)
WALLER, Landar? 62 (m) (B) (333)
WALLER, Marcellus C. 53, (364)
WALLER, Millie 50 (B) (327)
WALLER, Milton 21* (B) (400)
WALLER, Richard 28 (B) (400)
WALLER, Robert W. 30, (408)
WALLER, Samuel 27 (B) (364)
WALLER, Thornton 85* (B) (364)
WALLER, Tom 24 (B) (400)
WALLER, Wm. 24 (B) (333)
WALLER, Z. 100 (f) (B) (400)
WALLER, _. _. 31 (m)* (327)
WALLER?, John 55, (414)
WALLIS, Isaac 18* (B) (403)
WALLS, Abe 60* (B) (484)
WALLS, Anna 15 (B) (203)
WALLS, Annie H. 18* (356)
WALLS, Berry 30* (B) (415)
WALLS, Milton 12, (367)
WALLS, ____ 31 (m)* (B) (203)
WALS?, George 24 (B) (484)
WALSON, Lucinda 30 (B) (343)
WALTEN, Thomas 40 (B) (310)
WALTEN?, Laura 35* (315)
WALTER, Clarkey 73 (f)* (B) (304)
WALTER, Horace 22* (B) (361)
WALTER, Willis 20 (B) (384)
WALTERS, Ely 35* (320)
WALTERS, Samuel 62 (B) (402)
WALTERS?, Laura 30* (B) (416)
WALTON, C. 40 (m) (B) (498)
WALTON, Daniel 23 (B) (350)
WALTON, Fletcher? 9* (B) (320)
WALTON, George 72 (B) (405)
WALTON, Harris 28 (B) (317)
WALTON, Harris 28 (B) (342)
WALTON, Henry 28 (B) (386)
WALTON, Jacob 45 (B) (348)
WALTON, Jim 35* (B) (320)
WALTON, Joe 27 (B) (256)
WALTON, Lawrence 20* (B) (354)
WALTON, Mag 34 (f) (B) (347)
WALTON, Nelson 19* (B) (314)
WALTON, Samuel 21 (B) (386)
WALTON, Thomas 9* (B) (349)
WALTON, Wm. 24* (B) (405)
WAN?, Jake 29 (B) (402)
WANDREN?, Base 32 (f)* (B) (233)
WARD, Edward 30* (B) (351)
WARD, Henry 21* (B) (364)
WARD, J. W. 40 (m), (481)
WARD, Jack 96? (B) (399)
WARD, James 32 (B) (363)
WARD, Jenie 25 (B) (434)
WARD, John 55 (B) (379)
WARD, Mary 36* (406)
WARD, T. W. 23 (m)* (331)
WARD, Wm. 28 (B) (346)
WARDLOW, Louis 52 (B) (423)
WARDY, Walton 22* (B) (370)
WARE, Albert 17* (B) (285)
WARE, Charles 26* (B) (280)

WARE, Emma 27 (B) (177)
WARE, George 17* (B) (225)
WARE, John 23* (B) (221)
WARE, John 28* (B) (419)
WARE, Mattia A. 6 (f)* (261)
WARE, Wm. 23* (417)
WARFORD, Joe 23* (236)
WARMACK, Sam 22 (B) (405)
WARMONT?, Braxton 55 (B) (205)
WARNER, Jerry 54 (m)* (B) (482)
WARNER, Mack 35 (B) (274)
WARNER?, Rufus 12* (B) (390)
WARP, Wm. H. 26, (169)
WARR, Adam 40 (B) (364)
WARR, Americus 45 (m)* (392)
WARR, Amos 13* (B) (181)
WARR, Charles 22 (B) (362)
WARR, Charley 23* (B) (367)
WARR, Eliza 35 (B) (363)
WARR, Elizabeth 60 (B) (361)
WARR, Harriet 16* (B) (359)
WARR, Harriet 68 (B) (362)
WARR, Ike 50* (B) (162)
WARR, Jack 54 (B) (362)
WARR, Jacob 64 (B) (365)
WARR, James M. 36* (364)
WARR, John 30* (B) (364)
WARR, Lycurgus 37, (357)
WARR, Moses 26 (B) (361)
WARR, Olie 4/12 (m)* (364)
WARR, Sampson sr. 75 (B) (362)
WARR, Samuel 43 (B) (366)
WARR, Shadrack 55* (B) (366)
WARR, Shedrack 11* (B) (359)
WARR, Thomas J. 40, (357)
WARR, Wm. 54 (B) (363)
WARREN, Alex 25, (414)
WARREN, Bob 53 (B) (335)
WARREN, Chany 53 (f)* (B) (358)
WARREN, D. E. 57 (m)* (335)
WARREN, Douglass 54 (B) (307)
WARREN, Easter 75* (B) (326)
WARREN, Edward 33 (B) (175)
WARREN, Gilbert 50* (B) (326)
WARREN, Gilford 60 (B) (399)
WARREN, Grandison 22* (B) (172)
WARREN, Henry? 32 (B) (327)
WARREN, John 26* (376)
WARREN, John C. 60, (374)
WARREN, Lucinda 62, (408)
WARREN, Margaret 34* (B) (166)
WARREN, Moses 50 (B) (288)
WARREN, Nedd 22 (B) (398)
WARREN, Parker 22 (B) (418)
WARREN, Prince 65* (B) (247)
WARREN, Randal 32 (B) (328)
WARREN, Right 70 (m), (377)
WARREN, Tena 32* (B) (170)
WARREN, Wm. T. 34, (408)
WARREN?, Nathan? 18* (B) (326)
WARREN?, Tom? 33, (323)
WASH, Matilda 50* (B) (415)
WASHINGTON, Antony 33 (B) (175)

WASHINGTON, Boss 14* (B) (482)
WASHINGTON, Charles 61?* (B) (183)
WASHINGTON, Deb 20* (B) (405)
WASHINGTON, Ellen __ (B) (401)
WASHINGTON, Euly 35 (f)* (B) (370)
WASHINGTON, George 26* (B) (234)
WASHINGTON, George 26 (B) (457)
WASHINGTON, George 30 (B) (362)
WASHINGTON, George 35 (B) (351)
WASHINGTON, George 48 (B) (385)
WASHINGTON, George 62* (B) (259)
WASHINGTON, Henry 24 (B) (401)
WASHINGTON, Liza 35* (B) (270)
WASHINGTON, Melia 40 (f)* (B) (377)
WASHINGTON, Patty 39 (B) (354)
WASHINGTON?, J. S. 40 (m), (160)
WATERS, Patient 31 (f)* (B) (202)
WATERS?, ____ 43 (m)* (B) (391)
WATKINS, A. 17 (m)* (168)
WATKINS, Abe 60 (B) (475)
WATKINS, Alex 67 (m) (B) (475)
WATKINS, Andy 30 (B) (474)
WATKINS, Bettie 45 (B) (171)
WATKINS, Henry 54* (B) (414)
WATKINS, James 17* (B) (360)
WATKINS, Joe 25 (B) (474)
WATKINS, John T. 26* (236)
WATKINS, Laura 18* (B) (363)
WATKINS, Mager 33 (m) (B) (469)
WATKINS, Mollie 22* (B) (175)
WATKINS, Polk 31? (B) (250)
WATKINS, Robert 50 (B) (475)
WATKINS, S. K. 40 (m), (475)
WATKINS, Spence 23 (B) (498)
WATKINS, Sye 53 (m) (B) (475)
WATKINS, U.? P. 42 (f)* (168)
WATKINS, Wm. 46 (B) (236)
WATSON, America 45, (314)
WATSON, Benjamin 30 (B) (416)
WATSON, Chas. T. 40, (279)
WATSON, Dean 19* (B) (382)
WATSON, Gafford 25 (B) (367)
WATSON, H. E. 50 (m), (203)
WATSON, J. 30 (m)* (B) (367)
WATSON, James 26, (188)
WATSON, Joe 41* (B) (312)
WATSON, Lamb 40 (m)* (B) (311)
WATSON, MAttie 30 (f)* (B) (169)
WATSON, Nathan 53* (B) (290)

WATSON, Sal 54 (m)* (315)
WATSON, Tom 26, (227)
WATSON, W.? B. 37 (m)* (164)
WATSON, Wm. 32* (221)
WATSON?, Willy 53 (m) (B) (323)
WATT, W. M. 60 (m), (342)
WATTS, Issabella 40* (B) (437)
WATTS, Mitchell 50 (B) (451)
WATTS, Texanna 1* (427)
WATTS, Tom 20 (B) (394)
WATTS, Wm. 63* (427)
WAULER, Henry 25 (B) (379)
WAW?, Lavacca 4* (410)
WEATHERLY, Alax 25 (B) (237)
WEATHERLY, E. T. 64 (f)* (163)
WEAVER, Charley 25 (B) (468)
WEAVER, Green 25 (B) (379)
WEAVER, Green? 24 (B) (378)
WEAVER, Pat 28 (m)* (B) (393)
WEAVER, Washington 56 (B) (378)
WEBB, Allis 12* (B) (479)
WEBB, Charley 35 (B) (462)
WEBB, Charly 38* (B) (438)
WEBB, Edmon 56 (B) (238)
WEBB, Emsey 67 (m) (B) (345)
WEBB, Henry 35 (B) (395)
WEBB, Horace 28* (B) (401)
WEBB, J. M. 65 (m)* (268)
WEBB, Jacob M. 69* (165)
WEBB, Joseph 31* (166)
WEBB, Louisa 58* (267)
WEBB, Martha 40* (B) (347)
WEBB, Ruby 5* (461)
WEBB, Temp. E. 48 (f)* (328)
WEBB, Thos. 40* (440)
WEBB, ____ __* (195)
WEBB?, Alcy 24 (f)* (B) (186)
WEBB?, James 42, (196)
WEBBER, Eliza 11* (B) (389)
WEBBER, Jacob 32 (B) (361)
WEBBER, James 28* (B) (356)
WEBBER, Lee 38 (m)* (B) (356)
WEBBER, Peter 31* (B) (361)
WEBBER, Spencer 50 (B) (357)
WEBBER, Wm. R. 35* (361)
WEBER, A. 39 (m), (315)
WEBSTER, Dan 35 (B) (451)
WEBSTER, John 58 (B) (355)
WELCH, Frances? 41?* (222)
WELLS, Clarence 15* (292)
WELLS, Dick 55 (B) (287)
WELLS, James R. 61, (234)
WELLS, Jim 40* (B) (316)
WELLS, Joanna 38 (B) (287)
WELLS, Marcellus 33, (234)
WELLS, NElson 48 (B) (268)
WELLS, Rufus 18* (B) (317)
WELLS, Scott 17* (B) (422)
WELLS?, Isaac 35? (B) (181)
WESSEN, C. 30 (f)* (497)
WESSON, Joshua 40 (B) (396)
WEST, Edward 12* (B) (362)
WEST, Edward 19* (B) (267)
WEST, Matison 23 (B) (376)
WEST?, Brook R. 61 (m)* (342)
WEST?, ____ 62 (m), (417)
WESTMOLAND?, R. 45 (m)* (B) (255?) ·

WHARTON, Wm. 21* (B) (419)
WHATTAMORE, LAndon 49* (231)
WHEELER, Callie 24* (433)
WHEELER, G. T. 36 (m)* (488)
WHEELER, J. H. 20 (m)* (483)
WHEELER, Robert 27* (B) (388)
WHEELER, Robt. J. 60* (171)
WHIDBEE, Maria 60* (B) (345)
WHILMORE, E. 39 (m)* (263)
WHITACIR, John 48 (B) (385)
WHITAKER, Alf 21 (B) (489)
WHITAKER, Ben 39* (490)
WHITAKER, J. 36 (m) (B) (489)
WHITAKER, John 34* (490)
WHITAKER, Katy 19* (B) (169)
WHITAKER, Sue 14* (B) (177)
WHITAKER, ___ 25 (m)* (B) (489)
WHITE, A. 17 (f)* (B) (464)
WHITE, Adam 31 (B) (350)
WHITE, Allen 54* (B) (266)
WHITE, Anna 11?* (B) (160)
WHITE, Banks 62 (B) (255)
WHITE, Banks 65 (m) (B) (274)
WHITE, Dock 33 (B) (434)
WHITE, Ethel 6* (425)
WHITE, George 24* (B) (269)
WHITE, H. T. 26 (m), (207)
WHITE, Harrison 40 (B) (274)
WHITE, Harrison 45 (B) (254)
WHITE, John 22* (B) (340)
WHITE, John 32 (B) (346)
WHITE, John 58 (B) (355)
WHITE, Jordan 38 (B) (226)
WHITE, L. 12 (f)* (338)
WHITE, Martha 30 (B) (338)
WHITE, Millie 25 (B) (465)
WHITE, Milton 29 (B) (255)
WHITE, Milton 30* (B) (274)
WHITE, NEwton 52 (B) (214)
WHITE, Rozena 16 (f)* (B) (260)
WHITE, Sallie 20* (181)
WHITE, Sam 26 (B) (438)
WHITE, Shep 40 (m) (B) (233)
WHITE, Squire 60 (B) (266)
WHITE, Winnie 30* (B) (261)
WHITE, ____ 50 (f) (B) (208)
WHITEHEAD, Ann 55* (B) (474)
WHITEHEAD, R. 61 (m)* (474)
WHITEHORN, Z. M. 80 (f)* (207)
WHITEHORNE?, Ellen 47, (268)
WHITEMEADE, James 23* (422)
WHITES?, Paul 23* (B) (213)
WHITESIDE, Alexander 26* (B) (336)
WHITESIDES, Henry 25 (B) (405)
WHITFIELD, J. W. 37 (m), (275)
WHITICER, Own? 22 (m)* (B) (478)
WHITIKERS?, Strange 57 (m), (417)
WHITLEY, Ann 11* (289)
WHITLEY, Clabe 35 (m), (283)
WHITLEY, Lou 10 (f)* (490)
WHITMORE, Billy 20* (B) (228)
WHITMORE, Jim 38 (B) (266)

WHITMORE, Norris? 25 (f), (283)
WHITMORE?, Charles 65* (B) (267)
WHITNEY, James 26* (461)
WHITNEY, Sara 50* (426)
WHITTAMORE, Taylor 24, (239)
WHITTEN, Mason 67* (B) (496)
WHITWORTH, Sid 35 (m), (277)
WHIT____, John 21* (271)
WIGGINS, Arch 28 (B) (402)
WIGGINS, Bobb 40 (B) (402)
WIGGINS, Ferry 54 (m) (B) (294)
WIGGINS, James 48* (276)
WIGGINS, Murphry 24 (B) (279)
WIGGINS, Nathan 23 (B) (402)
WIGGINS, Ned 45? (B) (327)
WIGGINS, Peyton 35 (B) (294)
WIGGINS, Wiley 22* (B) (273)
WIGGINS, Wiley W. 62* (410)
WIGGINS, Willis M. 29, (410)
WIGGINS, Zang 33 (m)* (B) (397)
WIGGLESWORTH, Andrew J. 54* (361)
WILBORN, May 53* (437)
WILDER, W. L. 52 (m), (277)
WILES, Adam 59* (206)
WILES, Harvey 34, (196)
WILES, J. M. 22 (m), (204)
WILES, M. L. 25 (m)* (204)
WILEY, Ann 46? (B) (199)
WILEY, M. 16 (f)* (202)
WILEY, T. 20 (m)* (B) (489)
WILKERSON, Albert 74 (B) (240)
WILKERSON, Bill 50 (B) (474)
WILKERSON, David 40* (B) (235)
WILKERSON, Edmon 21* (B) (215)
WILKERSON, Maggie 23* (B) (467)
WILKERSON, Mary 60* (B) (484)
WILKERSON, Simon? __ (B) (240)
WILKERSON, Sye? 50 (m) (B) (467)
WILKERSON, Theop.? 50 (m), (443)
WILKERSON, Thos. 57, (443)
WILKERSON, Vina 16* (B) (495)
WILKERSON, Wesley 22* (B) (422)
WILKERSON, _. 28 (m)* (B) (484)
WILKES, A. 60 (f) (B) (500)
WILKES, G. 28 (m) (B) (500)
WILKES?, Letty 58 (f)* (B) (211)
WILKINS, Alax 52 (B) (239)
WILKINS, Alfred 50* (B) (162)
WILKINS, Henry 21* (B) (233)
WILKINS, John 22* (B) (260)
WILKINS, L. Grant 17* (B) (262)
WILKINS, Lucy 37 (B) (241)
WILKINS, Nancy 2_ (B) (160)
WILKINSON, W. B. 56 (m)* (179)

WILKINSON, Wiley 78* (B) (180)
WILKS, Andrew 28* (B) (479)
WILLBANKS, Wm. 54 (B) (219)
WILLEFORD, Mary C. 43* (182)
WILLET, George 60* (B) (224)
WILLET, John 24* (B) (224)
WILLIAM, Allen 40 (B) (397)
WILLIAM, J. F. 49 (m), (209)
WILLIAMS, A. 60 (f)* (280)
WILLIAMS, Adam 65* (B) (342)
WILLIAMS, Addison 6* (B) (360)
WILLIAMS, Alax 36, (234)
WILLIAMS, Albert 30* (B) (374)
WILLIAMS, Alfred 10* (B) (461)
WILLIAMS, Alfred? 10* (B) (236)
WILLIAMS, Allen 30* (B) (359)
WILLIAMS, Alx. 47 (m) (B) (478)
WILLIAMS, Ann 26 (B) (256)
WILLIAMS, Anna 80* (B) (428)
WILLIAMS, Benjamin 50* (389)
WILLIAMS, Betty 19* (B) (233)
WILLIAMS, Burton 23 (B) (358)
WILLIAMS, Butler 46? (B) (269)
WILLIAMS, Callie 30* (B) (442)
WILLIAMS, Ch____ 16 (f)* (B) (264)
WILLIAMS, Charley 45* (B) (339)
WILLIAMS, Daniel 70* (B) (217)
WILLIAMS, David 37 (B) (464)
WILLIAMS, Demcy 25 (m) (B) (389)
WILLIAMS, Don 35* (B) (326)
WILLIAMS, Dow 60 (m)* (B) (234)
WILLIAMS, Drew 50 (B) (345)
WILLIAMS, Ed 21* (B) (170)
WILLIAMS, Ed 26 (B) (332)
WILLIAMS, Ed? 34 (m)* (B) (496)
WILLIAMS, Edd 32* (B) (325)
WILLIAMS, Edward 27 (B) (358)
WILLIAMS, Elisha 66* (442)
WILLIAMS, Ennis 31* (B) (227)
WILLIAMS, Ester 50* (B) (301)
WILLIAMS, Fannie 38 (B) (234)
WILLIAMS, Frankie 70 (f)* (B) (254)
WILLIAMS, Ged 30 (m)* (B) (405)
WILLIAMS, George 22* (B) (480)
WILLIAMS, Gilfred 60 (B) (335)
WILLIAMS, H. 70 (m), (209)
WILLIAMS, H. R. 52 (f)* (205)
WILLIAMS, Hannah 25* (B) (323)
WILLIAMS, Hary 24* (B) (325)
WILLIAMS, Henry 22* (B) (482)
WILLIAMS, Henry 25 (B) (421)
WILLIAMS, Henry 26* (233)
WILLIAMS, Henry 27* (B) (369)
WILLIAMS, Henry 40, (357)
WILLIAMS, Henry 40 (B) (457)
WILLIAMS, Henry 60* (B) (290)
WILLIAMS, Henry __* (B) (416)
WILLIAMS, Horda 38 (m)* (B) (234)

WILLIAMS, Indiana 34* (195)
WILLIAMS, Ivin 49 (B) (342)
WILLIAMS, J. 27 (m) (B) (308)
WILLIAMS, J. H. 28 (m), (209)
WILLIAMS, J.? A. 51 (m), (336)
WILLIAMS, Jacob 65* (B) (254)
WILLIAMS, Jane 23?* (B) (243)
WILLIAMS, Jane 65 (B) (389)
WILLIAMS, Jef 22 (B) (234)
WILLIAMS, Jeff 43* (B) (421)
WILLIAMS, Jery 30 (m) (B) (389)
WILLIAMS, John 22* (B) (261)
WILLIAMS, John 24* (B) (261)
WILLIAMS, John 37* (B) (227)
WILLIAMS, John 52* (B) (500)
WILLIAMS, John 71* (195)
WILLIAMS, John F. 36, (410)
WILLIAMS, Josh 32 (B) (444)
WILLIAMS, Josie? 70 (f) (B) (465)
WILLIAMS, L. M. 40 (m)* (469)
WILLIAMS, Louis 40 (B) (290)
WILLIAMS, Marlow 10 (m)* (383)
WILLIAMS, Martha 1* (B) (267)
WILLIAMS, Martha 31 (B) (457)
WILLIAMS, Martin 48, (253)
WILLIAMS, Mary 18* (B) (434)
WILLIAMS, Mat 56 (m) (B) (325)
WILLIAMS, Matt 60 (B) (388)
WILLIAMS, Nathan 33 (B) (261)
WILLIAMS, Nelson 60* (B) (302)
WILLIAMS, Noah 26* (B) (349)
WILLIAMS, P. T. D. 29 (m)* (213)
WILLIAMS, Peter 48 (B) (358)
WILLIAMS, Pollie 35 (B) (468)
WILLIAMS, Rebecca 55 (B) (365)
WILLIAMS, Richard 54 (B) (262)
WILLIAMS, Richd. 57 (B) (233)
WILLIAMS, Sam 48 (m) (B) (334)
WILLIAMS, Sarah 30, (406)
WILLIAMS, Sarah 6* (B) (178)
WILLIAMS, Sarah 80* (B) (160)
WILLIAMS, Shade 35 (m) (B) (405)
WILLIAMS, Spencer 36* (B) (305)
WILLIAMS, Spencer 49 (B) (418)
WILLIAMS, Sylva 50* (B) (276)
WILLIAMS, Thomas 21 (B) (455)
WILLIAMS, Thomas 26 (B) (180)
WILLIAMS, Thomas 40 (B) (258)
WILLIAMS, Thomas 55* (204)
WILLIAMS, Thos. R. 59* (263)
WILLIAMS, Vina 60 (B) (375)
WILLIAMS, W. 7 (m)* (B) (270)
WILLIAMS, Wesley 43 (B) (347)
WILLIAMS, Wesly 35 (B) (331)
WILLIAMS, Willey 13* (B) (335)
WILLIAMS, Willis 40 (B) (444)
WILLIAMS, Wm. 59* (B) (426)
WILLIAMS, Wright 25? (B) (264)
WILLIAMS, ___ 51 (m)* (B) (165)
WILLIAMS, ___ 54 (m)* (B) (325)

WILLIAMS, ___ 32 (m)* (B) (341)
WILLIAMS, ___ 70 (m)* (B) (418)
WILLIAMS?, John 35 (B) (287)
WILLIAMSON, Aaron 55 (B) (354)
WILLIAMSON, Alfred 40* (B) (235)
WILLIAMSON, Allen 33* (B) (229)
WILLIAMSON, Alphis 25 (m) (B) (221)
WILLIAMSON, Alphius sr. 70* (B) (229)
WILLIAMSON, Ann 21* (B) (235)
WILLIAMSON, Annette 45* (B) (233)
WILLIAMSON, Arch 50 (B) (401)
WILLIAMSON, Asbery 24 (B) (240)
WILLIAMSON, Ben 26 (B) (166)
WILLIAMSON, Buck 43 (B) (230)
WILLIAMSON, Burell 50 (B) (164)
WILLIAMSON, Cambridge 24* (B) (356)
WILLIAMSON, Clay 36 (B) (242)
WILLIAMSON, Crawford 55 (B) (189)
WILLIAMSON, Dock 19* (B) (403)
WILLIAMSON, Edward 55 (B) (346)
WILLIAMSON, Emanuel 40* (B) (168)
WILLIAMSON, Emerson 19* (B) (240)
WILLIAMSON, Frank 50* (B) (346)
WILLIAMSON, George 33* (B) (180)
WILLIAMSON, Gilbert 24 (B) (187)
WILLIAMSON, Hardy 57* (B) (357)
WILLIAMSON, Horace 38? (B) (239)
WILLIAMSON, Isaac 66* (B) (203)
WILLIAMSON, J. 77 (m) (B) (471)
WILLIAMSON, JAck 56* (B) (254)
WILLIAMSON, James I. 60, (348)
WILLIAMSON, Jane 65 (B) (237)
WILLIAMSON, Jerry 40 (m) (B) (242)
WILLIAMSON, Jesse 42 (m) (B) (230)
WILLIAMSON, John 13* (B) (357)
WILLIAMSON, K. 20 (m) (B) (489)
WILLIAMSON, King? 60 (B) (489)

WILLIAMSON, Lark 19* (B) (339)
WILLIAMSON, Larkin 57* (B) (165)
WILLIAMSON, Leave 55 (m) (B) (234)
WILLIAMSON, Lucy 60?* (B) (258)
WILLIAMSON, MAtilda 56* (B) (169)
WILLIAMSON, Mag 43 (f) (B) (231)
WILLIAMSON, Mandee? 28 (m) (B) (358)
WILLIAMSON, Manuel 43 (B) (229)
WILLIAMSON, Mary 55* (B) (271)
WILLIAMSON, Mat 26 (m) (B) (233)
WILLIAMSON, Moses 31 (B) (259)
WILLIAMSON, Ned 34* (B) (238)
WILLIAMSON, Nelson 21 (B) (204)
WILLIAMSON, Orlando 29* (355)
WILLIAMSON, Patience 8* (B) (235)
WILLIAMSON, Richd. 24 (B) (177)
WILLIAMSON, Robin 55 (m) (B) (229)
WILLIAMSON, Sam 24 (B) (229)
WILLIAMSON, Sam 68* (B) (239)
WILLIAMSON, W. A. 66 (m)* (187)
WILLIAMSON, Wilson 29?* (B) (164)
WILLIAMSON, Woodson 29 (B) (354)
WILLIAMSON, huldy? 63 (f)* (B) (177)
WILLIMAS, Citha? 37 (f) (B) (286)
WILLINBERGER?, Henry 2_* (386)
WILLIS, Berry 30 (B) (442)
WILLIS, Ed 26 (B) (257)
WILLIS, Henry 75* (484)
WILLIS, JAmes M. 27* (221)
WILLIS, JOhn _7 (B) (243)
WILLIS, Sousan 18* (B) (375)
WILLIS, Wash 38* (B) (357)
WILLIS, William 20* (221)
WILLSON, A. P. 35 (m), (204)
WILLSON, George 27 (B) (394)
WILLSON, S. 39 (m), (412)
WILLSON, Willis W. 17* (406)
WILSON, Alford 30* (B) (382)
WILSON, Amelia 54, (424)
WILSON, Ben 21* (B) (242)
WILSON, D. S. 25 (m)* (342)
WILSON, Dennis 29 (B) (320)
WILSON, Dick 30* (B) (257)
WILSON, Eddie 19* (B) (307)
WILSON, F. A. _6 (m)* (315)
WILSON, George 55 (B) (422)

WILSON, Gin 21 (m) (B) (333)
WILSON, Harriet 24* (B) (356)
WILSON, Haywood 35 (B) (363)
WILSON, Henry 25* (B) (307)
WILSON, Henry 53* (B) (365)
WILSON, J. 33 (m)* (477)
WILSON, JAmes 47* (314)
WILSON, JAmes 66* (236)
WILSON, James 31 (B) (301)
WILSON, James 35, (478)
WILSON, Jason C. 60* (196)
WILSON, Jim 35 (B) (291)
WILSON, John 35* (B) (168)
WILSON, John 42, (299)
WILSON, Juda 40? (f)* (B) (236)
WILSON, Lake 27 (m)* (B) (429)
WILSON, Lou 45 (f)* (386)
WILSON, Louis 30 (B) (328)
WILSON, MAriah 60 (B) (262)
WILSON, Madison 33, (425)
WILSON, Mary 50* (484)
WILSON, Matilda 54* (B) (307)
WILSON, Matilda 57* (392)
WILSON, Mike 29* (425)
WILSON, Mollie 22* (B) (297)
WILSON, Moses 56 (B) (308)
WILSON, Ness 30 (m)* (B) (227)
WILSON, Ricahrd 23 (B) (380)
WILSON, Richard 28 (B) (382)
WILSON, Sam 27? (B) (425)
WILSON, Taylor 26 (B) (494)
WILSON, Taylor 47, (297)
WILSON, Tolbert S. 39* (168)
WILSON, Willis 24* (B) (308)
WILSON, _. P. 56 (f)* (470)
WILSON, ___ 21 (m) (B) (301)
WILSON?, D. S. 25 (m)* (317)
WINBORN, Caroline 25 (B) (164)
WINBORN, Henry 55* (B) (172)
WINBORN, JAne 23* (B) (161)
WINBORN, Lucinda 22* (B) (166)
WINDERS?, H. 18 (m)* (B) (494)
WINDMAN, JErry 25 (m)* (B) (241)
WINESBERRY, Amy 52* (B) (254)
WINFIELD, Anthony 25 (B) (390)
WINFIELD, Burrel 60 (B) (390)
WINFIELD, Even 27 (B) (423)
WINFIELD, Fannie 67* (B) (167)
WINFIELD, Henry 30* (B) (383)
WINFIELD, MArgaret 60* (169)
WINFIELD, McGain? 35 (m)* (B) (423)
WINFIELD, Sara 50* (B) (423)
WINFRED, Felix 16* (B) (257)
WINFREY, Arch 42 (B) (237)
WINFREY, Edmon 24* (B) (235)
WINFREY, Fed 55 (m) (B) (236)
WINFREY, Grandville 55 (m) (B) (238)
WINFREY, Granville 60* (B) (164)
WINFREY, Jesse 51 (m) (B) (238)
WINFREY, John 15* (B) (240)
WINFREY, John A. 40* (236)
WINFREY, Mariah 42 (B) (239)
WINFREY, Morris 20* (B) (233)

WINFREY, Napoleon 20* (B) (234)
WINFREY, Robert 17 (B) (234)
WINFRY, Aleax 15?* (B) (236)
WINFRY, Charles 50 (B) (237)
WINFRY, Donell 18* (B) (246)
WINGFORD, Jack 33 (B) (254)
WINRIGHT, Crocket 54* (B) (339)
WINSBERRY?, ____ 25 (m) (B) (257)
WINSET, Molly 22 (B) (187)
WINSETT, Robt. 74* (170)
WINSTED?, Virginia 48* (B) (460)
WINSTON, A. 45 (f)* (447)
WINSTON, C. 13 (f)* (B) (498)
WINSTON, Charley 24* (440)
WINSTON, Edmond 30 (B) (458)
WINSTON, James 25* (B) (365)
WINSTON, Mat 50 (m) (B) (459)
WINSTON, Peter 75 (B) (299)
WIRET?, Carrie 49* (255?)
WIREVA?, W. C. 40 (m)* (163)
WIRT, Ben 55 (B) (342)
WIRT, Callie 45* (B) (317)
WIRT, Callie 45* (B) (342)
WIRT, Charles 30 (B) (330)
WIRT, Clinton 29* (B) (235)
WIRT, Edmon 24* (B) (236)
WIRT, Eliza 39 (B) (162)
WIRT, Fereby 25* (B) (235)
WIRT, Finus E. 7_ (m), (248)
WIRT, Fletcher 24* (B) (172)
WIRT, Frances 70* (B) (235)
WIRT, G. A. 14 (f)* (B) (342)
WIRT, Harry 50 (B) (338)
WIRT, Isreal 24* (B) (236)
WIRT, James 35* (B) (186)
WIRT, Joe 30* (B) (236)
WIRT, Paul 22* (B) (236)
WIRT, Perry 26 (B) (237)
WIRT, Rasmus 33* (B) (235)
WITT, John 34* (B) (415)
WITT, Kitty 30 (B) (163)
WITT, Phillis 70* (B) (415)
WITT?, A. 1 (m)* (B) (416)
WITT?, Abraham 35, (440)
WI____, Leander 10* (B) (264)
WOLKER, Crofford 46 (B) (388)
WOOD, Cindy 28 (B) (329)
WOOD, Edd 14* (B) (329)
WOOD, John 35? (B) (448)
WOOD, Mack 65* (B) (244)
WOOD, Mollie 20* (B) (222)
WOOD, Moody 40 (B) (465)
WOOD, Paul 25 (B) (239)
WOOD?, James? 26* (B) (419)
WOODARD, Andrew J. 55* (375)
WOODARD, Marshal 11* (388)
WOODFORD, Ed 31* (B) (312)
WOODFORD, Jorden 68* (B) (313)
WOODRIDGE, Nelson 35 (B) (287)
WOODRUFF, JAmes 33* (B) (321)
WOODRY, S. F. 57 (m)* (165)
WOODS, Alex 27* (B) (267)
WOODS, Annie 12* (443)

WOODS, Annis 23 (f)* (B) (282)
WOODS, Bell 40 (B) (402)
WOODS, Charles 45* (B) (444)
WOODS, Charly 20* (B) (327)
WOODS, Jeff 25 (B) (396)
WOODS, Jessee 28 (m)* (B) (396)
WOODS, Leroy 39, (368)
WOODS, Morgan 53 (B) (455)
WOODS, Richard 40 (B) (294)
WOODS, Richard 45 (B) (463)
WOODS, Sarah 10* (B) (402)
WOODS, Sidney 24 (m), (253)
WOODS, Thomas 37 (B) (444)
WOODS, Thomas 60* (B) (390)
WOODS, Vina 45 (B) (443)
WOODSON, Bill 23* (B) (342)
WOODSON, Charly 25* (B) (470)
WOODSON, Eva S. 47* (B) (164)
WOODSON, Pattie 23* (B) (467)
WOODSON, W. T. C. 29 (m)* (168)
WOODSON, ____ 23 (m)* (B) (317)
WOODSON?, David 25* (B) (424)
WOODWARD, JAmes 30* (440)
WOODWARD, Samuel 24* (B) (365)
WOOD____, C. R. _ (m)* (296)
WOOLDRIDGE, Grandison? 38 (B) (271)
WOOLFORD, _. R. 44 (m), (407)
WOOLSY, Bob 50 (B) (221)
WOORLEY, John 48 (B) (420)
WOOTTON, Henry 59* (B) (394)
WORD, Cherry 68 (f)* (B) (323)
WORD, Finis 20* (316)
WORD, Finis 20* (344)
WORD, Fremeer? 24 (m) (B) (438)
WORD, Leanna 16* (B) (175)
WORD, Louisa 18* (B) (323)
WORD, Thos. 27* (162)
WORD, Wm. 49 (B) (312)
WORD, Wm. 52 (B) (298)
WORD?, Lance 17 (f)* (B) (169)
WORD?, Nannie 30* (169)
WORD?, Tobias 65* (B) (169)
WORDE, Perry 30 (B) (464)
WORDE, Prime? 66 (m) (B) (438)
WORDSWORTH, Jim 30 (B) (229)
WORL, Sam 27* (B) (218)
WORRELL, Benjamin 32* (191)
WORRELL, John 18* (B) (222)
WORTERS, George 30? (B) (370)
WORTERS, Sarah 18* (B) (388)
WO__DS, Charles? 50 (B) (479)
WRAY, Calvin 38 (B) (257)
WRAY, Charles 19* (B) (234)
WRAY, John A. 43* (234)
WRAY, M. G. 78 (f)* (178)
WRAY, Oliver 70 (B) (253)
WRAY, Rubin 60?* (252)
WRAY, Sam 14* (B) (247)
WRAY, Wm. 62 (B) (241)
WRIGHT, Ed 32* (487)
WRIGHT, George 23* (B) (382)
WRIGHT, John W. 21, (351)
WRIGHT, Joseph? 50?* (261)
WRIGHT, Lucy 23 (B) (366)

WRIGHT, Matilda 65* (B) (165)
WRIGHT, Randle 45 (B) (363)
WRIGHT, Thomas 40 (B) (355)
WRIGHT, Wilburn 48, (440)
WRIGHT, Wm. 42, (200)
WRITE, Ann 18* (B) (415)
WRITE, Richard 26* (B) (415)
WRITT, Sena 24* (B) (433)
WTASON?, Andrew 25 (B) (449)
WYART, Abe 65* (B) (476)
WYATT, Armisty 25 (m)* (B) (416)
WYETT, Martha 34 (B) (237)
WYLEY, Elizabeth 24* (B) (369)
WYLIE, James 33* (B) (363)
WYLIE, Samuel 29* (B) (418)
WYUT?, Willie 22 (m)* (B) (477)
YAMSEY?, R. H. 31 (m)* (309)
YANCEY, Abraham 62 (B) (350)
YANCEY, Algy 25 (m), (320)
YANCEY, Barbara 40* (B) (345)
YANCEY, Caroline 40 (B) (321)
YANCEY, Demus 40 (B) (350)
YANCEY, Dolly 15* (B) (349)
YANCEY, J. 30 (m)* (322)
YANCEY, Jack 75?* (B) (363)
YANCEY, Joe 29?* (322)
YANCEY, Joe 34 (B) (349)
YANCEY, Lucien 30 (B) (351)
YANCEY, Mary 40 (B) (485)
YANCEY, Mary 50* (B) (355)
YANCEY, Matthew 35* (B) (347)
YANCEY, Rachael 47 (B) (321)
YANCEY, Robert 26* (B) (352)
YANCEY, T. B. 37 (m)* (162)
YANCEY, Taylor? 58 (B) (446)
YANCEY, Thomas B. 38* (B) (351)
YANCEY, Wm. 70* (320)
YANCEY, ____ 34 (m)* (323)
YANCEY, ____y 17 (m)* (319)
YANCY, George 36 (B) (306)
YANCY, Peter 30 (B) (306)
YANCY, Richd. H. 24* (165)
YANCY, Samuel 24 (B) (310)
YARBROUGH, JAmes 23* (B) (240)
YARBROUGH, John 57* (B) (260)
YARBROUGH, Martha 52, (322)
YARROW, S. L. 36 (m)* (333)
YARROW, W. S. 40 (m), (327)
YATES, Ed 39 (B) (262)
YATES, Harry 60 (B) (282)
YERGER, Jeny 32* (163)
YOKELY, Milas 57 (B) (405)
YORK, A. A. 51 (m), (278)
YORK, John 20, (278)
YORK, S. S. 74 (m), (294)
YORK, Saml. 32* (276)
YOUNG, Annie 13* (B) (164)
YOUNG, B.? 25 (m) (B) (501)
YOUNG, David 27* (B) (251)
YOUNG, Gorge 25* (B) (214)
YOUNG, HEnry 30 (B) (485)
YOUNG, Jack 35? (B) (446)
YOUNG, James 22 (B) (455)
YOUNG, Mary 28 (B) (459)
YOUNG, Mary J. 47* (B) (360)
YOUNG, Mecca 12 (f)* (B) (392)

YOUNG, Moses 45 (B) (449)
YOUNG, Nicholas 35, (438)
YOUNG, Peter 34 (B) (278)
YOUNG, Thomas 46* (B) (263)
YOUNG, Tom 2_* (B) (259)
YOUNG, ____ 30 (m)* (B) (238)
YOUNG, ____ 24 (f)* (B) (390)
YOUNG?, John 11* (B) (422)
YOUNG?, Rubin 35 (B) (445)
YOUNG?, ____ 27 (m) (B) (445)
ZACKERY, Salla 65 (f), (489)
ZACKERY, T. _. 31 (m), (486)
ZELLNER, M. 62 (m), (302)
ZELLNER, Porter 19, (247)
ZENKER?, Simon 17* (B) (428)
ZIM?, Caroline 24* (B) (428)
ZIMMER?, Edd 50* (B) (485)
ZINN, Jim 25* (B) (433)
_ABIN, May 54 (B) (390)
_ARMONT?, John 15* (B) (218)
_ERSON, Armstead 25 (B) (211)
_EVEDAY?, Susan 45* (185)
_EWETTE, Berry 30* (B) (454)
_INES, J. R. 43* (327)
_OWLES, Johnie 10* (B) (325)
UNT, Henry 28 (B) (452)
__EITZ, ____ 7 (f)* (185)
__NE, Able 40* (B) (322)
__RREL, Fielder 28* (B) (382)
___WEN, Henry 21* (B) (325)
___WERS, James 30* (278)
____, Henry 36, (415)
____, Henry 40? (B) (391)
____, Peter 56* (B) (382)
____, Wm. 20 (B) (382)
____, ____ 55 (m)* (440)
___BROOK, R. A. 61 (m)* (317)
___LEWOOD, C. J. 27 (f)* (207)
____R, Daniel 20* (B) (213)
___SON, Patrick 27* (B) (167)
_____, Alford 50 (B) (218)
_____, Charles _* (B) (418)
_____, Ed 33* (B) (312)
_____, Edward _* (419)
_____, Elizabeth 1* (B) (324)
_____, George 25 (B) (261)
_____, George 31 (B) (434)
_____, Henrey 28* (B) (215)
_____, Henry 42 (B) (313)
_____, J. W. 68 (m), (474)
_____, MArtha 24* (B) (290)
_____, Mathew 45 (B) (418)
_____, Mattie 45 (m) (B) (449)
_____, Phillip 48* (B) (419)
_____, Richard 45 (B) (418)
_____, Samuel J. 65, (390)
_____, Thomas 57, (417)
_____, Vincent 28 (B) (432)
_____, Wm. 20* (B) (311)
_____, ____ 27 (m) (B) (418)
_____, ____ 53? (B) (391)
_____, ____ 60 (f) (B) (321)
____ER, J. W. 40 (m)* (330)
___IARD, ____ 34 (m), (417)
___ON, Wm. 28 (B) (283)
_____, Abram 50 (B) (416)
_____, Adam 55? (B) (390)
_____, Andrew 24 (B) (179)
_____, Charlie 23* (B) (191)

_____, Dick 30 (B) (204)
_____, James 50* (B) (382)
_____, John 10* (B) (263)
_____, Louis 25 (B) (264)
_____, Mabin 35 (m) (B) (390)
_____, Parille 35* (B) (416)
_____, _____ 28 (B) (390)